Diagnostic reading instruction in the elementary school

Diagnostic reading instruction in the elementary school

FRANK J. GUSZAK
The University of Texas at Austin

HARPER & ROW, PUBLISHERS
New York, Evanston, San Francisco, London

Diagnostic Reading Instruction in the Elementary School

Copyright © 1972 by Frank J. Guszak

Printed in the United States of America. All rights reserved. No part of this book may be used or reproduced in any manner whatsoever without written permission except in the case of brief quotations embodied in critical articles and reviews. For information address Harper & Row, Publishers, Inc., 49 East 33rd Street, New York, N.Y. 10016.

Standard Book Number: 06-042564-4

Library of Congress Catalog Card Number: 79-187047

Preface

Diagnostic Reading Instruction in the Elementary School was written in response to the current hope for at least a partial solution to our countless reading failures. During the last two decades the emergent theme of the most important research has suggested that teachers make the difference. The diagnostic reading teacher is unique in this respect, for she works in ghettos, disadvantaged rural areas, and other areas of high reading failure—with good results. She produces when others cannot.

The text began over six years ago as the author moved from the lecture-type reading course to the practicum-centered course. In working more intensively with children, we began to question many of the conventional approaches and see the need for specific learning systems. The systems were begun and have continued to undergo development, each one having been experienced, reexperienced, and evaluated by pre- and in-service teachers. Gathered together, all of these systems comprise the diagnostic reading program.

In presenting this material, a certain structure has been used that will hopefully enable the reader to derive as much benefit as possible in tailoring the program to his needs. The basic framework provides an understanding of the most crucial decisions regarding reading instruction, but that framework is flexible. Some parts of the book can be read very quickly and used only as needed in the future; other parts of the book may find immediate application, and still other parts may serve as a starting point for the development of new, individualized approaches to the problem of reading instruction.

Part One—Background: Diagnostic Reading Instruction reveals the problem of ever-increasing reading failures. The reader is taken on a whirl-wind tour of some of the common explanations of reading failure (no phonics, dyslexia, basal readers, etc.) in an effort to find precisely what can be done to overcome the problems. From there, he is whisked to Maple Hill School so that he can see a "modern reading program" in action. The Maple Hill reading program provides a crucial backdrop for the remainder of the text, so travel its halls slowly.

Part Two—What the Diagnostic Reading Teacher Knows operates on the hypothesis that those who teach reading skills must know such skills. Four chapters, dealing in turn with word recognition skills, comprehension skills, fluency skills, and motivational techniques should be read very deliberately, as these various skills will be subsequently diagnosed.

Part Three—What the Diagnostic Reading Teacher Determines guides the teacher toward a new era of accountability. Characterizing the new era will be the concern for individual learners and their unique needs. Teachers will be able to answer with accuracy the following three questions about every child in the class: What is *his most appropriate reading level*? What are *his specific skills needs* at that level? And, what is *his reading potential*?

Part Four—What the Diagnostic Reading Teacher Prescribes recognizes the importance of the proper prescription for the given malady. Specific skills needs and their prescribed treatments are discussed in great detail. Realizing that this type of instruction will stretch a teacher very thin in getting around to thirty children, it becomes necessary to assist the teacher in planning for *indirect,* pupil-managed learning tasks.

Part Five—What the Diagnostic Reading Teacher Organizes and Operates attempts something that is unique in reading methods texts. In this section we observe Mrs. Jones, a new second-grade teacher, as she goes about the task of implementing in her classroom the theory and skill of the previous chapters. We see, for instance, how she goes about testing her pupils' reading levels, how she manages to get more books, how she develops contracts, and does the myriad other things necessary to meet individual pupil reading needs.

Acknowledgements should not liable any of the following for "guilt by association." Teachers, colleagues, and friends who have contributed generously to my growth include Thomas Barrett, Miles Zintz, Thomas Horn, William Harmer, William Rutherford, Joe Frost, and Nancy Roser. Giants of the field of reading whose writing has spoken with much force to me include Kenneth Goodman, Albert Harris, Guy Bond, Miles Tinker, Nila B. Smith, Carl LeFevre, William Powell, William Gray, Constance McCullogh, Emmett Betts, Morton Botel, Jeanne Chall, Donald Durrell, Arthur Gates, Russell Stauffer, George Spache, and others. Bob

Palmatier helped tremendously in shaping specific points in the manuscript. Student assistants of extraordinary caliber who have contributed much to my education as they obtained their degrees were Richard Van Dongen, Judy Dettre, Joan Mortimer, Joyce Gipe, Lois Volchansky, Leon Williamson, Judy McHarg, Monta Akins, Jeannette Womack, Jerry Thomas, and still others I've forgotten to mention. Virtually hundreds of undergraduates (now teachers) at The University of Texas at Austin who have clearly shown me their dedication to children are due immense thanks. Still other hundreds of teachers in various parts of the country have helped me greatly. Without a patient, loving, and helping wife who shared the drudgeries known as manuscript preparation, I suspect I would still be typing Chapter 10. Children though, including my own four and the countless numbers I have worked with, have made it all a terribly exciting enterprise. Nearly all children have so much promise if we can do our jobs a little better.

Frank J. Guszak
March 1972

Contents

Diagnostic reading instruction in the elementary school

one Background: diagnostic reading instruction

The facts about reading failure are abundantly clear:

Over 8 million school-age children are not learning .to read adequately.

Sixteen percent of the enrollment in grades 1 through 12 require special instruction in reading.

In most large city school systems ... at least half the students are unable to read well enough to handle their assignments.

Each year some 700,000 youngsters drop out of public school. Studies show that the average dropout is at least two years behind his age group in reading and other basic skills.

There are more than 3 million illiterates in our adult population.

About 18½ million Americans lack the practical reading skills necessary to complete simplified application forms for such common needs as a driver's license, a personal bank loan. . . .

Statistics taken from U.S. Office of Education Reading Seminars Pamphlet, May 1971

It is equally clear from the findings of hundreds of research studies that the primary factor in preventing reading failure is the specially trained teacher who brings unique skills to bear in attacking the problem in the school. Because of the crucial significance of the teacher, the focus of this text is on those practical skills that are needed by what is often called the "diagnostic reading teacher." As a foundation for the skills dimensions of the teacher, we will concentrate in Part One on a brief survey of some of the most frequent explanations of reading failure, current reading program practices, and the emergence of the diagnostic reading teacher concept developed in this text.

Chapter 1, "The Explanations of Reading Failure," provides a brief examination of our numerous but often superficial explanations of "why Johnny can't read." Just as each of us is capable of calling better plays than the team quarterback or coach, we feel similarly talented in diagnosing the ills of our educational programs. Chapter 1 permits the reader to examine the most common explanations and assess their validity as well as their import for teaching. Chapter 2, "The Maple Hill Program," describes a mythical school program that is actually characteristic of many current reading programs. Reading materials (basals, supplementals), grouping arrangements, teaching strategies, and the impact of such instruction upon children are examined and discussed. Chapter 3, "The Concept of the Diagnostic Reading Teacher," briefly reviews some of the educational thinking leading up to a recognition of the importance of the teacher in learning to read and gives an overview of the rationale behind this book. The concept of the diagnostic reading teacher and what this teacher must know and do to obtain optimum results is introduced and explained so that the reader may fit the chapters that follow into a theoretical framework.

1

The explanations
of reading failure

When explanations of reading failure are offered, they most often take forms like these:

"Poor backgrounds; the parents don't care so the children don't care."
"They don't have the necessary intelligence to learn."
"They're dyslexic."
"They need glasses because they can't see correctly."
"Because they don't teach phonics anymore."
"They're not interested in those dull readers anymore."
"Poor reading teachers . . . ."

When these common complaints are tallied and organized into general categories, we find that the explanations center upon environmental concerns, physiological-psychological concerns, reading program failings, and teacher failings. Such categorizations cannot be discrete because of the difficulties involved in separating a child's inherent nature from his background conditioning or the teacher from the reading program she is given and expected to implement. Nevertheless, careful examination of the common explanations provides us with useful background for understanding:

1. The relative importance of each criticism
2. The efforts attempted and currently underway to combat each factor
3. The implications of these factors for us as we plan reading instruction

Environmental factors
There seems to be little argument with the thesis that environmental conditions can and do affect pupil responses to reading instruction—one has only to look at the far greater incidence of reading failure among so-called disadvantaged children in the large city school systems. Despite the magnitude of the failure rate, our strategy now should be to attack the problem more vigorously, for research findings clearly demonstrate that these failures can be overcome (Coleman, 1966; Cohen, 1970; Frost and Pilgrim, 1969; Fader and McNeil, 1968). Inspiring stories such as those of Kohl (1967), Fader (1966), Decker (1969), and others support what researchers such as Coleman (1966) have clearly observed: Dis-

advantaged children can obtain significant achievement gains under the direction of highly skilled teachers.

A prime example of a vigorous attack on the reading problems of delinquent, big-city boys is provided in Fader's exciting *Hooked on Books* (Fader and McNeil, 1968). By illustrating the power of building on these youngsters' reading interests, the author describes an apparently successful approach to what appeared to be an almost certain failure situation. Coleman's extensive research into the achievement patterns of disadvantaged and advantaged children documents the fact that unique school programs managed by unique teachers can be the determining factor in the success of the disadvantaged child, whereas home and peer inputs may be the significant determinants of the achievement of more advantaged children.

Our increased awareness of the plight of these children has led to a spate of government programs in recent years: Head Start (Economic Opportunity Act, 1964), Project Follow Through (Title II of the Economic Opportunity Act), Title I and Title III projects of the Elementary and Secondary Education Act, the Right to Read Program (U.S. Office of Education, 1969), and *Sesame Street* (Children's Television Workshop, 1969) are some of the better-known federal efforts. Behind many of these programs is the realization that to be effective, help must be given early. The huge gaps in experience from which disadvantaged children suffer must be filled if they are to learn to read. But Cohen (1970) suggests that we are sometimes prone to use environmental deficits as the scapegoat for poor instruction. My own observation supports this contention; we must be wary of explanations that hang all the blame on the child's background.

Physiological and psychological factors
Poor readers are poor because

Of low intelligence
Of dyslexia
They need glasses

Or at least these are the reasons we often hear and use. Let us look more closely at what lies behind these assertions.

Low intelligence
Recent research suggesting that race affects intelligence as measured by IQ has set off a fierce exchange within the ranks of behavioral scientists. The battles have become so violent that the National Academy of Sciences overwhelmingly refused to urge

expansion of federally funded studies in this area. But just as environmental backgrounds are utilized as a scapegoat, there is evidence that laymen and educators are using tenuous assumptions about intelligence as the scapegoat for what may be primarily instructional failure.

While most of us possess similar mental skills (and are commonly classified as average), there are on either side of us intellectually those who are geniuses as well as those who are retarded. These categories are valid and helpful under certain circumstances, but they become stumbling blocks in the classroom when we mistakenly assume that some children cannot learn to read because of the results obtained on an IQ test. The fact is that they can if given the proper kind of instruction. The important thing for the teacher to remember in making reading-program decisions based upon intelligence test data is to *be wary of jumping to conclusions*. Highly specialized testing and training should be sought if the available means do not seem productive, but no child should be prematurely written off because of low scores on standard intelligence tests.

Dyslexia

This term originated in the medical profession in the 1960s as a description of the reading problems of individuals who were unable to perform certain functions with written materials because of a neurological dysfunction (Lerner, 1969). Frequently the term is applied to children with normal orientation problems (e.g., who haven't established a pattern of left-to-right eye movement in reading) which work out in due time. At other times orientation problems that cause children to invert letters and numbers are presumed to be symptoms of dyslexia. Definitions aimed at clarifying the specific nature of dyslexia have led to more confusion. For example, if we define dyslexia as "A disorder of children, who despite conventional classroom experience, fail to attain the language skills of reading, writing, and spelling commensurate with their intellectual abilities" (Gunderson, 1969), we obscure the issue, because many children without neurological problems fail to achieve in accordance with their abilities for other reasons. The definitions are so unclear that the use of the term for labeling reading problems seems curious. If it meant that all children who are not achieving up to expectation would then be provided with special assistance to enable them to achieve, the labeling would be valuable. Unfortunately, this is seldom the case. The term is used to mask instructional failures by focusing on the pupil's disability rather than on a search for program deficiencies.

Labeling may have some value if it gives the child and/or his parents who think he is "mentally retarded" some dignity and hope to realize his problem is caused not by deficient intelligence, but by a condition that can be remedied. The release from their guilt at having passed on "poor material" often enables parents to face a child's problem more objectively and go about securing help. But then the problem manifests itself in these terms: *What do you do to help dyslexics learn to read*? If the means for sending them to a special program, are not available—as is the case in most schools, the diagnosis may only give the teacher an excuse to stop trying. A search of the literature yields a plethora of materials and methods (Money, 1966), but no program. We seem to have a label with no clear referents for differentiating and treating specific kinds of reading disabilities.

Visual problems

When a child fails to read properly or to respond to instruction, the teacher's first thought is often: "He needs glasses." Since reading is a near-point visual task (for sighted people), the concern about vision is certainly logical. Teachers need not be eye specialists to make incidental evaluations of visual functioning; they may simply look around and note certain possible symptoms, such as:

Squinting

Craning forward toward the book or bringing it unusually close to the eyes

Rubbing of the eyes

Such behaviors, if persistent, are sufficient reason for referring children to the school nurse or some other skilled operator of a binocular screening instrument such as the Telebinocular (Keystone) or the Ortho-Rater (Bausch and Lomb). Problems uncovered by such an examination should be referred to an eye specialist. But the curious thing about visual problems is that they are seldom the single causal factor in reading disability (Bond and Tinker, 1968; Harris, 1970). The teacher must almost always assess a combination of interrelated factors if the child is to be successfully helped.

Poor reading programs

Although the term *reading programs* suggests variant approaches to teaching reading, over the last three decades it has come to mean *basal* reading programs. Because reading instruction is so dominantly basal instruction, critics of reading failures have maintained an unceasing attack on the perceived shortcomings of the published materials with which teachers are forced to work. The major criticisms are these:

Too little phonics
Too much meaning emphasis
Story materials too stilted
Paucity of good children's literature

The following list, arranged according to frequency, gives criticisms and publishers' responses.

Attack 1 / Basic code-breaking skills (phonics) are not sufficiently emphasized (Flesch, 1955; Chall, 1967). Chall's criticisms have produced an effect in terms of an increase in the phonic materials content and organization of all the major basals. Whether the phonic emphasis will be supported by improved reading results may never be known, however, because of the necessity to consider the effects of other changes in the reading materials as well.

Attack 2 / Vocabulary controls and syntactical patterns are too restricting and thus result in uninteresting reading materials (Veeatch, 1966; Walcutt, 1961; Trace, 1961; Strickland, 1964). Vocabulary and syntactical controls have changed considerably, and there is now much greater leniency in the materials for the middle grades (Ginn 360 Program, 1969; Scott, Foresman Reading Systems, 1971). The use of linguistic advisors for each major reading series suggests that publishers are now making use of linguistic findings in determining such elements as syntax (word order in sentences) and lexicon (word meaning).

Attack 3 / Story situations have depicted only idealized types that bear no relation to the life situations of many children (Klineberg, 1963). As an initial concession to this criticism, some publishers merely darkened the faces of a few children in the illustrations for reprint editions. Now, however, multi-ethnic editions that depict a wider variety of life styles and situations have appeared (Macmillan, 1965; Scott, Foresman, 1968; Ginn, 1969; Houghton Mifflin, 1970).

Attack 4 / The basal formats are so highly structured that they kill interest (Veeatch, 1966; Hunt, 1967; Chall, 1967). The newest editions of the major publishers contain reduced amounts of directions for teachers.

Attack 5 / The accompanying skills materials (usually workbooks) are frequently of little value in skills development (Doctor, 1962; Black and Whitehouse, 1961; Chall, 1967). Publishers are making attempts to organize skills pads and workbooks in formats rather different from some of their earlier efforts. Whereas before pupils would do a lesson with several skills after a teacher-directed lesson, the children are now provided with pages that more nearly accommodate their particular needs.

Attack 6 / There is very little good children's literature (Klineberg, 1963). In the mid-1960s publishers began to obtain as much of the so-called good children's literature as they could. Guiding this process for each major publisher is a children's literature consultant.

Attack 7 / The pictorial material is so extensive it may actually defeat the purpose of teaching symbolic material. Pictorial materials appear to be as prominent as before in the major programs. In certain programs, most notably the *Merrill Linguistic Readers* (Fries, 1966), publishers have completely eliminated pictures from their beginning programs or made them far less significant (Basic Reading Series, SRA, 1964).

In general, it appears that the major publishers have been sensitive to criticisms of their products and have responded with changes. But the effect of the changes upon reading failure has not been readily apparent (Bond and Dykstra, 1967).

Poor reading teachers
How many of these have you heard?

"If he just gets Mrs. Smith in the first grade, I know he'll learn to read."
"I'll tell you why he can't read. It was the teacher in the . . . ."

These parental hopes and frustrations focus on the teacher. If the child reads well and all other things go all right, the teacher is a good teacher. If things do not go well and the child encounters reading problems, more than likely the same teacher will be blamed. Although some teachers receive simultaneous praise and blame, parents, teachers, and administrations usually have strong feelings about which teachers are the really good reading teachers and which are not. Because these perceptions are quite often accurate, we will try to describe more accurately just what it is that appears to be causing the difference.

Educational research in teacher performance has not provided us with as many answers as we think we would like; we have no quick appraisal form that will tell us the teacher's likelihood of success. Devices such as the National Teachers Examination and the Minnesota Teacher Attitude Inventory are seldom considered useful measures of actual or potential teaching effectiveness. Research begun by Turner and Fattu (1961) was aimed at seeking determinants of teaching skill via the problem-solving criterion. Using situations in which the teachers are given simulated problems to solve, the researchers and a number of their students have carried out experiments in reading as well as in other skills areas (Burnett, 1963; Wade, 1961). The reading problem-solving simulations ask teachers to determine the specific nature of several reading problems and plan practical prescriptive programs. Although far from complete, such leads provide attractive measurement possibilities for the future.

Research results so far have not given us a valid, reliable instrument for measuring teaching quality, but the findings do support these assertions:

1. Effective teachers are perceived as helpful by children (Hamacek, 1969).
2. Teachers' perceptions of children's abilities appear to affect the ways in which they handle and direct the children's learning (Rosenthal and Jacobsen, 1968).
3. If we believe in the child and communicate this belief to him, it is likely that he, too, will believe in himself (Combs, 1965).
4. The good teacher is flexible (Hamacek, 1969). This dimension is crucial for the diagnostic reading teacher, who must be able to explore and examine.
5. Teachers who perceive themselves positively will more than likely be perceived positively (Combs, 1965).

Continuing research into the specifics of pupil reading behaviors in schools and how teachers relate to them should eventually enable us to describe the productive techniques and strategies that are the hallmark of the excellent teacher.

2 The Maple Hill reading program

We have looked at some of the factors involved in reading failure; now let us look at all these elements in working combination. We will do our research in current reading instruction at Maple Hill Elementary School, where 720 children enter some twenty-four classrooms each day in the following configuration:

Grade 1:	Mrs. A	30 children	Grade 4:	Miss M	30 children
	Mrs. B	30 children		Mrs. N	30 children
	Miss C	30 children		Miss O	30 children
	Miss D	30 children		Mrs. P	30 children
Grade 2:	Mrs. E	30 children	Grade 5:	Miss Q	30 children
	Mrs. F	30 children		Mrs. R	30 children
	Mrs. G	30 children		Miss S	30 children
	Mrs. H	30 children		Mrs. T	30 children
Grade 3:	Mrs. I	30 children	Grade 6:	Mrs. U	30 children
	Mrs. J	30 children		Mrs. V	30 children
	Miss K	30 children		Mrs. W	30 children
	Mrs. L	30 children		Miss X	30 children

Reading program materials

A tour of Maple Hill prior to the classroom visit reveals the presence of the XYZ Basal Reading Program, which was chosen from among five such programs offered by the state four years ago. Although Maple Hill could have split its adoption and taken books from each of the publishers, the administration, like that of nearly all the neighboring schools, chose to purchase the single series. The XYZ Reading Series had been in use in the system for some twelve years in earlier forms; the teachers liked it and had built charts to correspond to it.

In addition to the basal program materials, Maple Hill also has supplementary readers, supplemental phonics program materials in the primary grades, and XYZ Reading Laboratories in the intermediate grades, primarily for comprehension skills practice (see Table 2-1). Let us make a quick survey of the reading materials.

Basal program materials

Copies of each teacher's manual, pupil's text, and pupil's workbook have been laid out by the principal for our inspection.

Table 2-1 / Typical reading program materials

Grade	A total basal reading program component		Supplemental readers	Supplemental phonics	Supplemental comprehension
	Readers	Workbooks			
	Readiness	X			
	Preprimer		Several	X	
1	Preprimer	X			
	Preprimer				
	Primer	X			
	First reader	X			
2	2¹ reader	X	Several	X	
	2² reader	X			
3	3¹ reader	X	Several		X (SRA Reading Lab Type)
	3² reader	X			
4	4th reader	X	Several		X
5	5th reader	X	Several		X
6	6th reader	X	Several		X

The teacher's manual / The manual for each text is rather thick and incorporates (1) an explanation of the reading program and its objectives, (2) a set of specific instructions for each major unit and story in the pupil's copy, and (3) a copy of the pupil's text. A close inspection of the instructions for each lesson reveals the following teacher-directed tasks:

Building backgrounds / This segment provides the teachers with suggestions for "getting the group ready for the story." In other words, the teacher is supposed to generate some excitement as well as specific knowledge before the story is read.

Introducing new words / In the primary editions, the suggestions for introducing new words provide the teachers with sentences and notions for getting new sight vocabulary programmed into the children before they encounter the words in the story. In the higher grades, this section focuses more on word meaning, since it is assumed that children will not have too much trouble sounding out the words.

Guided reading / In the early preprimers, the teachers are provided with many questions to ask the children before, during, and after reading virtually every sentence. As the books progress in difficulty, the questions seem to taper off in frequency. Apparently, the strategy is based on the notion that if children do not read things with specific meanings in mind, they will not do much more than look at or call the words.

Oral rereading / On the second or third day with the story, the teacher is directed to have the students reread parts or all of the story orally to determine (1) word recognition skills, (2) specific comprehension skills, (3) intonation patterns, and so on.

Extending skills / This task seems to have two distinct parts. The authors have written in a skills lesson for the teacher to teach at the beginning of the group meeting or at the end before the children work on the given skill in their individual workbooks. The second part of the task, of course, is the pupil workbook task which children take back to their seats for quiet work.

Extending interests / In this section the teacher is provided with directions for building from the content of the story just read in the group to other similar stories. Suggestions for various other books that can be read are provided.

Pupil copies / The pupil copies are in extraordinarily good condition. After four years, it would seem that they would be pretty well torn up and dog-eared. There is not a great deal that can be said to describe the pupil texts for someone who has not seen them. They begin with a series of paperback preprimers that tell the story of a family of three children, a mother, a father, a cat, and a dog. These characters carry the primary action through vividly illustrated materials in the first grade; the stories expand into other areas in the second grade and above.

In the primary grades, the vocabulary loadings of new words are as follows:

Grade	Book levels	New words	Cumulative words
	Preprimer 1	15	
	Preprimer 2	15	30
First grade	Preprimer 3	17	47
	Primer	100	147
	First reader	150	297 + attack words
Second grade	Second reader (2^1)	300	597 + attack words
	Second reader (2^2)	350	947 + attack words
Third grade	Third reader (3^1)	450	1397 + attack words
	Third reader (3^2)	450	1847 + attack words

At the back of each reader, the grade level is given along with the page numbers indicating where new words are introduced. It is possible to see at a glance how quickly new words occur as well as the nature of the words.

Pupil workbooks / Each pupil is given a consumable workbook corresponding with the level of his reader. As indicated previously, the workbook tasks correspond to story units from the reader. Certain pages are designated for testing purposes to determine how well each pupil is doing with a given skill.

Unit mastery tests / In the teacher's file are copies of special mastery tests that are given at the completion of the various units and texts to determine whether or not the child has gained the various skills. At Maple Hill, the teachers write these scores on a record card for each pupil so that each new teacher will know how well the child has done on previous tests.

Supplemental readers
In each classroom there are three or four supplemental readers that are supposed to be within the realm of the reading skills mastered in that specific class. Frequently, though, the supplemental readers will be too difficult or too unrelated to the basals to provide added skill. As in the case of the basals, many supplementals may be readopted every four years or so.

Supplemental phonics
The principal explained that the TVOP Phonics Program was purchased for use in the primary grades because of general concern over the failure of the basals to teach phonics. According to the principal, phonics instruction in the supplemental program was started early in the first grade. Generally found in workbook or duplicator form, these phonics supplements provided seatwork practice for the children. The immediate connection to connected reading was difficult to assess.

Supplemental comprehension
XYZ Reading Laboratory programs were purchased a number of years ago because the materials were well liked by teachers and children. The materials were mainly brief stories written on cards, color-coded, and placed in a large box. The children could individualize their reading by a test that placed them at the proper reading level or color. After determining their scores on the placement tests, the teachers would place the children with the appropriate booklets (usually color-coded in accordance with difficulty level). The principal indicated that interest was not as high as it had been earlier, although some children still liked to use them.

Grouping plans
Anticipating his visit to the Maple Hill reading program, the observer questioned Mr. Jones, the principal, about the grouping arrangements for reading. Mr. Jones' reply went something like this:

Mr. Jones: When I first became principal fourteen years ago, we would simply take all the children's names in a given grade and put them in a hat. I'd invite the various teachers at that grade level to come in and draw their classes randomly from the hat.

Observer: In other words, you grouped heterogeneously?

Mr. Jones: Yes, we did at that time. However, later after this Sputnik

(Russian space achievement that heightened interest in American education), it seemed like everybody was going to ability or achievement grouping.

Observer: Do you mean homogeneous grouping?

Mr. Jones: Yes, where you would take your students and put the most able in one room, the next most able in another room, and so forth down to the low group.

Observer: How did that work?

Mr. Jones: I'm really not too sure. There was always difficulty in getting someone to teach the low group. But I don't think that was as bad as the screams from the parents.

Observer: You mean the screams of the parents of low group children?

Mr. Jones: I mean the screams of parents from all groups. Low group parents yes, but also from the parents of the kids just below the top class. It was pretty hectic.

Observer: What did you do?

Mr. Jones: Well, for the last five years we have grouped the children heterogeneously into their homerooms in all the grades, but at reading and math periods they get up and move to the class on their level.

Observer: You mean a Joplin Plan?

Mr. Jones: Well, sort of, except that only the children in a given grade level exchange within that grade level. For instance, in the second grade, the best readers go to Mrs. E, the next best to Mrs. F, the next to Mrs. G, and the lowest to Mrs. H.

Observer: Is Mrs. H the newest teacher in the grade?

Mr. Jones: Yes, she's a first-year teacher, but a very good one or we wouldn't have put her with that group.

Observer: For the most part, how do your teachers seem to like the arrangement?

Mr. Jones: They seem to like it very much. They say it helps them to plan better for the children.

Observed practice

It's nearly 9 A.M., the time when the children are supposed to leave their homerooms and regroup for reading instruction. Standing near the second-grade rooms, we begin to see children trickling into the halls on their way to other classrooms. We see them halt and wait outside the receiving classrooms. The time is 8:55. As the minutes pass, we see more and more children filling the hall, most of them accompanied by their teachers. At 9:20 the last child disappears into one of the classrooms. The regrouping has taken some children 25 minutes.

The transition complete, we move into Mrs. F's class (second grade, second-highest reading group). After some people and paper shuffling, children hand out readers to each child in the class. Soon, the teacher is in the process of introducing a new story to the group. Some 15 to 20 minutes elapse as the children discuss the situation, use the new words in sentences, and so on.

We then move two rooms down to Mrs. H and the low group, where we find two different reading groups. At the front of the room, Mrs. H is apparently guiding 14 of the children through an oral rereading of the story. Each child in turn reads a few sentences or a paragraph. For the most part there is silence and a great deal of lethargy evident in the group. We listen:

Mrs. H: O.K. Johnny, your turn.
Johnny: (Begins reading aloud) One day where . . .
Mrs. H: There.
Johnny: One day there was someone . . .
Mrs. H: Something.
Johnny: One day there was something—I don't know that word.
Mrs. H: Else.

Strangely enough, it appears that Mrs. H must provide a great number of words to over half the children in the group. The book they are using is the same second-grade reader we had seen in Mrs. F's class; the only difference is that Mrs. H's children are not as far along in the book. Our strongest impression is that perhaps Mrs. H's children are much further along in book pages than they are in skills. After what appeared to be an agonizingly long period of time, Mrs. H's oral group left the circle and returned to their seats to work in the basal workbook. They were replaced in the circle by the other group. This group was even less able; the children were struggling with the first reader they had apparently had last year but still could not read.

Subsequent visits to the other classes and grades revealed minor differences, but still the same pattern of:

1. Children in low groups being asked to do tasks beyond their skills means.
2. Higher-group children doing things that appeared neither to tax nor interest them.
3. General lethargy in all groups, varied only by the personality of the teacher who could generate enthusiasm over anything.

The verdict
This script is enacted daily in the best and poorest schools across the country. Only the names have been changed to protect the guilty. Reading instruction as described in this sequence appears to be a "joyless, mindless existence" for many children (Austin and Morrison, 1963; Barton and Wilder, 1963; Frost and Rowland, 1970; Goodlad, 1969; Silberman, 1970). In rendering a verdict of guilty, our intent is not to chastise individual teachers who conscientiously labor at trying to teach children to read, but rather to

stimulate objective examination of what is going on in the name of reading instruction. Just as teachers should not be chastised un-duly, the authors and publishers of basal readers should not be blamed as the sole cause of the trouble. Often they produce good materials, but there is no way of ensuring that they will be used correctly.

The answer
The responsibility—and the opportunity to change this dreary pat-tern—lies really with the individual teacher. One way of altering the pattern is for teachers to develop the skills presented in this text. Let us go back now and look again at the Maple Hill pro-gram with a critical, analytical eye, and with particular attention to the crucial decisions in terms of reading program materials, grouping plans, and observed practices.

Critique
Materials
1. The decision to purchase a single basal reader (and the one they already had) instead of a combination of readers immediately limited the reading possibilities for the various levels. Using the old, familiar book was comfortable for teachers, but there were then no alternative books for very good and very poor students.

2. The rigid structure of the basal strategy was too compelling, as shown by the boring sessions we observed. The teachers needed to be able to move out of the strategy and use techniques tailored to their children.

3. The "good condition" of the pupil copies indicates lack of use. At Maple Hill, as at so many other schools, these readers were probably passed out only when the children met in the read-ing circle. Conceivably, many of the more able readers could have finished such books quickly on their own if they had been allowed to read them, take them home, and so on.

4. The TVOP Supplemental Phonics program was required be-cause of the pressure of the times; nobody really seemed to know what its effect was on word attack. Many such programs are pur-chased, used for a while, and then pushed back in the closet when the pressure is off.

5. The XYZ Reading Laboratories for comprehension provided some multileveled reading and comprehension checks in short story formats. A heavy diet of such materials without longer and more varied types of reading soon becomes tedious and distasteful.

Grouping plans
1. The principal's explanation revealed a good deal of the his-tory of reading grouping in this country, a circling pattern of

heterogeneous to homogeneous, and vice versa, and the recent combination of heterogeneous homerooms and homogeneous reading classes.

2. The assumptions of commonality on which the various groups were based would not be supported if the children's abilities were closely examined. The reading differences would be greatest in the low and high groups, as shown in Table 2-2.

3. The assignment of groups on this basis gives teachers a tempting opportunity to take the easy way out and give one type of reading instruction for all children, regardless of need. We observed one teacher who had done this as we listened to children struggling to read materials at a grade level that was obviously inappropriate.

4. New teachers or the teacher with the lowest rank or seniority most often draw the low-group assignments. Although they

Table 2-2 / Reading ranges in regrouped reading classes, Maple Hill

Grade	Section	Reading level of pupils in each section	Books in use in sections
1	Top	$2^1, 2^2, 3^1, 3^2, 4$	First reader (1^2)
	High av.	P, $1^2, 2^1, 2^2$	First reader (1^2)
	Low av.	PP2, PP3, P, 1^2	Primer (P)
	Low	RR, PP1, PP2, PP3, P	Primer (P)
2	Top	$2^1, 2^2, 3^1, 3^2, 4, 5$	Second reader (2^2)
	High av.	$1^2, 2^1, 2^2$	Second reader (2^2)
	Low av.	PP3, P, $1^2, 2^1$	Second reader (2^1)
	Low	PP1, PP2, PP3, P, 1^2	First, second reader
3	Top	$3^1, 3^2, 4, 5, 6$	Third reader (3^2)
	High av.	$2^1, 2^2, 3^1, 3^2$	Third reader (3^2)
	Low av.	$1^2, 2^1, 2^2$	Third reader (3^1)
	Low	PP3, P, $1^2, 2^1$	Third reader (3^1)
4	Top	$3^2, 4, 5, 6, 7, 8$	Fourth reader
	High av.	$3^1, 3^2, 4$	Fourth reader
	Low av.	$2^1, 2^2, 3^1$	Fourth reader
	Low	PP3, P, $1^2, 2^1, 2^2$	Fourth reader
5	Top	5, 6, 7, 8, 9, 10	Fifth reader
	High av.	4, 5, 6	Fifth reader
	Low av.	$3^1, 3^2, 4$	Fifth reader
	Low	P, $1^2, 2^1, 2^2, 3^1$	Fifth reader
6	Top	6, 7, 8, 9, 10, 11	Sixth reader
	High av.	5, 6, 7	Sixth reader
	Low av.	4, 5, 6	Sixth reader
	Low	P, 1^2, 2, 3, 4	Sixth reader

may be best qualified to handle them, the pattern of assignment suggests that the low group is something to be avoided. Presumably, the finest teachers should be assigned the most demanding learning tasks.

Teaching practices

1. Although it may appear insignificant, the amount of time spent by children waiting for classes to change can eat into learning time. Some children spent 25 minutes waiting for the complete regrouping. If a similar amount of time were wasted at the end of the reading period, these children would be spending nearly an hour a day simply changing classes.

2. Teaching practices appear to ignore individual differences. The result is tasks that are either too difficult for many or too easy for others.

3. Reading time seems to be greatly restricted because of largely trivial group activities and questionable workbook assignments.

Maple Hill enters the seventies

With the emergence of new reading programs from the major and minor publishers, we might expect a very different picture for Maple Hill in the near future because of developments such as the following:

An increase in the levels of materials that may remove some of the emphasis from using a given book or two only in the grade with the corresponding number (see Table 2-3)

A decrease in the amount of teacher directions for guiding each story lesson and increasing use of annotated pupil editions for the actual guidance of specific lessons

Increased use of visual aids and devices so that pupils can work on skills in contexts other than that of the workbook

Improved assessment tools so that teachers can see individual progress in skills more clearly

Improved materials for home use so that parents can assist children with specific, well-defined reading tasks

There is, however, no reason to expect that reading instruction in the seventies will be different unless there are far-reaching changes in materials procurement policies and teacher skills. Many, many books of all levels must be available if children's widely varying needs are going to be met. The adoption of a single series will not permit the necessary variation. If, however, a wide array of reading books and materials are developed, the most important element of

Table 2-3 / Relationship of Scott, Foresman reading systems to previous reading grade levels

Previous level	New reading system
Prereading	1
Preprimer 1 Preprimer 2 Preprimer 3	2
Primer	3
First reader	4
Second reader (first)	5 6
Second reader (second)	7 8
Third reader (first)	9 10
Third reader (second)	11 12

all—the teacher with diagnostic reading teaching skills—can move into the program and tailor it to individual needs. The thesis of this text is that the publishers' materials are not nearly so important as the teachers who will carefully plan their use.

3 The concept of the diagnostic reading teacher

Reading researchers long preoccupied with measuring the best types of reading programs must now turn to the key ingredient of any successful reading program—the teacher. The message from evaluators is unmistakable: "It is necessary to train better teachers of reading rather than to expect a panacea in the form of materials" (Bond and Dykstra, 1967). But before we can train better teachers, we must determine what better teachers do.

Strategies for developing diagnostic teachers

Although numerous strategies can be proposed for developing highly effective diagnostic reading teachers, two approaches appear basic. The first means would be to go to successful teachers and seek to identify the characteristics unique to this group and logically related to observed pupil success. These elements could then be incorporated into pre- and in-service teacher preparation programs. The second strategy is an interim one that would be built on a logical model of the behaviors that appear to be effective in teaching reading to children of differing abilities and viewpoints. Just as in the first strategy, its merit would be determined using pupil achievement as the criterion.

This text is largely based on the latter strategy, although elements of the other have been used where the research findings are available. The plan for the development of the diagnostic reading teacher offered here, then, is one grounded in a set of logical assumptions and research findings that I have been testing for five years in both pre- and in-service reading programs. This is surely not the only concept of diagnostic reading instruction, but I feel that to report all the possible positions would be to repeat a great deal of information already available in most texts and to avoid giving the teacher the practical guidance she needs for her own day-to-day work in the classroom. Many teachers are frequently just confused by texts that are comprehensive in terms of reporting positions, but vague in terms of spelling out basic guidelines for action. The rationale for the diagnostic reading teacher offered here will become in later chapters the description of the *means* for diagnostic reading instruction *in the classroom.*

Rationale for a diagnostic reading teacher

The diagnostic reading teacher I envision is not to be classified as a "reading specialist" or one who works solely with cases of "reading difficulty" or "reading disability." Rather, this teacher is the director of the normal classroom at any grade level or non-graded grouping. This teacher will work with a wide variety of reading abilities that span the range from "gifted" to "remedial" levels, because it is not at all certain that exceptional children can or should be pulled out of normal classrooms.

Because so much is expected of the diagnostic reading teacher, she must be a person who possesses extensive knowledge and the skill to diagnose, prescribe, and organize. Let us look more closely at each of these prime requisites.

What the diagnostic reading teacher knows

The diagnostic reading teacher knows at what her pupils should be aiming. In other words, such a teacher knows:

The large objective of reading instruction
The intermediate objectives of reading instruction
The specific objectives of reading instruction

Observation of reading instruction often causes one to wonder where the pupils are going in terms of skills. One critic was moved to remark that "education is aiming at nothing and hitting it most of the time." Although this may be too strong a statement, there is certainly evidence that reading teachers do not always really know what kinds of readers they want to develop and the specific skills necessary for such development. Testimony to the lack of skills knowledge is offered by the results of numerous studies of teacher understandings in which both practicing and future teachers have been found lacking in basic skills knowledge (Aaron, 1961; Spache and Baggett, 1961; Emans, 1965; Burnett, 1963; Wade, 1961). Teacher knowledge of the following types of skills (intermediate and specific) seems essential:

Word recognition
Reading comprehension
Reading fluency

A thorough understanding of these skills, their relative sequence of development, and the interrelationships among them permit the diagnostic teacher to progress to the next area—determination.

What the diagnostic reading teacher determines

The term *diagnose* suggests a clinical situation in which a physician notes specific symptoms and then names a specific disease. If you apply this term to reading, you may have a mental image of having to test a pupil with every conceivable type of diagnostic reading instrument, and then to gather the results into a specific definition of the reading problem. The prospect of developing so much technical knowledge and skill may appear staggering.

What we intend, however, is that the diagnostic teacher be capable of making a sequence of relatively simple determinations of a pupil's reading achievement level, his achievement potential, and his prominent skills needs. With increased experience, insight, and reading, the quality of these determinations should improve considerably. Although it is an oversimplification, the following example illustrates the nature of such determinations about 8-year-old Mary Smith, a new third-grader in your classroom:

What is the highest level on which Mary can read with enough skill so as to understand most of the material and not be frustrated? / You may find that the third-grade text is too difficult, and through subsequent checks of her reading in first- and second-grade readers, that she can effectively read the second-grade reader.

What kinds of errors does Mary make in the second reader? / If you find that she cannot sound medial vowels, you might determine that she needs work in this area in order to achieve by reading more accurately.

What is Mary's listening comprehension (potential) level? / By reading third-grade stories to Mary and then asking her questions, you might be able to determine whether or not her inability to read them is caused by her failure to understand them or her inability to attack the words.

Through determinations such as these, the teacher can make intelligent decisions about the kinds of work to prescribe for individual children.

What the diagnostic reading teacher prescribes

Prescription in reading is much like prescription in medicine; several drugs or treatments may be used in the hope that one or a combination may solve the problem. After the prescriptions are applied, sufficient time must be allowed to elapse before we can determine whether or not the attempts appear to be successful. To conclude prematurely that they are ineffective can be almost as disastrous as waiting too long to decide. The teacher can sharpen her timing skill only through practical experience and close observation. The following table gives some examples of the kinds of prescriptions the reading teacher might employ.

Specific problem	Specific prescription
Mary waits to be told unknown words; she does not attempt them on her own.	Employ closure prompts; ask Mary to reread the sentence and try to guess what word belongs. In this way she is prompted to use the context as an aid to diciphering unknown words. Prescribe work on beginning consonants to offer her a phonic clue. Pair these two skills.
John tends to completely ignore periods at the ends of sentences as he reads orally.	Lay a piece of clear plastic or acetate over the page John will read. Tell him you are coloring the periods red with your marking pen (on the plastic to save the book) because they are his "stop" signs. Have him read, using the red "stop" signs. Remove the sheet and allow him to transfer the skill to unmarked pages.
When reading aloud, Tommy makes poor substitutions that do not make sense. He does not stop to repeat or correct.	Ask him to reread the material. Gradually condition the child to listen and think while he reads, so that he will stop and go back if something does not make sense. Also try closure tasks in which he must anticipate what the omitted words are; for example, some people think the moon is made of green_____.

What the diagnostic reading teacher organizes and operates

As a result of carrying out the tasks of diagnosis and prescription, the teacher must inevitably organize the materials and children into instructional matches. In other words, the more prescription is keyed to actual need, the more individualization of program there will necessarily be. Many attempts at individualizing reading instruction are initiated because people want to "individualize reading instruction," rather than because they want to meet the unique needs of the individual children. Although the two may appear to be the same, one is aimed at installing a process and is not goal-oriented; the other is oriented to the needs of the pupil. A program oriented to pupil needs will necessarily be more individualized.

In the final section of this book, the reader is offered a description of how the diagnostic reading teacher begins the move toward organizing her program to meet individual needs. There we will discuss the specific ways the teacher determines what she will do in terms of direct teaching tasks and what she will attempt to install in terms of pupil-managed learning tasks. At the very end of Part Four we will consider a class that has undergone a complete metamorphosis from traditional three-reading-group instruction (or single homogeneous group instruction) to a prescription-based program that fits the label "individualized reading program."

Behaviors of a diagnostic reading teacher

Like the farmer who only farmed about half as good as he could, we sometimes find ourselves teaching below our capabilities. The knowledge we have is wasted if we do not translate it into action. Because our primary concern is action, my intention is that the reader will take away more than a smattering of *knowledge*; he will take away and develop the behaviors outlined by Bloom (1956) in the *Taxonomy of Educational Objectives*: *comprehension* (an understanding of the concepts), *application* (the direct use of the concepts and suggestions with live pupils), *analysis* (the direct use of the concepts with children for the purpose of analyzing needs), *synthesis* (the putting together of observations about a pupil that gives an indication of what to do to help him), and *evaluation* (the constant testing of observations against logic and authoritative sources).

The reader will note a set of behavioral objectives at the beginning of each chapter. These should be read before, during, and after the reading of each chapter as a guide to the content. Although most of the behavioral objectives exercise the memory processes, some involve tasks that can only be accomplished by working with live subjects. It is through such direct contact that the reader will begin to understand the importance of the concepts we are presenting and the nature of the child's needs. If only we could include one live child with each copy of the book, some of our most difficult training problems might be made easier.

two
What the diagnostic reading teacher knows

Most teachers know whether or not a pupil can read, but many do not know whether or not he can locate specific places on a city map, point out illogical conclusions in an editorial, or synthesize the pertinent concepts in an explanation. These are specific reading skills that are often not developed because we are unaware of their importance or of the means to develop them (Austin and Morrison, 1963; Guszak, 1967; Smith, 1963). The diagnostic reading teacher must have a thorough knowledge of the various reading skills, their general sequence, and their interrelationships. At the same time, she must bear in mind the goal of the whole process—to train a mature reader. Perhaps it will be easier if we conceive of reading instruction in terms of three levels of objectives: overall, intermediate, and specific. The overall objective of reading is this: The development of an individual who reads widely and critically in such a way as to solve his problems in a reasoned manner, to entertain himself and others, and to gain a deep appreciation of the joys and hardships of living.

Although this major objective must be understood and sought, it does not provide much direction for the daily task of teaching reading. The means for its attainment are contained in the development of intermediate objectives, which are word recognition, comprehension, and fluency. As the following table shows, each of these major areas contains subcategories.

Word recognition	Comprehension	Fluency
Context analysis	Locating information	Oral
Sight words	Remembering	Silent
Phonic analysis	Organizing	
Structural analysis	Predicting and extending	
Dictionary analysis	Evaluating	

The specific objectives are the multitude of skills that contribute to these categories. Chapter 4, "Word Recognition Skills," presents the host of reading skills that permit children to recognize whole words and word elements. Chapter 5, "Reading Comprehension Skills," spells out the various types of comprehension. Chapter 6, "Fluency Skills," indicates the standards by which we determine whether or not children are learning to read smoothly and effectively in oral and silent reading.

As valuable as skills knowledge is, it can only be translated into results when the child is motivated to want to read. Consequently, we end this part of the book with Chapter 7, "Motivation Techniques." This chapter should assist the teacher in building up her stock of techniques to galvanize reluctant readers.

4 Word recognition skills

Behavioral objectives
1. List and define the five basic types of word recognition skills.
2. Detail the contents of each basic skill type:
   a. Context analysis
   b. Sight words
   c. Phonic analysis
   d. Structural analysis
   e. Dictionary analysis
3. Describe the approximate sequence of various word recognition skill inputs; for example, sight words in beginning reading.
4. Describe the important interrelationships between various skills; for example, the use of context analysis and consonant sound knowledge.

Effective reading requires the instant recognition of words and word parts. Such recognition appears to be largely the result of an intermix of four basic word recognition or word analysis techniques (the fifth, dictionary analysis, is not an instant technique). The sequence in which each of these major skills areas is discussed parallels their normal introduction pattern in most reading programs: context analysis, sight words, phonic analysis, structural analysis, and dictionary analysis (see Figure 4-1).

Context analysis
Context analysis is the skill of using the words and meanings surrounding an unknown word or phrase to determine the unknown element. Such analysis is considerably more than guessing, because the student is narrowing the possibilities by using the accumulated cues. For example:

Thomas: (Reading orally) The boy jumped on his—— (stops at the word *horse* and looks at the teacher for help).
Teacher: Yes, read the rest of the sentence and see if you can tell.
Thomas: (Reads orally) The boy jumped on his (slight pause) and rode away. Horse. The boy jumped on his horse and rode away.

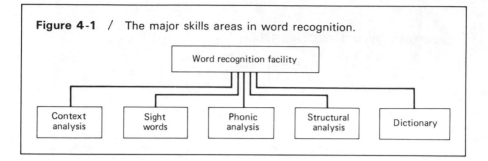

Figure 4-1 / The major skills areas in word recognition.

Children can often continue through a reading segment just as Thomas did and determine the unknown element logically. The process is one of effecting language or thought closure and stems directly from the individual's understanding of the language. Most children develop skill in oral language well before they enter school, and are able to effect closure orally, as shown by their ability to construct sentences with different modifiers, objects, action statements, and so on. If we play games in which they have to insert omitted words, they are capable of making a precise restoration or at least one that is close. When we try to keep them from following a conversation we do not want them to hear, we frequently spell certain critical words. To our surprise—and sometimes our dismay—we find they got the message anyway. Since they cannot spell the words, it is evident that they figured out the word from the context.

When written language corresponds to the child's oral language, it is logical to assume that the child will read such material with greater ease and meaning than he will read material that differs from his oral language. Ruddell's (1965) research provides empirical support for this assertion and further emphasizes the gains to be made by beginning reading instruction with children's own language experiences. The teacher records such stories on tagboard for the children to read after they have dictated them. It usually does not take long for most children to see the point of reading when they relate to it as the written version of what they have said orally.

After children transfer from language experience stories to the conventional basal stories, it is usually apparent that they are using their knowledge of context for word recognition. Goodman's (1965) study of the number of words missed by first-, second-, and third-graders when reading isolated words and words in context clearly reveals the power of context. In his study, primary-grade children could read many words in context that they could not read when the same words were presented in isolation. When we consider how many of our basic words contain irregular spelling patterns, we can conceive of the difficulty of the reading task if sight words and phonics are the major means of word attack.

Although most children develop contextual analysis skill intuitively, some do not because they fail to interact mentally with the reading materials (perhaps because of inattention to the story line, overanalysis of words, or other problems). Such children can be spotted immediately by their poor word substitutions. Teacher prompts can help these children toward greater and more skillful context usage.

In addition to prompting, the reading teacher can provide learning experiences that cause children to use their anticipatory skills. Some of the types of tasks that might be constructed can be seen in the classifications developed by McCullough (1955).

Definition / The descriptive context defines the unknown word. For example, Tom and Dick lived next door. They were_____.

Experience / Children use past experiences to complete the thought. For example, Jack gave his dog a_____to chew.

Comparison with known ideas / The unknown word is compared to something known. For example, you do not have to run, you can_____.

Synonym / The preceding context offers a synonym of the unknown word. For example, when the captain gave up, the crew had to_____too.

Familiar expression / Our language is literally filled with expressions that are meaningful to native speakers but confusing to those learning the language. For example, if he isn't careful he's going to put his foot in his _____.

Summary / An unknown word serves to summarize previous concepts. For example, down the street came the elephants, clowns, and cages. The _____had come to town.

Reflection of a mood or situation / The clouds were black. Scarcely any light came in the window. The house seemed very dark and_____.

These illustrations are indicative of some of the many ways that context can suggest word placement. You may wish to refer to the list in constructing specific context tasks.

The power of contextual analysis when paired with consonant analysis is illustrated by McKee (1966), the principal author of the Houghton Mifflin reading series. McKee's series is geared toward developing these two skills areas concurrently. As Figure 4-2 shows, closure can be realized when all the vowel elements are omitted.

Sight words

The terms *sight word teaching* and *look and say teaching*, as used in most discussions, refer to practices geared to teaching reading

Figure 4-2   /   Realizing closure when all vowel elements are omitted.

_nc_   _p_n   _   t_m_   th_r_   w_s   _   l_ttl_   g_rl

n_m_d   L_ttl_   R_d   R_d_ngh_d.   Sh_   w_s   g_ng   t_   h_r

gr_ndm_th_r's   h_s_.   Sh_   h_d   m_d_   s_m_   c_k_s   f_r   h_r

gr_ndm_th_r.

_n   th_   w_   t_   gr_ndm_th_r's   h_ _s_   sh_   m_t   a   w_lf.

initially by repeatedly telling pupils what given words are. As a rule, such instruction is usually given when the teacher holds up a picture or series of pictures and assists the pupils in recognizing the word associated with each picture. With the exception of a few widely used basal programs—for example, McKee (1966), McCracken and Walcutt (1963)—most such programs initiate instruction by sight word recognition (Chall, 1967). The rationale for this is that it permits students to participate from the start in reading as a process of getting meanings from printed materials. Rather than being forced to focus on fine sound-to-symbol relationships, the children begin reading vividly illustrated pages that contain few words (which are subsequently reinforced through much repetition). New sight words are added very slowly and supposedly in such a way as to provide a basis for generating future word attack. By directing attention initially to a series of words each with a picture referent, the designers of such programs anticipate that pupils will make some type of association between the symbol and its referent. Although the shapes of certain words (very long or very short, distinctive letters) offer total configuration clues, it is difficult to say just what this configuration learning contributes. Most often, it appears that young students tend to use both the shape and the first letter of the word as the primary association referents. When these first-letter learners hit subsequent words with the same first letter and shape, they are thrown for a loss.

Initial sight word instruction usually includes the names of the various story characters (human and animal) and the color and number words, all of which have convenient referents. Because a story line cannot be carried by the picture referent words alone, it is necessary to introduce children to some of the basic action (*come, look, run, jump*) and structure words (*the, at*). Generally, these words are chosen so as to offer a visual contrast with the referent words previously introduced, and the pacing is such that words are reinforced many times before new ones are added. It is undoubtedly because of the importance of the action and structure words that reading instruction has been so largely characterized by the look and say method. These so-called glue words occur so frequently that a mere 220 words constitute nearly half our ordinary reading vocabulary. When we look closely at these basic words (the Dolch Basic Sight Words, Table 4-1), we get an even better idea of why they are normally taught as sight words.

Obviously, if you set about teaching enough phonics generalizations to cover these 220 words, you would be busy for a long while. It therefore seems practical to have children learn to recognize many as whole units, a process that is not significantly aided by picture associations (only colors and numbers have ready picture referents). The significance of these glue words is readily seen in Table 4-2, which illustrates the percentages of the sight vocabulary in school textbooks. In addition to the Dolch list, there appears to be merit in teaching contractions as sight words. It seems sensible for the student to recognize the whole, because there seems to be no consistent explanation of why certain letters are omitted. As pupils discover some of the more unusual spelling patterns, the teacher assists them with the development of generalizations such as the following:

Sight word	Other similar words	Generalizations
black	rack, sack, track, chick	*ck* represents only one sound.
know	knife, knight, knee	In *kn-* the *k* is silent.
write	wrap, wring	In *wr-* the *w* is silent.
light	right, taught, bought	In *-ght* endings the *gh* is silent.
funny	pretty, bunny, witty, marry, carry, summer	When double consonants occur, only one is generally sounded.

By way of summary, most children begin reading by recognizing sight words that normally have picture referents. The recognition task is keyed by the recognition of the first letter. From words with picture referents, students progress to action and structure words. These words occur so often in English that they make up the biggest percentage of most people's reading, despite the fact that they number only a few more than 200 words.

Phonic analysis
Phonic analysis—phonics, as it is most often called—is the system (or systems) in which specific sound generalizations are keyed to

Table 4-1 / Dolch basic sight words

Preprimer	Primer	First grade	Second grade	Third grade
1. a	1. all	1. after	1. always	1. about
2. and	2. am	2. again	2. around	2. better
3. away	3. are	3. an	3. because	3. bring
4. big	4. at	4. any	4. been	4. carry
5. blue	5. ate	5. as	5. before	5. clean
6. can	6. be	6. ask	6. best	6. cut
7. come	7. black	7. by	7. both	7. cone
8. down	8. brown	8. could	8. buy	8. draw
9. find	9. but	9. every	9. call	9. drink
10. for	10. came	10. fly	10. cold	10. eight
11. funny	11. did	11. from	11. does	11. fall
12. go	12. do	12. give	12. don't	12. far
13. help	13. eat	13. going	13. fast	13. full
14. here	14. four	14. had	14. first	14. got
15. I	15. get	15. has	15. five	15. grow
16. in	16. good	16. her	16. found	16. hold
17. is	17. have	17. him	17. gave	17. hot
18. it	18. he	18. his	18. goes	18. hurt
19. jump	19. into	19. how	19. green	19. if
20. little	20. like	20. just	20. its	20. keep
21. look	21. must	21. know	21. made	21. kind
22. make	22. new	22. let	22. many	22. laugh
23. me	23. no	23. live	23. off	23. light
24. my	24. now	24. may	24. or	24. long
25. not	25. on	25. of	25. pull	25. much
26. one	26. our	26. old	26. read	26. myself
27. play	27. out	27. once	27. right	27. never
28. red	28. please	28. open	28. sing	28. only
29. run	29. pretty	29. over	29. sit	29. own
30. said	30. ran	30. put	30. sleep	30. pick
31. see	31. ride	31. round	31. tell	31. seven
32. the	32. saw	32. some	32. their	32. shall
33. three	33. say	33. stop	33. these	33. show
34. to	34. she	34. take	34. those	34. six
35. two	35. so	35. thank	35. upon	35. small
36. up	36. soon	36. them	36. us	36. start
37. we	37. that	37. then	37. use	37. ten
38. where	38. there	38. think	38. very	38. today
39. yellow	39. they	39. walk	39. wash	39. together
40. you	40. this	40. were	40. which	40. try
	41. too	41. when	41. why	41. warm
	42. under		42. wish	
	43. want		43. work	
	44. was		44. would	
	45. well		45. write	
	46. went		46. your	
	47. what			
	48. white			
	49. will			
	50. with			
	51. yes			

Table 4-2 / Percentage of the basic sight vocabulary in selected types of reading materials*

Level and/or type of material	Percentage of sight words
Second-grade basals	68 %
Third-grade basals	60
Fourth-grade basals	56
Fifth-grade basals	54
Sixth-grade basals	52
Daily newspapers	
Front page	48
Editorial	50
Sports	56

*As based on samples of currently used texts and 1970 newspapers.

specific letter symbols (either individual letters or groups of letters). A phonics system can be developed by anyone who wishes to set up a series of generalizations about the characteristic sounds of letters or groups of letters in the language. The term *generalization* is used because it is impossible to design a manageable system of rules that would describe with complete accuracy the infinite sound to symbol relationships of the English language.

Designers of phonic analysis generalizations are caught between the polar positions: That is, the more they strive for descriptive accuracy, the more they are forced into lengthy, unmanageable schemes; the more they strive for simplicity, the more they depart from descriptive accuracy. Table 4-3 represents one effort to achieve a compromise between the polar positions that will provide the diagnostic reading teacher with a manageable and accurate phonics syllabus. The basic divisions of the phonics program are consonants and vowels. As Table 4-3 shows, each major division is subdivided further. In the consonant division are single elements, blends, digraphs, and silent consonants; in the vowel division are single elements (long and short), *r, l,* and *w* controlled vowels, vowel digraphs, and diphthongs. We will discuss each of these in turn in the section that follows.

Consonants
For most readers, the meaning of the term *single* consonant is clear; these consonants stand alone rather than with another consonant. The terms *blend* and *digraph* may, however, need definition.

Consonant blend / Two- or three-letter consonant combinations that produce a blended sound of the component letters; for example, the blended sound of the *b* and *l* in *blend*.

Consonant digraph / Two-letter consonant combinations that do not produce the blended sounds of the participating letters, but rather produce a variant speech sound; for example, the *f* sound at the beginning of *phone*.

Single / Single consonants in the initial position (*D* in *Dick*, *J* in *Jane*, *S* in *Sally*) are important to beginning readers, who fre-

---

Table 4-3 / Phonic analysis components

Consonants				Vowels			
					R, L, W		
Single	Blend	Digraph	Silent	Single	Controlled	Digraph	Diphthong
b	bl	sh	-ig͟ht	Long	r(bar)	ai	au
c*	cl	ch	w͟rite	e		ay	aw
l	dl	th‡	kno͟w	i	l(always)	ea	oi
h	fl	wh	chic͟k	a		ee	oy
g*	gl	ph	bomb͟	o	w(awe)	ei	oo
t	sl			u			
w		qu					
m	br			Short			
d	cr	-nk		e			
s†	dr	-ng		i			
j	gr	-ck		a			
p	pr			o			
k	tr			u**			
y							
n	sc			y			
	sk						
	sm						
	sn						
	sp						
	st						
	scr						
	spr						
	shr						

*C and *g* have both hard and soft sounds. *C* tends to be hard when preceding *a*, *o*, or *u* and soft when preceding *i*, *e*, and *y*. *G* tends to be hard when preceding *a*, *o*, and *u* and soft when preceding *e* and *i* (*cake, city, go, gem*).

†*S* has three prominent sounds: (1) *s* sound in *so*, (2) *z* sound in *his*, and (3) *sh* sound in *sugar*.

‡The *th*- digraph represents two different sounds: *thin* and *then*.

**The short sound of *u* is also produced by other vowels when they occur in unaccented syllables; for example, hasten, charity. This is known as the *schwa* sound and is represented by the inverted ə.

quently look at the first letter as a visual cue to the word. Because they are instructed in the sound values of these letters, children have the additional advantage of knowing the first sounds of many words (175 of the Dolch 220 words begin with consonants).

Because of the high consistency between consonants and the sounds associated with them, most reading programs begin phonic decoding by focusing attention on the initial consonant sounds. After children have become skilled at identifying the sounds of beginning consonants, they are asked to identify the sounds of ending consonants—for example, ca*t*, ca*b*, ca*c*, ca*d*, ca*p*, ca*n*. As a result of such instruction, the reader should be able to attack both the beginning and the end of the word.

Blend and digraph / As students strengthen their associations between single consonants and their sounds, new words are introduced that contain blends of consonants; for example, *bl*ack, *gr*een, *sl*ow. The students are led to blend consonants together, first in combinations of two and then in combinations of three (*spr*ing). At the same time, they are taught the sound counterparts of such digraphs as *th*-, *ch*-, and *wh*-. Because words like *that, there, this,* and *they* enter as sight words so quickly, they may or may not be explicitly told that "these combinations are consonant digraphs and they make different sounds than you think."

After a child has acquired skill in identifying beginning and end-ing consonant elements, his attention is frequently (but not al-ways) shifted to the middle of the word so that he may learn to identify consonants in medial positions; that is, se*v*en, li*t*tle. Conceivably, most children can then parlay a knowledge of the sounds of consonant elements and contextual understanding into a strong word attack. For example:

Th_ _rr_nd G_rl

M_lly's wh_l_ f_m_ly w_s b_sy. H_r f_th_r w_s b_sy w_th r_k_ng th_ y_rd. Gr_ndf_th_r w_s w_t_r_ng fl_w_rs _nd v_n_s _r__nd th_ h__s_.

Some problems / Critics of consonant instruction that does not include vowels suggest that little is achieved by simply teaching a pupil to know the corresponding sounds of consonants. They point out that in order to attack words, the reader must necessari-ly blend the consonant (or blend or digraph) with a vowel element. Only when he does this can he avoid the unnatural habit of articu-lating an extra vowel sound. For example,

Teacher: Now how does this sound (holding up *b*)?
Johnny: Buh.
Teacher: Good. Then what would this word be (holding up the word *bat*)?

Johnny: Buh-at.
Teacher: Good.

To avoid such a situation, Durrell and Murphy (1964) and others believe in asking children to blend consonant elements with vowel or phonogram elements from the very start:

Teacher: This letter makes the same sound as the first sound in *ball*. Now we say the new word as *bat*. (Blends consonant with word element and avoids the sound of *b* in isolation.)

There appears to be much wisdom in the suggestion that students learn to perform the blending task in this way. Not only does it prevent unnatural sounding, it places the student well on the road to using phonics as an attack weapon. Although we will discuss this point in greater detail in subsequent chapters, it is pertinent here to indicate four rather unique developmental steps in phonics usage.

Step 1. Auditory discrimination / The pupil is able to distinguish between the sounds. That is, he realizes that *boat, big,* and *boy* begin alike. This type of distinction must be made with the basic consonants. If *bad* and *dad* sound the same to him, there is little use in working above this level.

Step 2. Visual association / The student can associate the letters with their distinctive sounds (*bad* begins with the letter *b* and *dad* begins with the letter *d*).

Step 3. Blending / The student can take the *b* and the *d* and any other symbol for which he knows the sound and blend it with a known word element; for example, he knows *cat*, so the teacher erases the *c* and changes it to *bat, dat, rat,* and so on, and the student reads the words.

Step 4. Contextual application / This is the real payoff, because now the student uses his previously developed skills to attack unknown words that contain the elements he has practiced.

Perhaps this sequence seems simple-minded, but hours of classroom observation indicate that many individuals neither understand nor develop these skills efficiently. There is often a tendency to become stalled on the first kind of task (auditory discrimination) because it is contained in a workbook. The result is unnecessary amounts of time spent teaching something that children already know.

In summary, it seems clear that the consonant elements should be the primary phonics focus for most beginning readers. The consistency of the consonant sound-to-symbol relationships, plus their great frequency in the beginnings of the most-used words, can leave little argument as to their importance. However, if the greatest attack potential is to be realized from phonics instruction, it is necessary to begin as soon as possible in tasks that require children to blend consonants with vowel elements in such a way as to achieve quick transfer to connected reading.

Vowels
The following are the vowel components (see also Table 4-3):

Single / *a, e, o, u, i* and sometimes *y* are the single vowels. These vowels sometimes represent long sounds and sometimes short sounds. Normally, when there is one vowel in the middle of a syllable or word, it has a short sound—h*a*t, m*e*t, f*i*t, t*o*t, b*u*t. When an *-e* is added to such words, the *-e* normally is not heard, while the previously short vowel becomes long—h*a*te, m*e*te, f*i*te, t*o*te, b*u*te.

Single—r,l,w controlled / Single vowels preceding *r, l,* and *w* often produce sounds that are neither long nor short, but unique. Because they are unique and we have no better name for them, we call them *r* controlled sounds, *l* controlled sounds, and *w* controlled sounds—b*a*r, *a*ll, *a*we.

Digraphs / One vowel of an adjacent vowel combination (*rain, gray*) receives the long vowel sound, while the other vowel is silent.

Diphthongs / Two adjacent vowels, each of which contributes to the sound heard (the vowel counterpart of the consonant blend). Common diphthongs are *au* in h*au*l, *oi* in b*oi*l, *oy* in b*oy*.

Schwa / Schwa is the name given to the sound often produced by vowels in unaccented syllables and is represented by the pronunciation symbol ə. For example, *a* in *about, e* in *taken, i* in *pencil, o* in *lemon, u* in *circus.*

Single / Precisely how to teach children to attack single vowel elements in words requires a number of decisions. Some of the most basic are made in response to questions like these:

1. *Should consonants or vowels be introduced first? Or should they be introduced together?* As we have indicated in the consonant section, the elements should be introduced together so maximum attack transfer may occur.

2. *Should long or short vowels be introduced first? Or should they be introduced together?* Our position is that the short vowels should be introduced first because of their great frequency in beginning reading materials, as well as their prominence in multisyllable words.

3. *When should the vowel elements first be introduced?* Since we interpret "introduction" as meaning the first task of auditory discrimination, we would suggest that parents of three- and four-year-olds attempt to draw children's attention to words that rhyme—for example, focusing the child's attention on words that rhyme with his name: *James, flames, dames, games.* The subse-

quent tasks of visual discrimination and blending should be reserved until the child has at least one sight word referent for the vowel—*cat* for short *a*. The procedure then is to teach the child how to recognize the familiar word part in new words by working with the complete phonogram *-at*.

4. *How should the single short- and long-vowel elements be introduced?* The introduction of short vowels is described above. From short vowels (introduced in phonograms), attention should be directed to long vowel sounds via familiar sight word referents. For example,

rat—rate
fat—fate
mat—mate
hat—hate

The student should generalize the silent *e* rule. After the basic generalizations dealing with short and long vowel sounds (as found in silent *e* words), we would suggest attention to the open syllable generalization, in which the long vowel sound is most often heard —m*e*, g*o*, r*o*bot, r*i*val, r*e*fine.

Up to this point, we have covered three of the basic vowel generalizations in English. More formally stated, they are as follows:

The closed syllable / When a word or a syllable contains a single vowel and ends in a consonant, the vowel is usually short—*at, bit, let.*

The open syllable / When a word or a syllable contains only one vowel and ends with that vowel, the vowel is usually long—h*e*, g*o*, d*e*fine.

The silent (or final) *e* / In words or syllables with two vowels, one of which is final *e*, the *e* is usually silent and the first vowel is long.

Single (*r, l, w* controlled) / These elements are best taught with the same approach as that suggested for the short vowels—namely, the use of a known sight word that contains the phonogram in question. Thus, when the child knows the referent words shown in the first line of each column below, we can build from them to the words that follow:

R controlled					L, W controlled	
car	h*er*	b*ir*d	f*ur*	c*or*n	*all*	s*aw*
bar	herd	third	turn	torn	tall	dawn
tar	nerve	whirl	burn	for	call	law
mar	serve	twirl	curl	shore	malt	draw

Adjacent vowels / Adjacent vowel pairs (which include such things as vowel digraphs and diphthongs) are the real phonic troublemakers. Studies by Clymer (1968), Emans (1965), Burrows (1963), Bailey (1967), and Burmeister (1968) have clearly pointed out the instability of the most widely known phonics generalization: *When two vowels go walking, the first one does the talking.* According to this rule, the first vowel has a long sound while the second is silent—for example, r*ai*n. Unfortunately, when the most-used vowel pairs are studied, it is apparent that this rule holds less than half the time.

Telling the reading teacher that his two-vowel generalization is of dubious value is of little solace to him; what he wants to know is how to help children attack this extremely frequent pattern (adjacent vowels). Thanks to the study by Burmeister (1968) of the phonemic behavior of the most common adjacent vowel graphemes, we appear to have a better attack means. Tables 4-4, 4-5, and 4-6 represent Burmeister's findings and give us indications of whether adjacent vowel pairs act most often as vowel digraphs, diphthongs, or erratics. Although the tables do not contain all the adjacent vowel combinations, they contain those that are commonly found in elementary reading vocabularies.

With regard to the "two vowels go walking" rule, the material in the three tables indicates that the prime offenders are:

1. Four pairs that act most often as diphthongs: *au, oi, oy, oo*
2. Two pairs that act in many ways: *ie, ei*
3. Two pairs normally called diphthongs, but which act more often as something else: *ou* (which most often produces a schwa sound as in *rigorous*), *ow* (which is heard as a digraph approximately half the time as in *own* and as a diphthong the remainder of the time, as in *town*).

From another angle, we can put the exceptions in order according to the first vowel. It seems apparent that the vowel elements beginning with the letter *o* create the largest number of exceptions to "the two vowels walking" rule. For example, *a—au, e—ei, i—ie, o—oi, oy, oo, ou, ow.* We might derive the following two-vowel generalization: *When two vowels go walking, the first one generally does the talking unless it is* au, ei, ie, *or a diphthong beginning with* o. The generalization might go like this if the teacher singles out for separate instruction the diphthongs and *ou, ow* (which he might treat as problem diphthongs): *When two vowels go walking, the first one generally does the talking unless it is* -ei-, -ie-, *or a diphthong.*

Table 4-4 / Adjacent vowel pairs that act most often as digraphs

Grapheme			Phonemic behavior		
Name	Frequency	Pronun-ciation key	Example	Frequency	Percentage
ai	(309)	$\bar{a}$	abstain	230	74.4
		$\tilde{a}$	air	49	15.6
		i	mountain	15	4.9
		ə	villain	9	2.9
		e	again	4	1.3
		$\bar{a}$	plaid	1	0.3
		$\bar{i}$	aisle	1	0.3
ay	(137)	$\bar{a}$	gray	132	96.4
		$\bar{i}$	kayak	3	2.2
		e	says	1	0.7
		i	yesterday	1	0.7
ea	(545)	$\bar{e}$	east	275	50.5
		e	weapon	140	25.7
		$\bar{e}$	ear	49	9.0
		û	earth	31	5.7
		â	bear	13	2.4
		ä	hearty	18	3.3
		$\bar{a}$	great	14	2.6
		$\bar{i}$	guinea	2	0.4
		ə	sergeant	3	0.5
ee	(290)	$\bar{e}$	sleet	248	85.5
		$\bar{e}$	peer	36	12.4
		i	been	6	2.1
oa	(138)	$\bar{o}$	road	129	93.5
		ô	broad	9	6.5

Source: Based on information reported in Lou E. Burmeister, "Vowel Pairs," *The Reading Teacher*, 21, 5 (February 1968), 447-448. Reprinted by permission of the International Reading Association and the author.

Phonograms

Phonograms or "word families" are word elements that contain both vowel and consonant elements to which can be added an initial consonant element:

-at	*-et*	*-it*	*-ock*	*-ug*
bat	let	bit	lock	rug
cat	met	fit	dock	lug
fat	fret	hit	mock	chug
hat	Chet	kit	frock	slug

Table 4-5 / Adjacent vowel pairs that act most often as diphthongs

Grapheme			Phonemic behavior		
Name	Frequency	Pronun-ciation key	Example	Frequency	Percentage
au	(178)	ô	auction	167	93.8
		ō	chauffeur	5	2.8
		ä	laugh	4	2.2
		ə	epaulet	1	0.6
		ā	gauge	1	0.6
oi	(102)	oi	moist	100	98.0
		ə	porpoise	2	2.0
oy	(50)	oi	convoy	49	98.0
		ī	coyote	1	2.0
oo	(315)	ōō	lagoon	185	58.7
		oo	wood	114	36.2
		ō	floor	9	2.9
		oŭ	blood	7	2.2

Source: Based on information reported in Lou E. Burmeister, "Vowel Pairs," *The Reading Teacher,* 21, 5 (February 1968), 447-448. Reprinted by permission of the International Reading Association and the author.

You will note that we have continuously stressed the value of blending consonant elements with vowel elements that occur in phonograms. This should take place after a model word has been learned as a sight word.

Perhaps you have had an opportunity to see reading programs that depend either totally or partially upon such blending tasks for initial reading instruction. Such programs are outgrowths of the thinking of the noted linguist Leonard Bloomfield (Bloomfield and Barnhart, 1961), who felt that children should be taught the systematic sound-to-symbol relationships first through carefully prepared materials featuring phonograms with varying initial consonants. The program, which was based on the alphabetic principle, featured initial story material such as the following:

> Nan can fan Dan.
> Dan ran a tan van.
> Can Nan fan Dan?

Beginning with material on the -an phonogram, the stories add new phonograms with the first consonant varied. Ultimately, the ending consonant is varied, and the students begin effecting consonant and vowel substitutions. Note that students are not taught the single consonants or vowels in isolation, but total words.

Table 4-6 / Adjacent vowel pairs that act most often as erratics

Grapheme			Phonemic behavior		
Name	Frequency	Pronun-ciation key	Example	Frequency	Percentage
ie	(156)	ē	thief	56	35.9
		i	lassie	30	19.2
		ī	die	26	16.7
		ə	patient	23	14.7
		ē	cashier	17	10.9
		e	friend	4	2.6
ei	(86)	ā	reign	34	40.0
		ē	deceit	22	25.6
		i	foreign	11	12.8
		ī	seismic	9	10.5
		â	their	5	5.8
		ə	sovereignty	2	2.3
		ē	weird	2	2.3
		e	heifer	1	1.2
ou	(815)	ə	rigorous	336	41.2
		ou	out	285	35.0
		ōō	soup	54	6.6
		ō	four	47	5.8
		u	touch	30	3.7
		oo	your	25	3.1
		û	journey	22	2.7
		e	glamour	1	0.1
ow	(250)	ō	own	125	50.0
		ou	town	121	48.4
		o	knowledge	4	1.6

Source: Based on information reported in Lou E. Burmeister, "Vowel Pairs," *The Reading Teacher,* 21, 5 (February 1968), 447-448. Reprinted by permission of the International Reading Association and the author.

Phonograms have long been used in other programs to teach children word families. Although the writers of such alphabetically principled programs as SRA's Goldberg and Rasmussen series (1965) and the Merrill Linguistic Readers (Fries, 1966) believe in the value of this type of reading, others suggest that the approach is not sound. Smith (1963) suggests that teachers avoid teaching "family words" because they occur so infrequently in our language. As the basis for her contention, she cites the work of Dolch, in which he investigated the twenty-six phonograms commonly taught in the primary grades as a means of sounding syllables:

This study indicated that the twenty-six phonograms which are commonly considered as "important" corresponded only to 11.6 percent of the 8,509 syllables in a sampling of fourteen thousand running words in elementary textbooks in arithmetic, history, and geography; that 6.8 percent of these were accounted for by the endings *-ing, -er,* and *-ed,* and therefore, only 4.8 percent corresponded to the remaining phonograms. This study implies that teaching the twenty-six phonograms in themselves is of small value. (Smith, 1963.)

While Smith may be correct in her assertion that teaching the twenty-six phonograms in themselves may be of little value, it would seem that if they were taught in such a way that the children could see the characteristic vowel patterns and consonant substitution possibilities, phonograms would be useful as an adjacent program for some pupils. Table 4-7 lists some of the more useful phonograms for an elementary reading program.

Phonic attack plan

It would seem that the best way to summarize the section of phonics would be to offer a means by which the pupil can use the various phonic skills to actually attack unknown words. The phonic attack plan that follows is both an organizer of the content and an actual tool that children should have as they confront unknown words.

Step 1 / Blend the sound of the beginning consonant, blend, or digraph with:

1. The *short vowel sound* of the letter in the middle; for example, *blaf.*
2. The *long vowel sound* when:
   a. There is a vowel-consonant *-e* ending; for example, *blafe.*
   b. There is one vowel and it is on the end of a word or syllable; for example, *be, no, go, bla.*
   c. There are two vowels side-by-side (except in the cases of diphthongs and *ie, ei,* which are likely to be irregular).

Step 2 / Blend the consonant and vowel elements into a whole word or syllable. If you do not know the word, try an alternative vowel sound.

Step 3 / If you still do not know the word, check its pronunciation in the dictionary or glossary (provided you have an understanding of the marking systems).

Structural analysis

A more rapid aid than phonic analysis to word recognition is structural analysis (Table 4-8). Here the student seeks larger structural elements that have corresponding sounds and, frequently, corresponding meanings. Included in structural analysis is morphemic

Table 4-7 / Phonograms

A	E	I
ack all an and ay	e(me) ed eep eet	ick ill in ind ip
ad am at ap ash atch	en et eed eek enny	ish it itch ittle
ade ake ame ane ank	erry ear eat ee end	ied ight ike ile
ard ark ast ave	ent ew ea each ead	ine ing ist ite
aw ace ag age ail ain	ean ear(bear) ell	ice ich ide illy
aint air ait alk ar	ept etter ever eg	ime ink ipe ive ize
arge arm art ate able	eam ense ess eal	ief ies(ties) ife
ange ass aster aze	ead(bead) eck ell	igger ix ift iss
aid airy amp ance	eer elves em est	inger(finger)
aper are arp arrow		inner inter
atter		

O	U
	ug ump un unny up
	ust ut uch uck ull(pull)
o(no) ock od og	urry udge ue uit unch
ot ob ond oo ool	url urn ud uff uffle
oop oot op ow own	ung unk utter
ox oat old ole ook	
oon ose ouch ound	
out ow(now) oy one	
ocket ong oom or ore	
oss other our ouse	
over own(grown) oad	
oast ollar ollow ony	
oor ope ought oan	
ove(love) owl(howl)	
obe oint oise oke	
oodle oth ower(flower)	

analysis, or the recognition of symbols that have meaning counter-parts; that is, plural -*s* as in *dogs*.

Structural units in the first four categories shown in Table 4-8 (roots, compounds, contractions, and endings) are met very early in the reading program. Among the earliest contractions are: *let's, can't, I'm, I'll.* The plural -*s* (as in *boys*) is usually the first ending studied. It is soon followed by the endings -*ed, -ing, -er.* Affixes are usually introduced in the second-year reading material through the teaching of prefixes such as *un-* (*unhappy*), *re-* (*rewrite*), and *be-* (*because*). The placement of prefixes and suffixes in the reading program has been based on research indicating the relative frequencies of usage of these elements. Among the more noteworthy studies were those of Stauffer (1942) and Thorndike (1941).

Table 4-8 / Structural analysis components*

Root word	Compound	Contraction	Ending	Affix	Syllable†
jump in	in to	let's	-s	*Prefix*	in/de/ci/sion
jumped					
	hen house	can't	-ed	be-	
instruct		I'm	-ing	re-	
in					
instructor		I'll	-er	dis-	
		she's	-est	*Suffix*	
		he'd	-es	-ful	
		it's	-d	-less	
		we've	-ly	-en	
			-s		

*Because of the vast number of structural elements, these are only illustrative examples.
†Structural unit containing vowel sound.

Stauffer found that the following prefixes accounted for most of the reading in the elementary school: *ab-, ad-, be-, com-, de-, dis-, in-*(into), *in-*(not), *pre-, pro-, re-, sub-, un-.* In a study of the most common features of the words in children's reading, Thorndike found the following suffixes to be most common: *-ion, -tion, -ation, -er, -y, -al, -ent, -ful, -ity, -ure, -ous.*

A syllable is a structural element that contains a vowel sound. While syllabication is undoubtedly an important skill in breaking up unknown multisyllabic words for attack, there is little certainty as to precisely how readers learn to perform this feat. Even though we as teachers may be convinced that they learn to do so by applying the rules we teach them, careful observation may reveal that the process occurs inductively as they apply previously attained knowledge sets about the sounds of certain structural patterns. The discussion thus points up two very different approaches to teaching syllabication skill. The first approach is that the process will occur naturally; all the teacher has to do is call attention to the structural units as the pupils inductively discover that such units can be tacked together into words. In the second approach, direct attention is given to providing the student with the basic generalizations for mechanically dividing multisyllabic words (visual dividing rules) and the subsequent generalizations concerning the characteristic sounds that can be anticipated of vowels in different syllable positions. The teacher-directed generalization process can be broken down into the following steps:

Step 1 / Auditory discrimination of syllable units. Pupils are sensitized through listening to the distinct number of vowel sounds they hear in a word; for example, ge-og-ra-phy.

Step 2 / Visual discrimination of the structural units that make up the sound units heard. Pupils go beyond the auditory syllable counting of the first step and visually note the structures that make up each of the syllables in ge-og-ra-phy.

Step 3 / Application of phonic generalizations to the sounds that can be expected of vowels in open and closed syllables. When there is one vowel in a word or syllable and the vowel comes at the end, it usually has a long sound; for example, va-ca-tion. When there is one vowel in a word or syllable and the vowel does not come at the end, it usually has a short sound; for example, bot-tle.

Step 4 / Application of the following visual division generalizations. (1) When the first vowel sound in a word is followed by two consonants, the first syllable usually ends with the first of these consonants; for example, bul-let, pic-ture. *Exception*: When the first vowel sound in a word is followed by *th, ch, sh,* and other normal consonant combinations, these combinations are not divided and go with the first or second syllables; for example, moth-er. (2) When the first vowel sound is followed by a single consonant, that consonant usually begins the second syllable; for example, sta-tion. (3) Prefixes and suffixes are generally separate syllables; for example, dis-trust, sugges-tion. (4) The endings *-ble, -cle, -dle, -gle, -kle, -ple, -tle,* and *-zle* usually make up the final syllable; for example, ap-ple, puz-zle.

Although not listed, accent (the degree of stress on a syllable) has an important bearing on where a word is divided and ultimately sounded. In a multisyllabic word, the syllable that receives the greatest stress is said to receive the primary accent. Other syllables may receive either secondary accent or no accent at all. Accent generalizations of high utility were isolated in a study by Winkley (1966). Because of their high utility, these generalizations might be useful to certain children who have difficulty knowing where to accent certain words.

1. When there is no other clue in a two-syllable word, the accent is usually on the first syllable.
2. In inflected or derived forms of words, the primary accent usually falls on or within the root word.
3. If *de-, re-, be-, ex-, in-,* or *a-* is the first syllable in a word, it is usually unaccented.
4. Two vowel letters together in the last syllable of a word may be a clue to an accented final syllable.
5. When there are two like consonants within a word the syllable before the double consonants is usually accented.

6. In words of three or more syllables, one of the first two syllables is usually accented.*

Dictionary analysis

Dictionary analysis as a word recognition technique is seldom used because of the time involved. Nevertheless, it is an important source of word recognition because it provides the reader with an independent means for finding the pronunciation of an unknown word. Most often, dictionary analysis (in a word recognition or pronunciation sense) is equated with the ability to use the pronunciation key symbols of a glossary or dictionary or the phonetic respelling of the word. There is, however, another instance in which young readers can use a dictionary, and that is to use a picture dictionary to identify unknown words.

Picture dictionary assistance in determining words is obviously a limited aid, but it can permit the child to seek out words that have picture referents. For example, (1) Pupil puzzles over word: I want an *apple*. (2) Pupil begins at a section and seeks to match the unknown word with a similar word in the picture dictionary. (3) Pupil finds word and notes referent: *apple.*

By the time pupils develop basic proficiency in reading multisyllabic words, they should be given instruction that will permit them to be independent in the use of the dictionary as a pronunciation guide. Such skill should be transferable to other pronunciation guides in content area books (science, geography). One such pronunciation key is shown in Figure 4-3. It is from the *Thorndike-Barnhart Beginning Dictionary* (1968).

Summary

Word recognition is the result of an intermix of context analysis, sight word recognition, phonic analysis, structural analysis, and—occasionally—dictionary analysis. Context analysis is the skill by which the reader uses the surrounding words for the identification of unknown words. Because reading is mainly concerned with communication, skill in this area is of primary importance. Sight word recognition is the recognition of word units by distinctive features or configurations. The prominence of some 220 high-frequency words indicates the importance of their instant recognition as wholes. Phonic analysis is the systems of word recognition that employ generalizations about the relationships of sounds to certain symbols (as used individually or in groups). Phonic analysis

*Carol Winkley, "Which Accent Generalizations Are Worth Teaching?" *The Reading Teacher*, 20, 3 (December 1966), 224. Reprinted by permission of the International Reading Association and the author.

Figure 4-3 / Thorndike-Barnhart pronunciation key. From the *Thorndike-Barnhart Beginning Dictionary*, copyright © 1968, Scott, Foresman and Company, Chicago. Reproduced with permission.

The pronunciation of each word is shown just after the word, in this way:
ab bre vi ate (ə brē′vē āt).
The letters and signs used are pronounced as in the words below.
The mark ′ is placed after a syllable with primary or heavy accent, as in the example above.
The mark ′ after a syllable shows a secondary or lighter accent, as in ab bre vi a tion (ə brē′vē ā′shən).

a	hat, cap	j	jam, enjoy	u	cup, butter
ā	age, face	k	kind, seek	u̇	full, put
ã	care, air	l	land, coal	ü	rule, move
ä	father, far	m	me, am	ū	use, music
b	bad, rob	n	no, in		
ch	child, much	ng	long, bring	v	very, save
d	did, red			w	will, woman
		o	hot, rock	y	young, yet
e	let, best	ō	open, go	z	zero, breeze
ē	equal, be	ô	order, all	zh	measure, seizure
ėr	term, learn	oi	oil, voice	ə	represents:
		ou	house, out		a in about
f	fat, if				e in taken
g	gp	p	paper, cup		i in April
g	go, bag	r	run, try		o in lemon
h	he, how	s	say, yes		u in circus
		sh	she, rush		
i	it, pin	t	tell, it		
i	ice, five	th	thin, both		
		ŦH	then, smooth		

deals with consonant elements (single, blend, and digraph), vowel elements (long, short, *-r* controlled, *-l* controlled, *-w* controlled, digraphs, diphthongs), phonograms, and silent letter spellings. Structural analysis is the instant recognition of morphemic structures such as root words, compounds, contractions, endings, affixes, and syllables. Dictionary analysis is the use of the pronunciation key (of a dictionary or glossary) and phonetic respellings for the determination of the sound of a word.

5 Reading comprehension skills

Behavioral objectives
1. Define reading comprehension skills.
2. List the five major types of comprehension skills and the specific skills involved in each.
3. Construct questions that measure pupil skills in the five major types of comprehension.

Defining reading comprehension

Reading comprehension skills are thinking skills that are applied prior to, during, and after the visual scanning task by which written language is converted into associated meanings. Pictures, titles, headings, and other elements serve as cues. If the reader is thoroughly familiar with the ideas they suggest, he begins the reading of the material with a much greater headstart, and the comprehension process is triggered before he has read many words. To a great extent, subsequent reading is a process by which he checks his anticipations. He reads carefully to see whether the information contained in symbols confirms, refutes, or adds to his information stock. After finishing certain phrases, sentences, or paragraphs, he frequently reflects on what he has read and then sees a previous meaning in a new way that alters all he has read and reconstructs the meanings.

As important as these actions are to reading, it is well to remember that they could not be performed with out the following elements:

Experiences
Concepts (and the vocabulary that translates them into language)
Language patterns
Meaning cues (semantic)
Skill in holding prior thoughts as new ones are added
Skill in relating experiences and concepts to those emerging in symbols

When you ask almost anyone, "What is reading comprehension?" you are likely to get answers like these: "Understanding"; "getting meaning from the printed page"; "comprehending." "Understand-ing" and "comprehending" do not explain what reading compre-hension is. Who can get meanings from a printed page without bringing meanings to that page? Thinking of comprehension in lump-sum entities seems to explain some of our difficulties in developing reading comprehension skills (Kerfoot, 1965; Smith, 1963). Because "comprehension" or "understanding" is usually equated with "remembering," most of us are satisfied when readers remember a certain amount of the material previously read (Aschner et al., 1965; Bellack and Davitz, 1963; Guszak, 1968; McDonald and Zaret, 1967). But students can remember a great many details and yet fail to make pertinent associations, spot faulty logic, and so on. The following example illustrates how poorly chosen questions can obscure our judgment of the pupil's comprehension of the story.

Pam ran for the ball.
She said, "Come here, Bob.
I can not see the ball.
Look for it, Bob.
Look for the ball."

Alice came with the ball.

Bob said, "Here comes Alice.
She got the ball for you.
Here she comes with it.
Come and play ball, Alice."

1. Who was in the story? *Bob and Pam and Alice.*
2. What were they doing? *Playing ball.*
3. What kind of ball were they playing with? *A rubber ball* (visible in picture accompanying story).
4. Who got the ball? *Alice.*

If the pictures that accompanied this story were included, it would show even more clearly our inability to determine what the child had obtained from reading the printed words. Every question could be answered by a casual look at the pictures. Beginning reading practices often get caught on such lines of questioning (Chall, 1967). In the higher grades, literal compre-hension questions also fail to hit the mark by concentrating on fact remembering (Guszak, 1968).

The situations that cause us to think of comprehension in these terms seem to be conditioned by: (1) the lack of a single set of skill descriptions, (2) unwieldy basal reader descriptions, and (3) a general lack of knowledge of the means for eliciting high-level comprehension skills. Almost every basal series has its own labels for the varied comprehension behaviors, and teachers therefore become confused by the variety. Sometimes the description of reading comprehension skills becomes so unwieldy that scarcely anyone can remember what they all are or why they are important. A prime example is the Scott, Foresman Basal Series (1965), in which some twenty-two basic comprehension skills are listed (see Table 5-1).

Table 5-1 / Reading comprehension skills listed by the Scott, Foresman reading series

---

Identifying the meaning of a word or phrase in specific context
Identifying story problem
Making and checking inferences about what is read
Grasping implied ideas
Anticipating action or outcome in a story
Perceiving relationships (analogous, cause-effect, general-specific, class, se-
    quence, time, place, or space, size)
Forming sensory images (visual, auditory, kinesthetic, tactile)
Sensing emotional reactions and inferring motives of story characters
Evaluating actions and personal traits of story characters
Following story sequence and plot
Recognizing plot structure
Comparing and contrasting
Interpreting figurative, idiomatic, and picturesque language
Identifying elements of style
Making judgments and drawing conclusions
Identifying author's purpose or point of view
Comprehending author's meaning
Organizing and summarizing ideas
Generalizing
Reacting to story content, linking it to personal experience, and applying
    ideas gained through reading
Using aids to memory:
        Association
        Sensory imagery
        Sequence
        Cause-effect relationships
        Size relationships
        Organization of ideas
Achieving effective oral interpretation, including sensitivity to pitch, intona-
    tion, stress, and rate

Source: "Reading Comprehension Skills," from the *Scott Foresman Basic Readers* by Helen M. Robinson, A. Sterl Artley, Ira E. Aaron, Marion Monroe, Charlotte S. Huck, and Samuel Weintraub. Copyright © 1965, Scott, Foresman and Company.

This sort of listing puts the teacher in the role of a recipe follower. Because the comprehension program is so diverse, the teacher's job may become one of following the teacher's manual by telling pupils what to read specific parts for (guided reading) and by asking the questions given in the manual. Neophyte teachers usually follow the directives closely whether or not they fully understand why they are doing so. As they become more familiar with the story content, they tend to use the manual less. Eventually, they seem "to play it by ear"—they impose their own patterns of questions and guidance. The "playing by ear" process can be a definite improvement if the teachers stimulate in-depth thinking about stories and obtain wide patterns of student response. Unfortunately, however, my own research and that of others indicate that the new patterns are often more limited than the textual patterns they replace. If this is indeed what happens, what is the solution to the problem of stimulating improved comprehension?

That there is no shortcut seems apparent; it does not seem likely that a single set of descriptive categories will be universally adopted in the next few years, nor does it appear that any startling new materials will reverse the current direction of comprehension instruction. Nevertheless, it is my conviction that teachers can sharply improve comprehension skills if:

They will thoroughly familiarize themselves with a particular description of comprehension (and know precisely what the observable behaviors of the various skills are)
They will seek to plan questions that call for the various behaviors in a systematic fashion

The most useful structure to learn would seem to be that of whatever basal program is used in the school (if its sequence is understandable). For those teachers who would like to consider the possibility of learning another structure, I would recommend *Barrett's Taxonomy of Comprehension Skills* (Clymer, 1968) or my own system, which is discussed in the balance of this chapter. Figure 5-1 shows this system in graphic form.

Before we discuss the components of reading comprehension, a word of explanation about the organization of the text is in order. Authors of reading texts generally make a distinction between the various reading skills and identify some as reading comprehension skills and others as reading-study skills. No such distinction is made in this text; since all reading is done for some purpose or combination of purposes, our major concern should be that of delineating these purposes as clearly as possible rather than establishing artificial dichotomies between skill types. Thus, in this chapter and

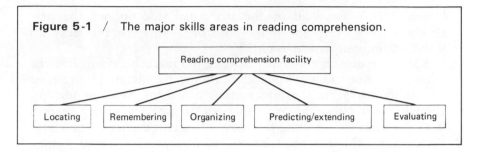

Figure 5-1 / The major skills areas in reading comprehension.

in the rest of the book, we shall focus on the tasks required of the skilled, effective reader, whether he be writing a research report or simply reading a story for entertainment.

Locating information

"Please point to the line that tells us the name of this story," says the kindergarten teacher.

"Who can find the sentence that tells us John is angry?" queries the second-grade teacher.

"Can someone," asks the science teacher, "quickly find out what an aardvark is?"

Questions and statements such as these guide pupils in the use of a multitude of locational skills. That such skills are critical to everyday life is apparent when we consider the consequences of not being able to locate telephone numbers, streets on a map, a special job assignment, advertising information, and so on. Because pupil competence in following both oral and printed directions is implicit in the development of locational skill, we have included this skill in the category of locating information.

Broken down into its major parts, the task of locating information contains the purposes or tasks of (1) locating specifics within written materials, (2) locating information with book parts, (3) locating information with reference aids, and (4) following written directions.

Locating specifics within written materials

These are the skills with which we identify specific conventions of written materials, such as phrases, sentences, paragraphs, pages, parts of a story, chapters, introduction, summary, and so on. A large part of beginning reading instruction is usually devoted to this skill area through the use of so-called setting purpose questions such as the following: "Read this page and find the sentence that tells the day." "Find the paragraph that tells what the house looked like." "Read all of the story and find out whether the children get to keep the money or not." "Where in the story do you first find out that he is old?"

Such questions are designed to give the teacher an indication of whether or not the pupil is understanding the material by tests of his ability to locate the information called for. More important, though, such questions are supposed to provide young readers with guidance for selecting the most important events of the story. Presumably, children must be guided to recognize salient points. Whether or not this viewpoint is valid can be argued. Although there definitely appears to be value in assisting children to outline the main ideas mentally before filling in the details, there is also a need for them to have opportunities to become engrossed in tangents or minor points. These "meanderings" are what give depth and breadth to reading for pleasure and critical evaluation.

Locating information with book parts
This skill opens the door to a variety of abilities we may take for granted, such as being able to use an index or a glossary. The book parts concerned are:

Locating titles
Locating stories
Locating the preface
Locating the introduction
Locating and using the contents
Locating publishing information (publisher, copyright)
Locating lists of illustrations
Locating specific chapters
Locating and using indexes
Locating and using bibliographies
Locating and using footnotes
Locating glossaries
Locating the appendix

Not only do pupils need to be capable of locating these book parts, they must also be skilled in using them for reference purposes that may be as simple as finding what page the next story is on or as complex as noting the dates and sources of the bibliographical references for purposes of critical evaluation. As pupils enter the stage of increased reading of content materials, they must be skilled in the *rapid* use of these skills. In Part Five we will discuss in greater detail the role of the teacher in structuring situations that enhance the attainment of these skills.

Locating information with reference aids
The achievement of this skill broadens the student's horizons: now he is able to use information from numerous sources. Some of these sources are as follows:

Dictionaries (picture and word, used as encyclopedias)
Encyclopedias
Atlases
Maps (physical, political, geological)
Globes (earth, lunar)
Telephone books
Directories
Newspapers
Magazines
Timetables (air, bus)

Using references involves, among other skills, alphabetization skills, ordering skills, and numerical protocols (taxonomies, spatial protocols). If the teacher is not cognizant of the prerequisite skills for, say, looking up a phone number in the yellow pages, she may not understand why some children may not be able to cope with the task. A teacher for example, asked a child to look up the word *precedence* in his dictionary. The child's efforts indicated that he could not go to the fifth letter in the location process and was utterly confused about the second letter. Teacher and pupil time could have been better spent on a more appropriate task if the teacher had realized the child's limitations and the difficulty of the task.

Remembering
As we have already seen, much research indicates that teachers tend to focus on the remembering skills of reading. The results of several studies have shown that teachers allot about two-thirds of their questions to this area (Aschner et al., 1965; Bellack and Davitz, 1963; Guszak, 1966; and McDonald and Zaret, 1967). The point, however, is not the number, but the quality of the questions. Remembering is certainly indispensable for all levels of higher thinking, yet evidence which indicates that many of our remembering questions are trivial leads us to the conclusion that the tasks we set children are not productive of the kinds of skills they need to learn.

Sanders (1966) aptly points out that "the more important and useful knowledge a student possesses, the better his chances for success in other categories of thought." But he qualifies this statement by drawing our attention to three important weaknesses:

(1) The inevitably rapid rate of forgetting; (2) the fact that memorized knowledge does not necessarily represent a high level of understanding; (3) the fact that some intellectual processes are learned only through practice.

Because the retention of certain facts is critical for the subsequent building of other reading and thinking skills, it is imperative that teachers determine the necessary amount of remembering and then turn their attention as quickly as possible to work on the higher levels of thinking (Taba, 1965). Here are some of the remembering tasks children need to master:

Remembering simple sentence content; for example, Dick can run. (What is it that Dick can do?)

Remembering the content of two or more simple sentences in sequence; for example, Jane likes to jump. Sally likes to run and jump. (What is it that Jane and Sally like to do?)

Remembering the factual content of complete sentences and complex sentence sets; for example, specific happenings or titles.

Organizing

Organizing skill emerges from the concept of "translation" as developed by Bloom (1956). The reader organizes when he translates the printed message into a different form of communication—verbal (paraphrase, summary, synopsis), pictorial, or graphic. Although the form varies, the communication remains the same. The reader may well wonder how the first set of organizing skills (retells orally the content of a simple sentence) differs from the first remembering skill (remembers simple sentence content). In substance, there is little difference at this level other than that in translation the child must respond in a parallel communication. The differences in the categories become sharper as the communications become broader in scope.

One of the very important forms of organizing is the pupil's ability to pare a story down to its essentials for an oral or written playback. By observing the child's playback, rather than the replies to sporadic questions, we have substantial evidence for determining his understanding of the total story. Because of the importance of this skill and its accurate measurement, one focal point in a study of teacher questions was to determine how often pupils had opportunities to translate or organize large units (parts within a story, whole stories themselves). The results showed, unfortunately, that the teachers sought such responses less than 1 percent of the time (Guszak, 1966). Conceivably, many children do not receive the necessary stimulation and practice in performing this vital skill, and the evidence of their subsequent skills deficiencies in summarizing and outlining further emphasize the need to remedy this situation. Some useful practice tasks in organizing skills that teachers can use following reading sessions are given below:

Child retells orally or in writing the content of
    A simple sentence (complex)
    A simple sentence set (complex)
    A simple paragraph (complex)
    A simple paragraph set (complex)
    A simple story (complex)
    An idiomatic expression
Child outlines orally or in writing the sequence of
    Sentence sets
    Paragraph sets
    A story
Child reorganizes communication into
    Picture
    Cartoon
    Graphic design
    Formula (boy + motorcycle = trouble)

Predicting outcomes and extending ideas

At the beginning of this chapter we indicated the importance of the anticipation element in reading. Since most of the basal series use picture cues as aids to beginning reading, much of the reading readiness program is directed toward sensitizing children to note picture cues that suggest or tell the story action. The children are then guided toward matching the title of the story with the initial pictures in order to predict what the story will be about.

That prediction is a valuable aid to subsequent reading comprehension is universally accepted, although the use of pictures in the process stirs much debate. Often, however, the prediction becomes a farce (with or without pictures) when something like the following occurs:

Background: The students have read about and see that Dick is holding
    something behind his back. Presumably, they do not know what it is.
Teacher: Now, what do you think that Dick is holding behind him?
Children: (in unison) An apple.
Teacher: Well, let's all turn the next page and find out.

Obviously, no prediction behavior was generated because the children already knew what was behind Dick's back. In order to obtain true prediction, the teacher should ignore suggestions in manuals that elicit simple observation rather than prediction.

Prediction means the ability to anticipate likely outcome, or convergent thinking, which we use in many areas of life as a form of self-protection. For example, we do not attempt to perform feats beyond our capabilities. In terms of reading, we think convergently to resurrect specific facts, generalizations, principles, and laws in response to the printed and pictorial cues we see before us. As we become more knowledgeable and apply such knowledge to the reading task, we begin to gain skill in anticipating the content of a given story, selection, novel, or text. With broad knowledge in specific areas, we can frequently anticipate the content of a book by scanning the contents pages. The rapid reading rates of certain individuals must be largely explained in terms of their ability to pool vast knowledge resources into convergent thinking strategies that enable them to skim the material and yet know the content.

Problems arise when individuals do not have the necessary conceptual (and vocabulary referent) backgrounds for making good predictions. Although the pupil may be able to pronounce all the words with a semblance of fluency, he may not understand the concepts and may experience abnormal difficulty with such material. Content-area teachers must make careful assessments to determine the backgrounds individuals bring to the total educational enterprise and to specific reading tasks. One of the best means for getting this information is through questioning (discussed in detail in Chapter 13), which indicates whether these children can generate convergent predictions from the cues given at the beginning of a story.

For those who have mastered the skills of convergent prediction, the task of divergent prediction remains. Often called creative thinking or creative reading, this skill concerns the individual's ability to envision the unexpected. Those who have sharpened this skill to a high degree are writers and people in advertising. Divergent thinking skills are vital for innovation and problem solving.

The skills components of the predicting/extending comprehension category are listed below:

Predicting convergent outcomes from pictures
Predicting convergent outcomes from pictures and titles
Predicting convergent outcomes from story situations
Predicting divergent outcomes
Explaining why story characters hold certain viewpoints
Generalizing from sets of information in a story (includes the task
    of identifying an unstated *main idea*)
Labeling the feelings of characters

Explaining the operations of gadgets in a story (when such explanations are not provided in the context)
Restoring omitted words in context (close items)

Evaluating critically
Children must be taught the skills of making careful judgments
about the plausibility of an idea, suggestion, innovation, and so
on. Before we can determine whether or not an idea as developed
in any form of communication is reasonable, we must test it
internally or externally. Internal evaluation is the process by
which we test the internal consistency of the communication as
measured by its logical accuracy and the absence of internal flaws
(Bloom, 1956). We study carefully all parts of the author's
communication to discover whether he consistently agrees with
himself, constructs his ideas upon sound premises, and so on.
External evaluation is placing a value on the communication only
after we have compared it with similar communications. We may
check the documented portions of the text, the underlying rationale, and other facets.

There is some question however, as to whether we should call
every judgment an evaluation. Because so many of our judgments
are made without careful consideration, Bloom (1956) feels, and
I agree, that they should be labeled "opinions." Teachers should
seek more than pupil opinions by consistently pushing for internal
or external supports of evaluations. Here are some of the practice
steps to developing the evaluative skill:

Making judgments about the desirability of
   A character
   A situation
Making judgments about the validity of
   A story description
   An argument by comparison with other sources of information
Making judgments about the validity of
   A story
   A description
   An argument by internal comparison for consistency, logic, and
      so on
Making judgments about whether stories are fictional or non-
fictional by noting
   Reality
   Fantasy
   Exaggeration
Making judgments about the author's purpose

Summary
Reading comprehension skills are thinking skills that are applied prior to, during, and after the visual scanning task by which written language is converted into associated meanings. For the sake of simplicity and understanding, these reading and thinking skills are also referred to as reading tasks or purposes. The tasks or purposes are classified under the headings of locating information, remembering, predicting and extending, and evaluating critically.

Locating information includes the tasks of locating specifics within written materials, locating information with book parts, and locating information with reference aids. Remembering skills are fundamental to higher-level reading and thinking skills because specific factual material is necessary for prediction or evaluation. An overemphasis on some of the less important aspects of remembering is a current criticism of reading instruction. Organizing skills or tasks are those that require the reader to translate the contents of his reading into a different form of communication; for example, a verbal summary, picture, or graph. Some evidence indicates a need for greater emphasis on this area. Prediction skills are those in which the pupil uses various visual cues to trigger his associated knowledge and experience to understand the material he is reading. Such skills are either convergent or divergent. Evaluation skills and tasks are used in situations in which pupils place values on characters, ideas, books, stories, and so on. Evaluating is a process in which the reader tests the communication by making internal or external comparisons. Internal comparisons involve the analysis of a communication's logical accuracy and absence of internal flaws; external consistency is determined by comparing the communication elements with similar elements available in other communications; for example, the description of the first shots fired at Bunker Hill as recounted by American, British, and French observers.

6
Fluency skills

Behavioral objectives
1. Describe the relationship between oral and silent fluency.
2. Name and describe the following determinants of oral reading fluency: correct pronunciation, proper intonation, clear enunciation, and proper rate.
3. Describe the principles pertinent to the teaching of oral fluency.
4. Name and describe the determinants of silent reading fluency.
5. Describe the principles pertinent to the teaching of silent fluency.

When reference is made to a pupil's reading fluency, some judgment is usually being made about the relative degree of "smoothness" with which he reads aloud; seldom is the term *fluency* used to describe the same pupil's silent reading, because we obviously cannot hear it. For the purpose of our reading program, however, it is important to deal with descriptions of both oral and silent reading fluency. Often, a failure to give both equal attention has resulted in readers who may lack skill in one or the other. Thus, in the following sections we will treat in turn the relationships between oral and silent fluency, oral reading fluency, and silent reading fluency.

The relationship between oral and silent fluency
Although this section concerns the relationship between oral and silent reading fluency, the first basic relationship concerns oral language and reading. The old adage that "reading is simply talk written down" seems appropriate here, because we can transcribe children's spoken sentences into their symbol counterparts (Chapter 4). As a result of the transcription, children see that, for example:

Their sentences can be read back orally.
Symbols are grouped together to represent words.

These symbol groups (words) are read in a sequence that proceeds in the same direction across a line.
Little dots (periods) tell you when to stop momentarily.

Because oral language is the base for the "talk that is written
down," it is advantageous if the teacher can utilize the children's
own sentences and allow them to learn the tricks of playing
back their own words, since these will be the most meaningful
materials for them.

In the initial stages of reading instruction, oral reading seems
to be important because of the auditory reinforcement. As we
shall discover in the next section, many cues must be resurrected
from an imperfect reading product; we often find ourselves reading particularly difficult elements aloud in an effort to clarify
the meaning. As soon as students build up a small stock of
instantly recognizable words (preferably through reading their
own stories), they should be asked to read certain sentences and
stories silently. The development of silent reading should begin
in the first grade, even though it often appears that children
have difficulty doing this with proficiency at that level. They
seem to need the auditory reinforcement in order to retain what
they read. The teacher's handling of individual situations can be
extremely crucial because (1) If complete dependence on auditory reinforcement is permitted (presuming the student is reading
at a very easy level—no word recognition or basic comprehension
problems), the student is likely to become a handicapped silent
reader. (2) If the emphasis on silent reading is premature and the
student is denied the auditory reinforcement, he may also become
a handicapped reader.

Unfortunately, it is difficult to give the exact level at which
the shift in emphasis from oral to silent reading should be
effected. The prime elements are the pupil's word recognition
and comprehension facility, his reading purpose, and background
for the material. If the teacher is knowledgeable about these variables, he should be able to recognize the opportune time for
shifting emphasis. Although normative data does not necessarily
tell us what behaviors should be expected, they can give us some
indications of what exists. In the area of oral and silent fluency,
the common denominator appears to be rate. Table 6-1 shows
one such set of minimal norms developed by McCracken (1966).
At first glance, McCracken's minimum speed suggestions appear
reasonable for the first five grades, but the silent reading expectations after that seem at rather great odds with other such measures
(Spache, 1963; Taylor et al., 1960). Spache's research for the
diagnostic reading scales indicates an average sixth-grade rate

Table 6-1 / Suggested minimum speeds of reading
in basal readers, grades 1 to 7 and above

Grade	Oral*	Silent*
1	60	60
2	70	70
3	90	120
4	120	150
5	120	170
6	150	245
7 and above	150	300

Source: R. McCracken, "The Informal Reading Inventory as a Means of Improving Instruction," in *The Evaluation of Children's Reading*, ed. T. Barrett (Newark: International Reading Association, 1967), p. 85. Reprinted with permission of International Reading Association and the author.
*Words per minute.

varying between 138 to 175 words per minute. Taylor and his associates in their work on the controlled reader found an average slightly higher than Spache's of 185 words per minute.

The relative patterns of oral and silent reading in the various grades are especially interesting. Seemingly, there is no difference at all in the first and second grades, and only a 10-word-per-minute rate increase between the oral and silent minimums. In the third grade, a rather significant increase is noted in both dimensions, but especially in the silent reading rate (120 words per minute, which nearly doubles the rate of the previous year). From the fourth through the seventh grade, the oral rate increases only 60 words per minute, whereas the silent rate increases to the point where 300 words a minute can be read. The McCracken figures also show the increasing speed of silent reading at the third-grade level, which is supposedly due to an increase in the eye-voice span (the ability of the skilled reading eye to travel much faster than the voice, which generally does not exceed 180 words per minute). Although it is certainly reasonable to explain the logic of permitting the well-trained eye the freedom to move ahead of the voice, there is no certainty as to what the skill level determinant should be.

Oral reading fluency
A pupil is judged to be reading fluently when his oral reading is characterized by the correct pronunciation of words, proper intonation, clear enunciation, adequate volume, and appropriate

rate. Of course, the fluency rating depends largely on the quality criteria established by the specific judge. If the criteria are too stringent, both teacher and child may experience unpleasantness and disappointment; if the criteria are too liberal, the student may be moved ahead more rapidly than is desirable for his reading skills growth.

Correct pronunciation

Oral fluency cannot and should not be expected in materials where the student does not know nearly every word instantly; not only should most words be known or easily attacked, but the student should have had a previous opportunity to read the material. Oral fluency is the frosting on the cake. That is, it cannot be expected until after the reading foundation is constructed. To emphasize fluency before the underlying word recognition skills are developed is tantamount to frosting the cake while it is still in the oven. In Chapter 9 the reader will be given more information concerning the types of word recognition or pronunciation errors that are vital to fluency facility.

Proper intonation

Although we have said that "reading is just talk written down," that is not precisely accurate. In our system of transcription we are not able to pick up such things as the precise intonation or feeling with which it was spoken. For example, when we read "This is a ball game," we do not know whether a university student is explaining to a foreign student what is happening, an excited fan is proclaiming that this is indeed a terrific ball game, or an unhappy fan is questioning whether such a debacle is a ball game at all. Intonation as well as facial expression might tell us. The importance of intonation is illustrated in the following passage:

Anyone who listens carefully to a segment of speech will hear not merely a stream of sounds but also the tune, the intonation pattern—the pauses between sentences or between major syntactic units within a sentence, often accompanied by a rising or falling of the voice, a change in pitch. Such pauses are known as terminal junctures. The listener also will observe stresses ranging from weakest to primary on different syllables and slight, almost imperceptible, pauses between words and between meaningful parts of words. These prosodic patterns are not mere ornament; they mark syntactic structures. (Newsome, 1964, p. 8)

The elements of intonation are junctures and terminals, pitch, and stress. We will discuss each in turn.

Junctures and terminals / A number of pauses in speech serve as signals to the listener. In the English language, there are four classes of junctures and terminals: open juncture, level juncture, and rise and fall terminals. *Open* juncture indicates the slightest interruptions that occur between some syllables within words and between words. Such breaks make it possible for us to separate distinct word elements auditorily. Certain speakers may be difficult to understand because they tend to run certain syllables and/or words together. Note how the junctures are necessary for understanding the following sentence: "The unit was not inactive, but rather in active pursuit." *Level* juncture describes the slight pause between parts of an utterance that does not require a rise or falling off in pitch (as in the preceding illustration).

Fade-rise terminals are the speech signals that terminate most questions; for example:

When are you leaving?   /———▸/

In reading orally, the reader must pick up the syntactic clue that he should raise the pitch in advance of meeting the question mark.

Fade-fall terminals are the most common concluding intonational pattern, because they signal the end of declarative statements; for example:

We are leaving at dawn.   /———▸ /

Pitch / Pitch describes four discrete sound ranges of spoken language. Ranging from the lowest to the highest relative sound, the four levels are designated as follows:

Levels	Usual code
Low	1
Normal	2
High	3
Highest	4

The pitch contours of speech can be graphically illustrated. Because pitch changes characterize fade-rise and fade-fall terminals, the examples given in the preceding section are repeated here with pitch contours added:

2 —— —— - ——   fade-rise
When did it happen?   /———▸/

2- —— ———— ——   fade-fall
We are leaving at dawn?   /——▸/

Normally, most sentences are initiated at the level 2 (normal) range. As you can see in the examples above, the meaning is indicated by the linguistic intonational signals. If we were to reverse the patterns, the meanings would be changed.

Stress / Stress is the amount of emphasis placed on syllables or words. There are four levels of stress: heavy, medium, light, and weak. Stress, like juncture and pitch, may be represented by punctuation, but often it is indicated by underlining or italicizing a particular word.

It is *nearly* summer time.
It is nearly *summer* time.

Clear enunciation

Enunciation is the clarity with which pupils articulate the various segmental phonemes (speech sounds). When teachers spend great amounts of time in trying to correct the enunciation patterns conditioned by environment, larger reading goals can suffer. Enunciation errors are often scored as reading errors (Rudorf, 1968), even though meanings may be undisturbed; for example, the child of Mexican-American descent may read *share* for *chair*. Teachers should ascertain whether students are getting the meaning and avoid labeling enunciation errors as reading errors.

Proper oral rate

Proper rate is a variable that depends upon pupil skills, selection difficulty, and many other variables. It does seem reasonable, however, to expect performance in generalized terms (when students are reading expository materials in basals and supplementaries). Table 6-2 gives some generalized norms developed by McCracken (1966).

Table 6-2 / Suggested minimum speeds of oral reading in basal readers, grades 1 through 7

Grade	Words per minute
1	60
2	70
3	90
4	120
5	120
6	150
7	150

Source: R. McCracken, "The Informal Reading Inventory as a Means of Improving Instruction," in *The Evaluation of Children's Reading*, ed. T. Barrett (Newark: International Reading Association, 1967), p. 85. Reprinted with permission of the International Reading Association and the author.

Principles for teaching oral reading fluency

Teaching efforts aimed at improving oral reading fluency should be based on the following principles:

Principle 1 / Fluency is the product of an intermeshing of many elements. If any one of these factors (as well as others) presents a difficulty, the student will not achieve fluency.

Individual skill in word recognition
Individual comprehension of the selection
Familiarity with the selection concepts
Individual speech patterns (phonemic and syntactic)
Individual anxiety at the time

Principle 2 / Fluency determinations must utilize flexible criteria. It is unfair to establish the same enunciation criteria for varying dialects. Similarly, it is unfair to expect all children to read at the same rate or with similar pronunciation skill (word recognition). Some of the best silent readers are poor oral readers because they process thoughts faster than they process individual words. The minimal rate criteria (as developed by McCracken) should be coupled with an estimate of the pronunciation deviations in reaching a judgment of fluency. Pronunciation deviations that do not adversely affect meaning should be considered reasonable and allowable.

Principle 3 / Fluency practice is most appropriate in materials that pose few word recognition and comprehension problems. This principle underlies the almost universal basal practice of silent reading before oral reading. The silent preview should solve problems that might interfere with oral fluency.

Principle 4 / Oral reading fluency should not be equated with the precise pronunciation of every word. More fluent readers usually have to make additions and minor substitutions. Such deviations should not alter meanings, however.

Principle 5 / Oral reading fluency is not one of the primary goals of reading instruction. Although one might think otherwise from observation, oral reading fluency is quite unimportant when compared to thinking behaviors.

Principle 6 / Overemphasis on oral fluency can result in handicapped readers. That is, readers may not be able to free themselves from the word-by-word emphasis of oral reading to be able to apply various comprehension sampling techniques and skills.

Silent reading fluency

Silent reading fluency is the efficiency with which silent reading tasks can be accomplished. Efficiency must be measured in terms of both product quality and speed of production; both comprehension and rate standards must be established for various tasks. For example, *task*: read a 400-word selection in two minutes; *comprehension standard*: correctly answer 7 of 10 questions; *reading rate standard*: read at a rate of 200 words per minute.

The student is tested initially on the comprehension standard. If he answers less than seven questions correctly, no judgment of silent fluency can be made. If, however, he answers the seven questions correctly after reading the selection in one minute, we can assume a rate of 100 words per minute. Because the fluency criterion called for 200 words per minute, the student did not reach the standard. It is necessary, of course, to know more in order to evaluate the standard of 200 words per minute. For example, what was the difficulty level of the material? What was the reading skill level of the student? What is an appropriate fluency expectation for students at this level with reading materials of the given level? If the student has been a third-grade-level reader and the material is rather normal third-grade expository material, we would (in looking at McCracken's rate norms for third grade) judge the performance as satisfactory. If, however, the student was a sixth-grade-level reader who was reading third-grade material, we would be rather unhappy with the rate.

Principles for teaching silent reading fluency

Principle 1 / Fluency is the product of an intermeshing of many elements. Silent fluency requires the same skills as oral fluency with the exception of the articulation components. Thus, if the student cannot solve unknown word forms and understand certain concepts and syntactic patterns, he will probably not attain substantial comprehension and speed.

Principle 2 / Fluency is directly affected by the reading tasks or purposes, the reader's background, the format and nature of the material, and the reader's motivation. Because of the complex operation of these variables, we will see a wide range of performance levels in fluency on various occasions with variant materials. When the material is familiar and well received, we may see total comprehension and rapid rate. Conversely, with less familiar materials we may see poor comprehension and speed.

Principle 3 / Because silent fluency is such a prominent goal of the reading program, its development should be stressed in many contexts. Students should be taught to vary their rates in accordance with comprehension tasks (see Table 6-3). Such variance may range from very low rates (for high comprehension) in concept-loaded selections to very rapid rates (for main points) in materials that can be digested rapidly.

Summary

Fluency is broadly defined as the "smoothness" of both oral and silent reading. Judgments of the smoothness of oral reading are based on pronunciation, enunciation, intonation, and rate; judgments of the smoothness of silent reading are based on varying rate standards that are applied after specific comprehension criteria are met.

Because oral language is primary, oral reading normally comes

Table 6-3 / Possible silent fluency goals

Task	Grade	Rates*
Expository reading	2	70
Expository reading	3	90
Remembering details	3	80
Locating specifics	3	100
Expository reading	4	120
Remembering details	4	100
Locating specifics	4	150
Preview	4	200

*Words per minute.

first. As their skill increases, children are able to subdue oral responses and move their eyes more quickly than their tongues. Decisions as to when to change the emphasis from oral to silent reading are difficult to make using arbitrary grade standards; they must be made on other bases.

Principles for teaching oral and silent reading indicate the ultimate primacy of the silent reading skill. They also show that both oral and silent reading fluency skills are a complex intermesh of skills, backgrounds, attitudes, purposes, speech patterns. The teacher must therefore establish different criteria to take these factors into account in given situations.

7 Motivation techniques

Behavioral objectives
1. Define motivation.
2. Describe the potential influence of the boredom drive on reading motivation.
3. Describe the influence of learned drives on reading motivation in terms of preschool and in-school motivators.
4. Give suggested changes for the competitive motivation system employed in graded and ability-grouped school programs.
5. Give specific techniques for fostering motivation in terms of
    Building positive self-concepts
    Assisting realistic goal setting
    Establishing listening sets
    Creating self-instructional attitudes
    Planning tangible rewards reinforcement

Every day we see children who seem to be able to turn themselves on to reading while others seem totally indifferent. What influences condition such different responses? What can be done to stimulate the disinterested?

There are no simple answers, but as we learn more about some of the elements involved, it will be possible to establish more effective motivation techniques—techniques that result in "the initiation and direction of behavior" (Moskowitz and Orgel, 1969).

The motivation process
Every response that we make is motivated by a reflex action, instinctive behavior, physiological drive, or learned drive. Because of the vast and complex nature of the subject, our discussion will center upon one aspect, learned drives.

The boredom drive
In recent years, psychologists (Fowler, 1965) have recognized boredom as a major drive in animals and humans. The so-called boredom drive seeks to explain our basic need for sensory stimula-

tion. Given the constant jangle of transistor radios, television sets, piped-in music, and other media, it seems apparent that we do have such fundamental appetites. Reading, however, is only one among many media that can satisfy that appetite, and it appears to be losing ground (Gallup Poll, 1968). There are even some who question whether it will be necessary in the future. From our vantage point, it seems that reading will always be a critical vocational skill as well as a sensory stimulation. When one thinks about the boredom drive and its motivating effect on reading behavior, the example of the physician's waiting room comes readily to mind. Trapped in such a boring environment, our only immediate means of stimulation are the reading materials placed in the room.

The USSR (Uninterrupted Sustained Silent Reading) program described by Hunt (McCracken, 1969) seems in part attributable to the need for sensory stimulation. Prepared as they are to sit quietly and sustain themselves with a given piece of reading material for a given segment of time, the children in the program have little access to outside stimulation apart from their reading materials. It seems logical that they would focus their attention on the materials to the point that they would become more adept at obtaining both stimulation and meaning from them. Although the prospect of forcing behavior in this way may be unappealing, it may be that such behavior formation is needed in a multimedia world that presents fewer and fewer reading models (mothers and dads, brothers and sisters) in the home. Extensive experimentation and research in this area seems eminently justified. This may turn out to be a legitimate way of "getting hooked on books" (Fader and McNeil, 1968).

Learned drives

Because most of our physiological drives are easily satisfied, learned or acquired drives assume greater importance in prompting behaviors. Drives for tangible goods, affection, self-esteem, prestige, and status result in continuing incentives that motivate us. Strong drives for tangible goods make the accumulation of money important. Because our drives are usually directed not toward the money itself, but rather toward what it can buy, the acquisition of money is an incentive. We frequently see pupils and workers alike pursuing the incentives of money or grades while they may have no interest in the development of specific skills or products.

Conversely, we see other people totally engrossed in their vocations or tasks to the point where they appear indifferent to the acquisition of money and the goods it can purchase. Often referred to as "intrinsically motivated" individuals, these people are seeking goals of affection, self-esteem, recognition. That such goal-directed, learned drives are important is self-evident. In this chapter we will see how some learned drives condition pupils to respond to reading instruction as a result of preschool and in-school influences.

Preschool motivators of reading behavior

Young children's power to initiate and direct experiences with books is closely related to their observation of book-reading models (usually parents and siblings), the availability of books, and a number of other factors. The book-reading family is a highly conducive situation for acquiring a drive toward reading, but such environmental circumstances are not easily simulated. Illustrated books can be effective starters of reading interest. One can watch children of all ages paging carefully through the vivid images in Richard Scarry's (1963, 1966) series of picture books. Many children get hooked on books initially through beautifully illustrated picture books as well as through pleasing experiences with both sight and sound like those in the Dr. Seuss books (1957, 1960). The importance of reading is often communicated through the warm relationships that exist between parents and children as the parent reads to the child. Not only does the child have access to greater sensory stimulation, he also has access to a relationship that provides much satisfaction for his affective needs.

While the values of parent reading models, visually stimulating reading materials, and parents reading to children have been proved, it unfortunately remains true that:

Most adults don't read a book a year (Gallup Poll, 1968).
Many parents seldom, if ever, read to their children.
Relatively few children use library facilities.
Relatively few children participate in story-telling programs.
School library facilities are too often inaccessible or inadequate.
Reading takes a back seat to television and nearly every other form
    of leisure time activity.

Perhaps the strongest hope for preschoolers lies in the development of preschool and television programs to stimulate children's curiosity through story-telling situations that will trigger independent followups. Programs such as *Sesame Street* (Children's Workshop, 1969) and *Captain Kangaroo* (Columbia Broadcasting System) seem to be worthwhile starts toward constructive uses of television.

In-school motivators of reading behaviors

Traditionally, schools have utilized a variety of specific motivators, such as:

Grades (designed to reward or punish ego)
Promotion or retention (designed to threaten, reward, punish)
Symbols (such as gold stars to reward or punish ego)
Praise and criticism (designed to verbally reward or punish ego)

In all these techniques, the emphasis is on the pupil's need for affection and self-esteem. To achieve them, the pupil must initiate and direct his behavior toward reading goals, and he must do these things *in competition with the other children in the class.* The child suffers his first setback (or attains his first reward) when the reading groups are formed in the first year of school. If he is placed in the lowest group, he has failed badly. If he is placed in the middle group, the failure is not so bad because there are others who are poorer. Top group placement means success. As reading instruction progresses within groups and the distance between the best and the poorest readers increases, the poor readers suffer further attacks on their needs for affection and self-esteem by drawing both verbal and nonverbal punishment (verbal correction of mistakes, low grades on report cards, and the condescending looks and actions of the better performers). Although many teachers provide verbal reward where possible to the low-achievement students, the system has already made it clear to such a child that he is a failure. The graded system operates almost totally in a competition system that largely preordains success or failure in accordance with ability.

Necessary changes in the system

Although such changes will be discussed in greater detail in the last section of the book, it is my opinion that motivational patterns cannot be significantly altered until the following steps are taken:

1. Graded schools are changed to truly nongraded schools in which the negative motivators of grade failure and unbalanced competition are removed.
2. Reading groups are constructed according to individual pupil skills need and are not an arbitrary division into three reading groups.
3. Competition is centered on the individual and his attainment of personalized reading goals.
4. Praise and criticism are measured in accordance with the individual's attainment of his personalized goals.

5. Tangible rewards are based on the individual's attainment of his personalized goals.

Truly nongraded schools do not simply produce alternate graded structures (nine reading levels instead of three), but rather provide skills sequences that are adapted to individual pupils. Thus, labels and single adoptions are eliminated, and in their place a wide variety of reading materials is assembled. Reading groups are necessarily small because pupils' needs are different. As needs are met, the composition of groups can actually change, whereas they seldom do in the three-reading-group system. Competition is based on the individual's attainment of certain well-marked goals. Sustaining the competition is the student's perception of delayed reward, which may be teacher praise, promotion, and so on.

Techniques for fostering motivation
As social creatures, most children already have "self-initiating and directing behaviors" going for them. It is our task to foster their full development by:

Building positive self-concepts
Assisting realistic goal-setting behaviors
Establishing listening sets
Creating self-instructional attitudes
Planning tangible rewards reinforcement

Building positive self-concepts
"The children who come to the reading clinics are, almost without exception, unable to read because they believe they cannot read" (Combs, 1965). Children believe they cannot read because they experience a string of failures in their reading instruction. Although, as we shall see later, much of this is due to inappropriate reading placement, assignments, and pacing, there are other things we inadvertently do that condition such feelings. We can correct much of the damage or prevent it initially in the following ways:

Step 1 / Praise the child's efforts and accomplishments generously, and allow opportunities for delayed reinforcement as the child develops. Praise is essential to the development of a positive self-concept, which in turn permits good mental health and an openness to learning. Ginott (1965) feels that such praise should always be centered on the child's efforts and accomplishments, rather than upon his personality or character. According to Ginott, saying "You're really a good boy" may make the child feel insecure when he feels that he does not measure up to the praise. Presumably, through praise of his efforts he can draw his own conclusions about his worth.

Step 2 / Avoid criticism that reflects on the personality of the individual.

Statements such as "Are you going to be a baby all your life?" or "Why don't you ever listen?" attack the child and cause him to wonder about his worth.

Step 3 / Criticism can be useful to the child if it focuses on what has to be done and omits negative innuendos about the child himself. This is easy to say and difficult to do, but it is done by effective teachers and parents who ease the child's tensions and self-doubts by attacking the problem rather than the child. For example, *Teacher*: (noticing that Jack is stuck) "This one is really tough. Now let's see what we can find out about it. What is the first thing that we might try?" Such followup requires time and patience, but that is the whole idea of teaching. If we cannot follow up in careful, patient ways, perhaps criticisms should not be given.

Assisting realistic goal setting
The affection and praise of the teacher, while extremely powerful in the motivation process, will not afford sufficient satisfaction if the child perceives no challenge in the task or senses great frustration. Thus, one of the most important teaching behaviors concerns assistance to the child in establishing realistic short- and long-term goals. Realistic goals are those the child can attain with a reasonable amount of effort. Because it is difficult to predict precisely how quickly a child will master certain skills, it seems well to check progress at short intervals initially and adjust the goals in accordance with the findings. Such adjustment presumes that the child is making a reasonable effort and that the goals are appropriate. Actually, the efforts or the goals might be far less or more than anticipated. The student's introspective report of his effort as well as his evaluation of the task difficulty should therefore play an important part in the establishment of revised goals.

Long-term goals in reading are things like finishing a given book, learning a list of words, and learning certain sound-to-symbol relationships. Although it is often discovered that the goal will be attained easily or not gained at all within the time limits set, such projections give the pupil a valuable perspective on his progress. Often, neither students nor teachers clearly envision where they want to be on a given date. Specific feedback that may be the result of the teacher's evaluation or the student's own inspection of his skills progress serves to reinforce the learner and aid him in adjusting short- and long-term goals.

Establishing listening sets
Children are bombarded with words. From morning until night they are asked to "listen" and "do." Although in the school situation the greatest portion of the day is presumably spent in listening, it really is not. It would be more correct to say that most of the activities are listening activities, but that children are not listening

most of the time. Why should they? Who could process so much talk meaningfully? Rather than having children listening most of the time, we need to motivate them to listen carefully on specific occasions. Techniques or suggestions for creating such listening sets follow:

Step 1 / Develop a special attention getter that signals mandatory listening.   A specific phrase such as the Navy's "now hear this" will suffice, provided that it is not overused, and that efforts are made to make sure all eyes and ears are "up front."

Step 2 / Structure concise but precise directions that require immediate action on the part of the listener.   Often, when we sit down to structure such a communication and strive for the most effective means of saying it, we decide it really is not ready for communication or is not that important after all. When we do make the statements, we should make them slowly and carefully. In the time that follows the directive, the teacher should make a visual inspection to see that the communication has been received and acted upon. If it has not, the teacher should make individual followups and ask these children to repeat the directive in order that she may determine whether the problem is one of attention or understanding.

Step 3 / Plan listening situations in which students make responses via cards or other such devices. All students thus make a response that can be immediately assessed by the teacher. An example of such a situation would be to give children letter cards and ask them to show the letter that begins each word the teacher pronounces.

Step 4 / In a nonthreatening manner, seek spontaneous summaries, evaluations, or oral responses to your oral directives. If this is a fixed pattern that is bounced from child to child, children will not peg the listening session as a "teacher talkathon." Their participation will compel them to listen.

Creating self-instructional attitudes

In many instances, cultural influences prevent children from directing their own learning and achievement; many children grow up physically but not behaviorally. Effective self-instruction is obviously a learned behavior that rests heavily on the development of:

Achievement attitudes
Persistence attitudes
Self-control attitudes
Self-reinforcing attitudes

We often point to certain children and praise them because of the care they take in doing tasks, but neglect the fact that such an attitude of concern (or indifference) did not just happen; it was conditioned by such things as verbal and emotional rewards for such behaviors and attitudes of care or indifference exhibited by parents and teachers. That such attitudes are subject to manipulation by teachers is clear, for we all know of children who seem to be virtual Jekyll and Hydes, depending on which teacher they are with.

Persistence attitudes / These are intertwined with achievement attitudes, for the child perseveres in order that he may achieve. Whether the child stays at the task, of course, will depend on his past success in attaining goals as well as the subsequent goals to which he is directed. Realistic goal setting is therefore extremely important, but in addition, the student must be reinforced in meaningful ways. The reinforcement must be frequent in the initial stages of development, but can be tapered off as the child becomes more capable of accepting delayed reward. It is difficult to prescribe a precise schedule for delaying rewards; it depends on the sensitivity of the teacher in the given situation.

When children quickly become frustrated with tasks that seem within their range of accomplishment, we sense a lack of self-control. Evidently, such self-control or its lack is largely the result of a positive or a negative self-concept. If children do not develop confidence in their ability to achieve and consequently keep the task in focus, we must ensure that they see a self-controlled model (the teacher) as he struggles with a task unsuccessfully and learns how to stop and analyze a problem with his background knowledge. Nothing destroys self-control and self-instruction more quickly than hasty teacher criticism. Certain difficulties must be anticipated from time to time; it should not necessarily be assumed that the child "goofed off."

Self-reinforcing attitudes / These are the necessary motivators that enable children to find satisfaction in completed tasks. Most frequently called intrinsic reward or intrinsic motivation, this behavior is the result of much previous extrinsic motivation. We must bear this in mind when we expect children to do tasks that are not especially appealing for no reward or a long-deferred reward which is often meaningless at the time.

Planning tangible rewards reinforcement

Tom: How is it that your son makes such good grades, Joe?

Joe: Well, I'll tell you. Ever since he was in the first grade I've given him a dollar for every A he gets on his report card. It sure cost me a lot of dough, but I think it's worth it.

Sue: (to Joe's wife Ann) I see where your son has the best grade average in the school. How did you ever do it?

Ann: I'm not really sure. About all I know is that Art just simply can't stand to be second to anybody.

Jon: How do you do it, straight A's every time?

Art: By organization, man. I organize everything presented into a framework that's usually better than the one used by the teacher.

Really, how does Art do it? Does he do it to get his dad's
dollars, to be top man, or what? We really do not know. He does
it, and that is what counts. Why Art achieves is not our concern
here, but rather why Alex, Mary, Jane, and thousands of others do
not achieve.

Suppose low-achieving Alex had received a promise of a dollar
for every A when he began the first grade. He may or may not
have been motivated by such a reward. Usually, such a prospect,
although appealing, is too long-term to keep a young child going.
Often, it is neither necessary nor desirable, for most youngsters at
this age respond to approval and praise more than to monetary
rewards. Praise and approval are such powerful incentives that
their incremental increases alone can produce significant reading
achievement (Clark and Wahlberg, 1968). Unfortunately, in classrooms in which praise and approval cannot always be meted out in
the necessary doses (in terms of both frequency and timing), we
need to provide real motivators to children who are in great need
of them. These are the children who arrive in our classrooms as
underachievers, indifferent to many of the tasks we wish them to
do in reading, and who no longer respond to some of the forms of
group praise they once basked in as first- and second-graders.
Tangible rewards, on either a *fixed* or *occasional* basis, become
appropriate means to reading ends with such children.

Fixed rewards / Fixed rewards are those which are specified in
advance of a behavior; for example, "If you do all five of these
correctly, you can have a candy." Such rewards can be highly involved systems in which children can get candy, toys, books,
sporting goods or virtually anything of reasonable value that
appeals to them. Fixed rewards have value in the sense that they
can clearly be seen as the rewards for specific behaviors. Such
behaviors have to be limited so that the student can know precisely
what he has to do in order to obtain the reward. These rewards can
have negative results when the student (1) cannot complete the
task and subsequently gain the reward, (2) is asked to perform
other behaviors without reward, or (3) performs the task and gains
the reward, but does not retain the behavior.

Occasional rewards / Occasional rewards seem to be less meaningful in initiating a regular pattern of behavior but more useful in
sustaining established behaviors. The sporadic award may not
occur frequently enough for the student to really associate the
reward with the behavior. In time, as the student clearly sees his
behaviors and becomes more capable of judging them, he can

more readily see why he received an occasional reward. Whereas fixed rewards become monotonous, occasional rewards enable the child to sustain himself for increasingly long periods of time and delay gratification for his work. This may explain why painters, authors, and composers can sustain themselves through years of work on a single project.

Bribes / Ginott (1965), talking primarily to parents, warns against the use of bribes that are frequently associated with fixed rewards, because they spur children toward a goal. As Ginott points out, such things communicate doubts about the child's ability, persistence, and endurance and tend to promote blackmail and other sorts of unpleasant behaviors. If teachers perceive of fixed rewards as broad attainments (such as finishing a reader in a given amount of time, learning 200 words) that will be rewarded on completion, they are setting up bribe situations rather than fixed reward situations. Fixed rewards must be based upon small, readily achievable elements so that the emphasis is positive rather than negative.

Some pros and cons / Although a system of fixed rewards (such as tokens that can be accumulated and redeemed for prizes) can be built into any reading program at any point, it seems of dubious value in learning situations in which the extrinsic approval motivators are working successfully and the child is meeting success in appropriate tasks. When the teacher's verbal approval takes on minimal value because of previous failure, pupils need to have new motivators for trying.

Many case studies describe the positive motivational effects of tangible rewards (fixed) on delinquent children, underachievers, and retarded readers of various sorts (Staats et al., 1968). One of the most interesting case descriptions is that recorded on film by Wortman and Kirtz (1969), because it reveals the metamorphosis of a wild, underachieving group of Detroit inner-city children into a task-oriented group. The film was made to reveal the changes that can be effected when the usual motivators of grades, praise, and enjoyment of work, which have lost their effectiveness, are replaced by tangible rewards (candy, toys, books, sports equipment). The tangible rewards are placed in a display case in the room and can be earned by points given as the result of completing individual assignments of given point values. This part of the program should be noted because each child was given what was considered to be work appropriate for his skills, a factor which itself might be extremely motivating to children previously frustrated by inappropriate assignments.

Wittes and Radin (1969) describe how this group is slowly rewarded for working quietly and effectively on small segments.

From 5-minute periods of silent, sustained work at the beginning, the children work up to 30-minute periods by the end of the six-week period. At the end of the second week, Wittes and Radin indicate that the children start coming early to work on their assignments even though they are not given any reward for this. The authors conclude that "self-reinforcement replaced external reinforcement" as the work itself became rewarding. Such examples should encourage teachers of groups that seem to be in need of special kinds of motivators. Obviously, such motivational schemes are not panaceas or substitutes for effective teacher stimulation, appropriate curriculum, and proper provisions for individual differences. Fixed rewards schemes can succeed only with careful planning, and we encourage any teacher entertaining such notions to study the following questions carefully:

Question 1 / What reasons do you have for establishing such a system of rewards? As suggested earlier, your response must demonstrate that you have made appropriate curricular adjustments, attempted praise in varying amounts, and so on.

Question 2 / What are the potential effects of your system on the children who are not working in such a system? (those in other classrooms, other groups, and so on)

Question 3 / What will be the tangible rewards? Groups and their conceptions of valuable rewards will vary. If the rewards are not perceived as valuable, their motivation power will necessarily be limited.

Question 4 / What will be the reward schedule? If the schedule is not geared to a legitimate amount of work or accomplishment, the consequences can be disastrous. Children with easy tasks may clean out the rewards before some children get any. Children who achieve rewards too slowly may be more discouraged than motivated. Small-scale rewards can be useful at first to determine individual attainment speeds.

Question 5 / What will the pupil's role in goal-setting (and subsequent reward) be? Although there is danger that a pupil's goal-setting perspectives might be distorted by his desire for reward and notice of other's rewards, it seems important that he learn to make some realistic assessment of what he can accomplish in given time segments.

Summary

Motivation is defined as "the initiation and direction of behavior." Most reading behaviors are initiated by learned drives, although some are influenced by the boredom drive. Preschool and in-school learned drives significantly affect pupils' responses to reading. Children with reading models and books in the home frequently develop motivation for reading behaviors. After children reach school, they are conditioned to seek grades, promotion, and praise. When they receive these rewards, pupils usually achieve well, but when they do not, they sense failure and seek to withdraw from the competition that frustrates them.

Changes in the traditional system that would lessen the effects of unfair competition include nongraded structures, individualization of reading instruction, competition in which the individual competes with himself, and praise and reward based on individual attainment of individual goals.

Techniques for fostering motivation concern the building of positive self-concepts, realistic goal setting, establishing listening sets, and creating self-instructional attitudes. Positive self-concepts provide pupils with the necessary self-confidence to pursue legitimate goals. Such self-concepts are developed through careful use of praise and criticism on the part of the teacher. Realistic goal-setting skills are guided by teachers who assist pupils in checking their progress at short intervals and adjusting subsequent goals in terms of their findings. Listening sets are built through careful teaching procedures that place a premium on specific behaviors. Creating self-instructional attitudes largely rests on the development of the following types of pupil attitudes: achievement attitudes, persistence attitudes, self-control attitudes, and self-reinforcing attitudes.

three

What the diagnostic reading teacher determines

Probably no other teacher's determination skills are so visible as those of the superior or inferior football coach. On display are his successes in developing a multitude of specific skills—blocking, tackling, running, catching, kicking. Reading teachers, although charged with much more important diagnostic skills and subsequent behavioral changes, are seldom held as accountable for losses as are their football counterparts. There are few hangings in effigy because pupils did not learn to read. Reading failures are generally blamed on a wide variety of things—children's backgrounds, phonics, poor basals, dyslexia, and so on.

Despite the differences in accountability, it is our feeling that winning teachers of all kinds are alike in that they possess precise knowledge of the skills they desire to build and are subsequently able to measure their individual pupils against these skills goals in order to determine the work that has to be done.

With the skills goals in mind (Chapters 4, 5, 6), we are now ready to turn our attention to the basic determination tasks of the diagnostic reading teacher: reading readiness, reading achievement, reading potential, specific reading skills.

The fact that a child has reached his fifth or sixth birthday by a given date does not necessarily means that he is ready for reading instruction. Rather, the teacher must make determinations of specific capabilities, lest the child be propelled into meaningless tasks (Chapter 8, "Reading Readiness").

Just as every student is not ready to begin formal reading instruction at the same time, every student is not to be confined to the reading difficulty of his assigned grade. In order to make correct reading placement, it is imperative that teachers find each pupil's reading achievement level, whether it be below, on, or above grade level (Chapter 9, "Reading Achievement Levels").

Often, students have the ability to read above their actual achievement level. Knowledge of such power or reading potential can be useful to the teacher in making judgments about pupil programs and goals (Chapter 10, "Reading Potential"). Sometimes, such measures also reveal that pupils are achieving at their potential even though it may not be at the grade level. In such cases, the child should not be pressured to do work far beyond his capability.

Having determined each pupil's reading achievement level (or state of readiness for reading instruction), reading potential, and the relationship of the two, the teacher must then determine specific skills needs in order to stimulate growth (Chapter 11, "Specific Skills Needs").

8 Reading readiness

Behavioral objectives
1. Contrast the definition of reading readiness given here with those of other authors.
2. List the primary factors involved in reading readiness and outline their contents.
3. Name a standardized readiness battery and describe its content and predictive value.
4. Name a standardized partial battery and describe its content and predictive value.
5. Describe reading readiness skills that can be developed through the language-experience story approach.
6. Be able to administer formal and informal measurement instruments and interpret pupil skills in the physical, understanding, and adjustment areas of reading readiness.

Reading readiness! What is it? Reading readiness is:

... when he [the child] has attained a certain stage of mental maturity, and possesses a background of experience and the personal and social adjustments which make it possible for him to progress at a normal rate in learning to read when exposed to good classroom teaching. (Tinker, 1952, p. 24)

... a state of general maturity which, when reached, allows a child to learn to read without excess difficulty. (Harris, 1970, p. 21)

... when the child can learn to read. (Unidentified teacher, 1970)

Each of these definitions suggests a stage, state, or time when the child can respond to reading instruction without undue difficulty. Many educators feel that reading readiness is a clearly defined condition that can be measured precisely by a reading readiness test. There may be an optimum moment when the child can learn to read most effectively, but our means for determining that moment are surely lacking. As indicated by research, reading readiness tests are far from reliable in predicting success; they are also quite limited in telling us precisely what to do in order to assist specific children to reach the desired stage, state, or time.

Reading readiness, to me, is a complex of skills that enables a child to respond effectively to selective reading tasks. If the task is one in which the child is to learn to recognize his name when it is presented to him in manuscript form, it is essential that he possess:

The visual and perceptual skills that permit him to recognize the distinctive shape of the image so that he can differentiate his name from similar configurations

The adjustment skills of being able to focus his attention on the task for the necessary time required to be able to retain the image

Because it is important to understand the components of this complex of skills, we must know both the selective reading tasks and the various skills factors. We have dealt with the reading skills in other chapters; here we will focus on the reading readiness factors and the formal and informal means for assessing skills development.

Reading readiness factors

A description of every factor that affected each child's response to specific reading tasks is impossible, because we simply cannot describe the intricacies of such a complex operation. An explanation of the related research and findings alone would fill volumes. Consequently, the following section has been structured to convey a brief, practical description of certain skills factors that are crucial to young children's abilities to respond to specific reading tasks. Figure 8-1 shows the organization scheme in graphic form.

Physical factors

We often hear about children who stay up late at night and come to school apparently worn out. When such children fail to respond to reading instruction, there is a good possibility that we fault the rest patterns or the parents who permit them. Similarly, if a child is virtually starved and unable to concentrate on instructional concerns, we wonder what his response might be if he had a good breakfast each morning. These illustrations concern but two isolated factors that might affect readiness; there are many more that we will touch on briefly in the following paragraphs.

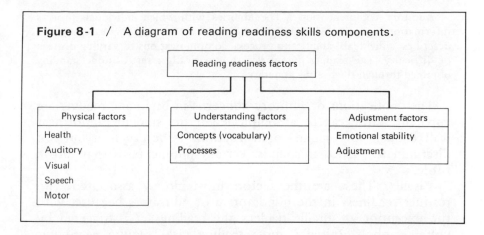

Figure 8-1 /   A diagram of reading readiness skills components.

Reading readiness factors

Physical factors	Understanding factors	Adjustment factors
Health	Concepts (vocabulary)	Emotional stability
Auditory	Processes	Adjustment
Visual		
Speech		
Motor		

Health / The plight of tired and hungry children frequently strikes a responsive chord in teachers; so do a host of other health factors such as sickness and low energy levels. Concern with health is so great that most colleges give a course on health information for all elementary education majors, and schools develop special policies and programs to combat the physical deterrents to learning—free lunch programs, physical examinations, and so on. The area of health is one that has received the appropriate amount of attention, so we need not dwell on it here.

Auditory / These are the factors concerned with the process of obtaining sounds through the hearing mechanisms. Because such sounds are subsequently organized into meaningful communications, it is often difficult to separate the physical act of hearing from the psychological act of understanding. We shall treat them as a unit here. The addition of descriptive words to the base word *auditory* gives us a useful set of terms for determining important readiness skills:

Auditory acuity / The keenness of the hearing organs in noting various levels of pitch and tone. Acuity can be tested with machines such as the Audiometer (Beltone Company).

Auditory perception / The ability to perceive (hear and make some mental association) different sounds in the environment.

Auditory discrimination / The ability to auditorily discriminate between different sounds—for example, *cat* and *bat*. Some children have problems in hearing the differences in certain sounds. The classic joke about the auditory discrimination difficulties (and pronunciation problems) of Orientals, for example, illustrates their difficulty in hearing and saying the sound of *l*: "Rots of ruck."

Auditory comprehension / The abilities with which individuals process information mentally. This skill belongs to the understanding category and describes individuals' abilities to process communications of varying degrees of difficulty. The reading potential test is basically a test of understanding obtained through the hearing apparatus.

The implications of auditory concerns in beginning reading are apparent. Little can be accomplished if the student cannot hear well enough to respond to instruction. If he can hear but not discriminate particular sounds, certain phonic tasks may prove futile.

Visual / These are the factors most closely associated with reading readiness in the minds of most educators because, with the exception of Braille readers, the reading act is triggered by visual symbols. Initially, most reading tasks require *near-point vision* and *accommodation*. The eyes must adapt in such a way that both images fuse into a single image or the child may receive a double image or a single one that is blurred. Measurement instruments such as the Telebinocular (Keystone Corporation) are useful for measuring fusion and accommodation processes. As the child reads on, he must make successive fixations (where his eye takes in the visual stimuli) in a left-to-right pattern. This left-to-right movement skill is referred to as *directionality* and is a learned skill. At the end of the various lines of print, the pupil must make the *return sweep* to the next line. Often, young children have difficulty in managing this return; they reread the line, skip a line, or simply become lost. As the student is carrying out these steps, he is making determinations of words by their unique shapes or forms (*form perception*). In other words, specific associations are made to the various forms, whether through the processing of whole words or of separate letters (in synthesizing words from their letters).

Speech / These factors are quite important in phonic-centered programs in which strong links are made between sound production and the symbols that represent the various sounds. Some teachers mistake the difference between speaking and reading and consequently subject children with speech problems to poor speech therapy when they should be receiving reading instruction. A child does not have to be able to pronounce a word accurately before he can read it; efforts to force him to articulate the correct sounds are not the concern of reading instruction.

Understanding factors

Two common descriptions of reading are these: Reading is just talk written down; reading is thinking. The statements are important because reading is thinking in the sense that ideas are being conveyed through written language which is, largely, talk written down. Because it is difficult to separate language from thought, we know that children can learn to read language more easily when it is their spoken language. Ruddell's research (1965) has indicated significantly better achievement with reading materials that parallel the children's own language.

But how often do reading materials actually parallel children's language? Strickland's study (1962) indicated what we all knew— that the language of beginning reading series was quite different from the oral language of all children reading such materials. Since that time, efforts have been made to write materials that better match the language patterns of the children who read them. Yet, when we consider the various deviations from standard American English, it is apparent that many, many different language patterns must be incorporated into texts. There is also recognition of the need of dialect groups to be able to read and understand the so-called standard dialect materials. For initial reading, though, there seems to be a strong argument for using the natural language of the child in the only type of program that provides for any variation—the language-experience program. In such a beginning program, the child's spoken thoughts become the reading material, as in the following story, which replaces the "Look, look Dick. See Spot" variety of beginning reader.

The rockets
Tom said, "We said that we is the best ones."
Gene said, "They say that it ain't so and we better prove it."
George said, "We prove it. We beat the hell out of them."
Rocco said, "The Rockets is best always."

Although the language of the story may offend some readers, it is *their* language. If reading instruction is going to mean anything, it seems obvious that children must read both thoughts and words they understand.

Vexing questions beyond the determination of the most efficient means of instructing children in reading concern the larger language problems that handicap millions of Americans. If these citizens are going to have a reasonable chance for a better life, we must determine how to assist them in obtaining additional oral and written language skills.

Concepts / These are man-made organizers that can be used for communication and interpretation when they have vocabulary referents (as well as similar real referents). We think of the concepts of "big" and "little" as simple elements without realizing that they are relative to situational variables; for example, to a 6-foot man, another who is 6 feet 4 inches is big, while to a college basketball coach, a 6-foot-4-inch forward is certainly little. What is your concept of "basketball"? Perhaps you think of a round object, a hoop on the garage, a complex game, and so on. Think for a moment of your concept for each of the italicized words in the following sentences:

Lay flat on the *floor until* the *Jerries pass over.*
I shall *get up before breakfast tomorrow* and do *five push-ups. three chins*, and *ten side-straddle-hops.*

These things probably communicate rather specific meanings to most of you, but imagine the difficulties of the pupil who has not grown up in the setting in which they are used. It is easy to confuse children who are unsure of seemingly everyday meanings such as *tomorrow, until, ten*, and so on.

Processes / How the mind performs its miraculous functions remains a mystery to man. Psychologists have long theorized about its functions, but they have not moved us significantly closer to a precise understanding of the mental processes. Nevertheless, the work of individuals such as Inhelder and Piaget (1958), Bloom (1956), Guilford (1959), and others has provided us with some comprehensible ways for thinking about the processes and the means toward their development. The system that appears especially useful was developed by Bloom and others as a means for organizing the various kinds of cognitive behaviors into taxonomic form. These processes, as modified by Sanders (1966), include memory, translation, interpretation, application, analysis, synthesis, and evaluation. The reader will see in the discussion which follows that these processes relate directly to the purposes of reading as described earlier under the categories of locating information, remembering, translation, predicting/extending, and evaluating critically.

Memory / Initially, understanding of language involves the storage and retrieval of a multitude of elements.

Translation / The individual cannot only store and retrieve, he can organize the information into a parallel communication through summarization, illustration, and so on.

Interpretation / The individual adds meaning to something by drawing from his experiences something he perceives to be a pertinent association. Interpretation may be either convergent or divergent.

Application / The individual can apply previously learned information to the solution of an actual problem.

Analysis / Skills that enable the person to break a communication down into its constituent parts in such a way that the organization of ideas and their relationships are made clear. Critical thinking and reading are largely analytical in nature prior to the judgment stage.

Synthesis / The individual can produce some unified whole from various parts. For example, determining a person's position on an issue by analyzing and synthesizing his previous statements into a position statement that was not clearly apparent before the synthesis.

Evaluation / Judgment behaviors in which we place values on things. Judgment behaviors are influenced by internal and external comparisons.

Adjustment factors

Even though a pupil may be eminently ready for reading instruction according to physical and understanding factors, it is conceivable that he may still not be ready if:

He defies his teacher and will not respond to direction.
He fears the other children, teacher, and principal to such an extent that he cannot function.
He becomes unduly upset at the slightest error or difficulty.

These are the behavioral results of emotional instability and/or adjustment sets that are conditioned by environmental factors too complex and extensive to describe here. Although understanding of background situations and causal factors *might* influence teacher actions in such a way as to assist the pupil in adjusting, I am not so sure. Regardless of how much we know, we are seldom able to control the outside variables that influence a child. It seems more sensible to spend our energies on creating the type of supporting classroom environment that will allay fears and construct positive attitudes. Rather than accurate psychoanalysis, what is important is behavioral modification.

Formal means for assessing reading readiness

The requirement for formal readiness assessment is a standardized reading readiness test. Standardized simply means that it has been given to large numbers of children who supposedly represent the various socioeconomic groups in our nation, and that some normative performance data have been derived in the process. Normative data tell us how well the various children did on the test. As a result, when we give the test to Joey, we can compare his score with the norms and determine how well he did. Usually, such tests indicate performance in terms of descriptive ratings (superior, good, average, poor, very poor) and percentiles (Joey's score ranks at the 60th percentile, which means that his score was better than 40 percent of the children in the normative sample). The rating and percentile scores of readiness tests are also supposed to give a prediction of the child's likelihood of success in initial reading instruction. Each of the test makers has made a series of systematic observations of the reading performance of the norm group children to determine the predictive value of the test. The formal assessment means discussed in this section are the full readiness battery and the partial readiness battery.

Full readiness battery

A full readiness battery is a composite of readiness measures grouped together in a single examination. Among the more commonly given readiness tests (full battery) are the following:

Harrison-Stroud Reading Readiness Profiles (Houghton Mifflin Company, Boston) / This examination consists of a single form that requires 76 minutes for completion. Skills measured include symbol usage, visual discrimination, context usage, auditory discrimination, combined use of auditory and context cues, and letter naming.

Metropolitan Reading Readiness Tests (Harcourt Brace Jovanovich, New York) / Probably the most widely used readiness test, the Metropolitan has two forms and requires approximately 60 minutes for completion. Skills measured include word meaning, listening, matching, number names and knowledge, letter names, pattern copying, and a draw-a-man test.

Murphy-Durrell Diagnostic Reading Readiness Test (Harcourt Brace Jovanovich, New York) / This test has one form that requires approximately 95 minutes for completion. The test is divided into three parts. Contained in the first part of the test are the following subtests: auditory discrimination, visual discrimination, and learning rate (which is partially individualized in administration).

Although not listed as one of the most commonly used readiness measures because of its recent development, the Clymer-Barrett Prereading Battery (Clymer and Barrett, 1967) has been found to have a correlation of .66 with subsequent reading achievement (Barrett, 1966), which ranks it high among readiness batteries in terms of predictive value. The test represents the utilization of some of the most recent research on visual and auditory discrimination predictors of reading success. All the preceding tests are designed to be administered to groups of children, although most test makers recommend group sizes no larger than twelve pupils. The batteries usually contain these elements: a teacher's manual (containing directions for administering, scoring, and interpreting), pupil test copies, and a scoring key or template. Included in the various batteries, but not necessarily in any single battery, are subtests measuring vocabulary, listening, visual discrimination, motor skills, auditory discrimination, and alphabet knowledge (which is actually visual discrimination and visual memory).

Vocabulary subtest / The students are directed to groups of pictures and asked to mark the one the teacher names in each group; for example, "Put a mark on the boat."

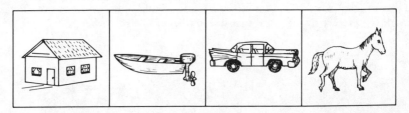

Listening subtest / Pupils are asked to mark the one picture in a group that best describes what the teacher reads; for example, "Tommy went to the store and bought milk, eggs, and cheese."

Visual discrimination subtest / Pupils are asked to match the figure in the left box with one of the figures on the right; for example, "Mark the figure that is just like the one in the first box."

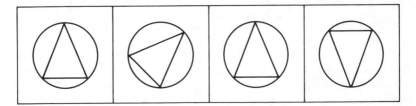

Motor skills subtest / This test requires that the student reproduce each figure in the available space in the box.

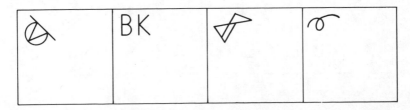

Auditory discrimination subtest / This test requires that the pupil differentiate between beginning consonant sounds and/or ending sounds (usually rhyming phonograms).

Teacher direction / Listen carefully as I pronounce three words so that you can hear the sound with which each word begins: *bat, ball, glove.* Two of the words begin with the same sound, but one doesn't. Please mark the picture of the word that doesn't begin like the others.

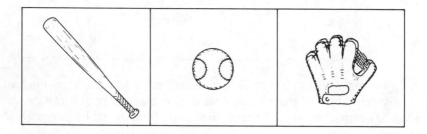

Teacher direction / Listen carefully as I pronounce three words so that you can hear the sound with which each word ends: *can, bun, cat.* Two of the words end with the same sound, but one doesn't. Please mark the picture of the word that doesn't end like the others.

Alphabet knowledge subtest / The students are directed to mark a given letter in a box that is usually identified by an object with which the child is familiar; for example, Mark the *y* in the box with the apple."

Information obtained from batteries containing subtests such as the foregoing is usually totaled in a score that is subsequently measured against some standard of readiness; for example, superior, high normal, normal, low normal, low. From such ratings, pupils are often given their first label as a reader. No one has apparently done with the readiness tests what Rosenthal and Jacobsen (1968) did with their bogus test results (determine the extent to which teacher expectations conditioned by such scores can actually preordain a pupil's success or failure), although there are important questions about the validity of using standardized readiness batteries.

Is the reading readiness test a reliable instrument? / After studying the available research, Dykstra (1967) concluded that the reading readiness test, as a whole, was a reliable instrument. Reliability suggests consistency, and it was determined that such tests were rather consistent in their judgments. Of course, a measure can be consistent or reliable and still not be valid.

What is the predictive value of reading readiness tests? / Dykstra found that a positive relationship did exist between the scores of pupils on readiness tests and their subsequent achievement in beginning reading. Despite the positive relationships, however, there were still numerous exceptions (primarily in terms of pupils who demonstrated better reading achievement than their readiness test prognosis suggested). A further finding indicated that the predictive validity of the reading readiness battery was not superior to a number of other measurements; for example, primary group intelligence tests, human drawing tests, and specific subtests of the total battery. With the exception of a study by Lee (1934), most research results indicate that teacher judgments of readiness are quite similar to those obtained from readiness tests.

What should the full readiness battery be used for? / Full readiness batteries are intended to predict likely success in reading as well as the specific readiness needs of the children who take the tests. From my interpretation of the available literature, there is some question whether the full batteries do well enough on either count to justify the money and time expended. Prediction of reading success can be obtained as well initially with one or two subtests that take only a few minutes and cost very little. There is also the question of whether or not the tests provide the teacher with information about the specific readiness needs of children. I would agree with Dykstra that not much of a case can be made for their use for differential diagnosis.

Partial readiness batteries

In the first-grade reading studies discussed at the beginning of the book, the best single subtest predictor of reading achievement was the Letter Names Subtest of the Murphy-Durrell Diagnostic Reading Readiness Test (Murphy and Durrell, 1964; Dykstra, 1967).

This subtest correlated .52 with the criterion, which is as strong a correlation as that achieved by most full batteries. In light of the predictive value of pupil knowledge of the alphabet, there is a strong case for using such tests for readiness prediction if teachers want some empirical support for their subjective judgments. The tests can be teacher-constructed, using the descriptive information supplied previously for the alphabet knowledge subtest of the formal readiness battery.

Informal means for assessing reading readiness

Many teachers will want to use varied means for measuring each pupil's readiness for reading. Among them should be informal assessments that can be taken during language-experience story tasks as well as other specific skills measurement tasks.

Language-experience story tasks

One of the most direct means for finding out whether someone can do something is to let him try it. For this reason, it makes sense to let children "try" reading through carefully structured language-experience stories in which they tell and read their own words as transcribed into print by the teacher. Language-experience sessions are conducted with small groups (probably no more than six children) so that the teacher can manage the dialogue and ensure responses from all group members. In the course of such sharing and reading sessions, the teacher can make pertinent observations about each pupil's development of understanding and adjustment skills. For example:

Understanding skills

To what extent do individual children demonstrate understanding of the various concepts (space, time, color, number, value)?
Do certain children display difficulty in following the line of thought?
To what extent do individuals interpret from logical positions?
How well do the various individuals respond to oral directions?

Adjustment skills

Do certain children show signs of emotional instability (undue crying, extensive demands for attention)?
Do certain children relate poorly to the other children, specific children, the teacher?
Are certain children not responsive?

The teacher might then wish to single out children for further observation and checking. Moving from oral sharing to the development of the language-experience story is done when the teacher suggests that the group make up a story about a certain experience. In building the experience, the teacher does the following:

Step 1 / She attempts to elicit a story title that will be pleasing to the group. Often, such titles may be the names of the principal story character.

Step 2 / She seeks to build the story in such a fashion that every child contributes a sentence to the story:

Spot

Billy said, "Spot is a funny dog."
Mary said, "He is silly because he jumps all the time."
Thomas said, "I like Spot."
Susan said, "I have a dog that looks like Spot."
Karen said, "My dog is much bigger than Spot."

Step 3 / She reads each word clearly as she prints it on the tagboard.

Step 4 / After completing the transcription, she reads the story, using her hand as a guide to indicate the sequence of left-to-right and the return sweep. She reads in natural phrases and does not pause for each word.

Step 5 / The class is then invited to read the story with the teacher.

Step 6 / After group-sharing experiences, individuals are allowed to read their own sentences. The teacher helps so that they are not under pressure to perform.

Step 7 / Those children who wish to read more than their own sentences are allowed to read others.

As the children participate in this experience, the teacher has the opportunity to observe physical, understanding, and adjustment factors. We have already described understanding and adjustment observations; let us look here at physical factors.

Auditory

Do certain children turn their heads in such a fashion as to indicate hearing difficulty?

Visual

Which students have difficulty in following as the group reads in unison?

To what extent do students have difficulty in making visual discriminations among the words (beginning with the most simple discrimination, their own name)?

To what extent do some students tend to drop momentarily from the chorus when the return sweep is made?

Speech

Which pupils substitute sounds or fail to note sounds that the others are making—for example, beginning digraph sounds, endings?

Which pupils have difficulty speaking in unison?

These are but a few of the observations that a teacher can make while students sample the actual reading act. Other observations can be made of whether or not pupils realize that:

Reading is just talk written down.
When they know code, they can play parts back selectively—for example, the parts prefaced by their own names.
Reading proceeds from left-to-right across the line from word unit to word unit (the concept of letters separated by spacings).
At the end of the line, one drops to the next line and makes the left-to-right trip again.
Groups of letters make up words.
Capital and small letters are used.
Capital letters are used for names, and so on.
Little marks that are not letters have certain meanings (punctuation).

It is my opinion that such activities allow not only for testing but for building readiness. Research reported by Dykstra (1967) indicates that many readiness programs often result in less subsequent reading achievement than plunging supposedly unready children into reading instruction (usually in basals). This does not mean that all readiness programs are valueless, but rather that actual task experience cannot be simulated with activities that are not readily transferable to the tasks. Because there is so much transfer potential from language-experience stories, they seem to have great value.

There will be children who, while profiting from the oral language portions of the language-experience approach, may benefit little from the written chart because of poor form perception, directionality, ocular motility, and so on. These children's needs must be pinpointed through further testing and met with appropriate tasks outside the language-experience story activities described.

Specific skills measurement tasks

Whether before, during, after, or in lieu of language-experience stories, it is well that teachers be aware of means for measuring and building specific physical and understanding skills. The following assessment techniques can also be used as development techniques.

Visual discrimination / The degree to which pupils can perform perception and movement tasks often needs careful assessment.

Ocular motility / The coordinated movements of the eyes as they follow an object should be noted.

Movement / The teacher should assess the visual movement

that must be performed in the reading act; that is, the child's eyes must work as a paired set so he can effect a series of fixations in left-to-right order and then the return sweep:

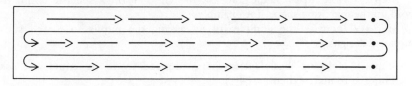

To assess whether the child can move his eyes in unison, note the following:

Whether the child's eyes can follow the path of a ball swinging to and fro about 2 or 3 feet in front of him at eye level.
Whether the child can follow the path of the ball as it is swung in an orbiting fashion.

These are not alternatives for a careful medical examination of accommodation and convergence, but informal tests that enable a teacher to discover conditions that might require examination by a specialist.

Form perception / The pupil's skill in perceiving increasingly intricate configurations should also be assessed. Children who have not had much (or any) symbol experience in their early years may have difficulty in differentiating letters of the alphabet. Determining form perception must therefore begin with gross geometric objects and tasks such as the following which may be developed by the teacher or purchased (The Fitzhugh Plus Program, Fitzhugh, 1968; Perceptual Achievement Forms, Winterhaven Lions Research Foundation, 1964).

Oral directions / Put a mark on the figure that is like the one in the first box.

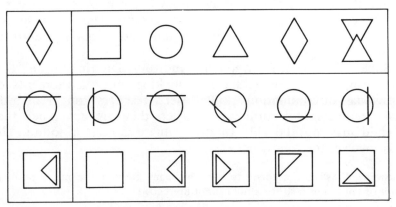

Another informal means of testing small groups is the following:

Step 1 / Give each child a set of the basic geometric shapes.

Step 2 / Hold up a shape and ask the children on a specific count to hold up the matching shape, for example, O.

Step 3 / Increase the complexity by asking the pupils to match such modeled designs as △ +

Step 4 / Hold up basic letter shapes derived from the circle and ask the children to match them. d b p

Step 5 / Continue with other letter families until all capital and small letters have been covered.

The final level of form perception involves actual word discrimination. At this point, the student identifies words by their unique configurations, distinctive characteristics, and so on. A determination of the student's understanding of the visual discrimination of word elements can be made in this way:

Step 1 / Ask the students to draw lines between the individual words in a group of words; for example, "Look here Dick."

Step 2 / Ask the students to circle the words in phrases; for example, "See me run, Jane."

Auditory discrimination / This is a normal concomitant of learning to listen and speak. If a pupil articulates the various sounds of his language correctly, we must assume he can discriminate fine shadings of sound or he never would have been able to articulate so well. If, however, a pupil cannot articulate all the sounds of his language, we may assume that he has not developed the auditory discrimination skill to hear the differences or that he has developed the auditory discrimination skill, but not the articulation skill. If we determine that he cannot hear the differences, we can attempt auditory training to sensitize him to them. If we determine that he hears but cannot articulate the differences, we may wish to refer the problem to a speech therapist and lessen the emphasis on undeveloped sounds in his phonics program.

Such tests as the Wepman Auditory Discrimination Test (Wepman, 1958) are valuable in making quick assessments of individual discrimination skills. Alert teachers can frequently make on-the-spot informal tests when they are concerned that a child may not be able to discriminate a certain sound. The task involves the following:

Step 1 / Ask the student to turn his back to you (or put a book in front of your mouth so the child cannot lip-read).

Step 2 / Ask the student to tell you whether the words you pronounce are the same or different.

Step 3 / Develop sound pairs that contain the sound in question and a
similar sound; for example:

Initial	Final	Medial
bat—dat	cat—cak	man—men
dat—that	bat—baf	kin—kan
what—but	bit—bet	bad—bed
chair—share	watch—wash	ban—ben
these—dese	which—witch	got—gat

Understanding skills / It seems evident that language is the
critical means for measuring understanding. From the very first
discernible naming words uttered by infants (*ma-ma*, *da-da*),
children learn the appropriate language referents for concrete
entities. From this stage they progress to the point at which the
concepts are more abstract and involve increasing syntactical
units; for example:

Me go.
Me go town.
Me go to town.
I go to town.
I want to go to town.

For the great majority of our children, the necessary understanding skills as illustrated in spoken language are well developed
before they begin formal instruction. For children who speak
another language or whose circumstances are different from the
prevailing life style, such concepts and the syntax for housing
them may be largely unknown. It is for this latter group of children that we suggest the checks shown in Table 8-1, which may
be made in addition to or in lieu of formal readiness measures.
In addition, pupils must demonstrate understanding of larger
patterns of language by successfully responding to listening-
thinking tasks that parallel reading-thinking tasks. These are
shown in Table 8-2.

Summary

The term *reading readiness* implies complex skills sets that
enable children to respond effectively to the selective reading
tasks. Physical, understanding, and adjustment factors contribute to such readiness. Measures of reading readiness include
formal and informal instruments. Formal instruments most often

Table 8-1 / Checking vocabulary understanding

Space relationships	Time relationships	Number relationships	Colors	Conditions
around	before/after	none/all	black	hot/cold
away	never/always	few/many	white	wet/dry
by	once/always	either/both	blue	soft/hard
far/near	now/then	little/much	brown	awake/asleep
here/there	yesterday/today	one	green	warm/cool
in/out	today/tomorrow	two	red	old/new
off/on	never/soon	three	yellow	alike/different
open/close	morning/night	four	orange	fast/slow
to/from	if/then	five	purple	empty/full
up/down	why	six		
front/back	how	seven		
front/middle	because	eight		
middle/back		nine		
top/bottom		ten		
inside/outside		short/tall		
first/last		short/long		
before/after		big/little		
high/low		small/large		
above/below		narrow/wide		
under/above		thin/fat		
right/wrong				
good/bad				
pretty/ugly				

Table 8-2 / Listening-thinking skills

Predicting/ extending	Locating information	Remembering	Organizing	Evaluating
Predicting convergent outcomes from pictures, titles, oral descriptions	Locating objects Locating pictorial elements (see Table 8-1)	Remembering simple sentence, sentence content, paragraph content, story content	Retells sentence, sentence set, paragraph, story Outlines sequence orally Reorganizes communication into a logical sequence, cartoon, picture	Making judgments about the desirability of a character, situation Making judgments about the validity of of a story description, argument, by making comparisons with other sources of information (external)
Predicting divergent outcomes				
Explaining story character actions				
Explaining gadget operations				
Restoring omitted words				

utilize total batteries that measure, among other things, vocabulary, listening, visual discrimination, motor skill, and alphabet knowledge. Certain subtests of whole batteries, notably the alphabet knowledge test, appear to predict subsequent reading achievement as well as the total battery. Informal measures center upon teacher observations, which may be of a general or specific nature. General observations of readiness can be obtained through language-experience story activities in which the teacher notes the presence or absence of certain skills. Specific observations of physical, understanding, and adjustment factors can be focused with checklist-type guides.

9 Reading achievement levels

Behavioral objectives
1. Describe what is meant by *formal* and *informal* measures of reading acheivement.
2. Describe the general contents of standardized reading achievement tests.
3. Describe the contents of informal tests of word recognition and comprehension.
4. Construct, administer, score, and interpret the results of informal word recognition, comprehension, and combination (word recognition, comprehension, fluency) tests.

"Before I can help you Johnny, I must find out where you are," explains Mrs. Smith to new student Johnny Jones. This is the initial task of all diagnostic instruction, whether it be reading, spelling, mathematics, or hog calling. She is telling Johnny that (1) there is a ladder or progression of reading levels (and concomitant skills) and (2) she must find precisely where he stands on this skills ladder (see Figure 9-1).

The means for locating Johnny's standing are many, but essentially they involve either formal or informal measures of reading skill (which include combinations of word recognition, reading comprehension, and fluency measures). In the sections that follow, formal and informal measures and their use are described.

Formal measures of reading achievement
Formal measures of reading achievement are those which have been devised and tested in such a way that an individual's score should reveal how his ability compares with that of the representative group of students on whom the test has been standardized. Thus, if a student has a composite reading score of 3.5, his score compares with the average score of pupils in the fifth month of the third grade. Of course, the validity of the comparison rests on the assumption that the test administration and scoring instructions were followed exactly; if a teacher gives more detailed explanations, allows more time than specified, prompts during the exam, and accepts incorrect score responses, the norms will be of

Figure 9-1 / A reading skills ladder based on word counts of representative basals.

	New Words	Total Words
7th (Vocabularies continue expansion)		
6th Sixth reader	2500	8394
5th Fifth reader	2000	5894
4th Fourth reader	2000	3894
3² Third reader (two)	500-600	1894
3¹ Third reader (one)	400	1294
2² Second reader (two)	350	894
2¹ Second reader (one)	350	544
*1² First reader	100	194
Pri Primer	50	94
PP 3 Preprimer three	20	54
PP 2 Preprimer two	17	34
PP 1 Preprimer one	17	17

*Johnny's standing on the skills ladder as subsequently determined by Mrs. Jones.

little value. Formal or standardized reading achievement tests appear in the forms of general achievement tests and specialized reading achievement tests.

General achievement tests

Near the beginning or the end of the school year, nearly every child in the public schools takes a general achievement test battery such as the Stanford Achievement Test (Kelley et al., 1965), the Metropolitan Achievement Test (Durost et al., 1962), or the SRA Achievement Series (Thorpe et al., 1964). In more affluent school districts, each child may take such a test at the beginning of the year and an alternate form at the end of the year. These tests measure achievement in the broad curriculum, but all have a reading achievement portion that usually contains subtests in the areas of (1) word reading, (2) paragraph meaning, and (3) vocabulary.

Word reading / These tests measure the student's word recognition skill by asking him to find and mark the word that tells what the picture is; for example:

Oral directions / Mark the square by the word that names the picture in each box.

□ car	□ boy	□ hand	□ saw
□ boat	□ girl	□ arm	□ was
□ house	□ saw	□ leg	□ has
□ sow	□ ball	□ ankle	□ see

On the basis of wide testing, the test developers can make some generalizations about which answers students in the various grades select. In this way, the teacher can get some idea of how individual pupils compare with other pupils (in the normative group) on this particular skill.

Paragraph meaning / These tests measure the pupil's skill in understanding connected reading in short paragraphs. Although some children may be able to sound out the words, they may not be able to understand connected reading. Conversely, some children will miss many words in isolated reading, but be able to read fully developed paragraph material.

Paragraph meaning tests are graduated in difficulty from simple items that correspond with the abilities of beginning readers to difficult paragraphs that sample skills at more advanced levels. Students are generally asked to respond to such tests by selecting a single word to complete a sentence from among several possibilities. For example:

Oral directions / Put a mark under the word or phrase that best fits in the paragraph.

Cows give _____.

   book   milk   eggs   money

Bill is a _____.

   girl   book   boy   toy

The boat is new. It can go _____.

   fast   run   catch   up

Because of the primacy of connected reading skill, most teachers attach more importance to this subtest score than to those of word knowledge and vocabulary.

Vocabulary measures / These tests measure both the student's understanding of key vocabulary and his ability to decipher (recognize) the word. Some examples follow:

Oral directions / I will tell you about one thing in each box. You mark the word in each box that tells what I'm talking about.

Mark the word that tells what we use to eat our supper with.

fork
bed
room
out

If the light bulb fell on the floor, it would probably _____ .

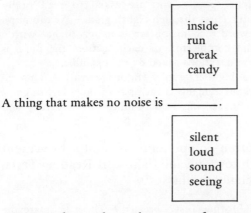

inside
run
break
candy

A thing that makes no noise is _____ .

silent
loud
sound
seeing

Strengths and weaknesses of general achievement tests (reading) / General achievement reading subtests are designed as a gross measure of program effectiveness. They (1) generally consume a relatively small amount of instructional time, (2) usually can be scored rapidly and impartially by machine, (3) provide schools and teachers with normative data about their pupils, and (4) sometimes provide diagnostic profiles of individual needs. The trouble starts when the test information is misused—for example, as a criterion for placing students in reading groups. Because the tests contain relatively few samples, it is inevitable that pupils who depart most from the level for which the test was built will have the least reliable scores. For example, teachers may be distraught when some of their highest achievers seem to show a decline from the first to the second test. They do not realize that because these students were at the top end of the battery in both instances, a single miss could make a major score difference. The opposite situation occurs when teachers are jubilant over the high scores of slow readers. There was actually a similar failure to sample, because the batteries used did not dip far enough down to really sample extremely limited reading skills. Perhaps the greatest disasters occur when teachers place slow students in accordance with their standardized test scores. Numerous studies (Botel, 1968; Harris, 1970; Bond and Tinker, 1968) testify to the fact that overplacement and subsequent frustration can result.

Specialized reading tests

These are not the broad spectrum of diagnostic tests, but rather those tests that purport to measure pupil achievement level via oral, silent, and combination oral and silent reading tests.

Oral tests that have been widely used for measuring reading achievement are the Gilmore and Gray tests.

Gilmore Oral Reading Test (Harcourt Brace Jovanovich) / This test is administered to individual pupils who are asked to read orally paragraphs of increasing difficulty (first through eighth grade). As the pupil reads, the examiner marks the word recognition errors in accordance with a specific marking system. At the completion of each section, the pupil is told to respond to comprehension questions asked by the examiner.

Gray Standardized Oral Reading Paragraphs (Bobbs-Merrill) / This individual test consists of paragraphs ranging from first- through eighth-grade difficulty. Pupils read orally, and scoring is determined by accuracy and rate.

Silent reading tests are often components of total achievement batteries. Illustrative of such tests are the California Reading Tests, which are sold as separate silent reading tests.

California Reading Tests (California Test Bureau) / These tests are designed as separate batteries for the following levels: Lower primary, grades 1 and 2; primary, grades 3 and 4; elementary, grades 4 through 6; and junior high, grades 7 through 9.

Combination oral and silent tests include the following:

Durrell Analysis of Reading Difficulty (Harcourt Brace Jovanovich) / This is an individualized diagnostic test designed for grades 1 through 6. The oral and silent reading tests take into account word recognition skill, literal and imaginative comprehension, and oral and silent reading rate. In addition, there are tests of listening comprehension, word recognition and word analysis, letters, visual memory of words, sounds, spelling, and handwriting.

Diagnostic Reading Scales (California Test Bureau) / Designed for administration to individual pupils, this test measures oral and silent reading skills from first through eighth grade. The test measures an instructional and independent reading level (in ways that differ from other tests); it also includes a test of auditory comprehension (reading potential) and six phonics tests.

Standard Reading Inventory (Klamath Printing Company, Klamath Falls, Ore.) / This individualized test measures reading skills from the preprimer to the seventh-grade level via a series of increasingly difficult story selections followed by comprehension tasks. The test indicates independent, instructional, and frustrational reading levels in terms of vocabulary (isolated and contextual), word recognition, comprehension (after oral and silent reading), and rate (in oral and silent reading).

All these tests are well-developed instruments and have unique strengths for reading assessment, the Standard Reading Inventory (McCracken, 1966) seems especially useful for a teacher who wants to obtain measurements of various connected reading skills. In the Standard Reading Inventory, the student first takes a test on isolated word lists. Depending on his performance in this test, the student is asked to read, first orally and then silently, selections at increasing levels of difficulty. After each selection, the student's comprehension is tested in terms of tell-back ability, recall, and inference skill. The results are graphed onto the profile sheet reproduced in Figure 9-2. Teachers may find it advantageous to administer a test such as the Standard Reading Inventory or any of the other tests described. However, for normal situations, it seems doubtful that such individualized tests should or could be administered to each pupil in a class.

Informal measures of reading achievement

Sunny Decker (1969) describes her anger at a boy who would not answer questions based on a book the class was reading and discussing. After asking him to leave the room, she discovered that he could not read. Although this incident occurred in high school and one might understand her assumption that everyone can read, it seems incredible that *any* teacher would not only not know whether a student could read, but how well or poorly he could read. Unfortunately, this is not an isolated example.

One might think a casual perusal of the student's cumulative folder or achievement test data would suffice, but as we have seen earlier, Sunny Decker's student could have scored better on the achievement battery than he was really capable of performing because standardized tests often do not accurately measure very deviant achievement levels. The conclusion that seems evident from all of this is that *the most powerful means for determining individual achievement levels are informal tests.*

We must determine (1) which students can profit from instruction in the assigned texts, (2) which students need more advanced texts, and (3) which students cannot profitably work in the assigned texts because they are too difficult. Student reading abilities vary so greatly within a given grade level or room (as we saw in Chapter 1) that it is imperative to have many levels of books available. The teacher then must decide which books fit which children. It is this determination of fit that involves the most sophisticated diagnostic skills, because if the book is too easy, it may not provide growth opportunities; if it is too difficult, the result may be the disaster of complete failure.

In order to diagnose informally, the teacher needs criteria of appropriateness. It is to these that we now turn our attention.

Criteria for informal reading assessment

The idea that there is some optimum level of reading instruction can be traced back to the 1920s (Beldin, 1969). It was based on the hypothesis that the level must be easy enough so as to not

Figure 9-2 / Profile sheet used in the Standard Reading Inventory.

Name_____ Date _____ Grade _____ School_____ form B

GENERAL SCORING SHEET - STANDARD READING INVENTORY

		frustration	questionable	instructional definite	independent
PRE-PRIMER	VOCABULARY context	. . . .	8 or less	9 —— 21	22 - 23 - 24
	isolation	. . . .	5 or less	6 —— 13	14 - 15
	ERRORS word recognition	7 or more	6 5 4	3 2	1 - 0
	total	11 or more	10 to 5	4 3 2	1 - 0
	COMPREHENSION oral	0 or 1	2	3 4	5
	SPEED oral (seconds)		60 or more	59 —— 48	47 or less
PRIMER 1-1	VOCABULARY context	. . . .	5 or less	6 7 8	9 - 10
	isolation	. . . .	11 or less	12 —— 22	23 - 24 - 25
	ERRORS word recognition	7 or more	6 5 4	3 2	1 - 0
	total	7 or more	6 5	4 3	2 - 1 - 0
	COMPREHENSION oral recall . .	0 to 5	6	7 8	9 - 10
	silent recall . .	0 to 5	6	7 8	9 - 10
	total interpretation . .	. . . .	0 1 2	3 4	5 - 6
	SPEED oral (seconds)	. . . .	65 or more	64 —— 49	48 or less
	silent (seconds)	. . . .	65 or more	64 —— 49	48 or less
FIRST READER 1-2	VOCABULARY context	. . . .	5 or less	6 7 8	9 - 10
	isolation	. . . .	11 or less	12 —— 23	24 - 25
	ERRORS word recognition	7 or more	6 5 4	3 2	1 - 0
	total	7 or more	6 5	4 3	2 - 1 - 0
	COMPREHENSION oral recall . .	0 to 5	6	7 8	9 - 10
	silent recall . .	0 to 5	6	7 8	9 - 10
	total interpretation . .	. . . .	0 1 2	3 4	5 - 6
	SPEED oral (seconds)	. . . .	69 or more	68 —— 49	48 or less
	silent (seconds)	. . . .	69 or more	68 —— 49	48 or less
SECOND READER 2-1	VOCABULARY context	. . . .	5 or less	6 7 8	9 - 10
	isolation	. . . .	12 or less	13 —— 23	24 - 25
	ERRORS word recognition	8 or more	7 6 5	4 3 2	1 - 0
	total	8 or more	7 6	5 4 3	2 - 1 - 0
	COMPREHENSION oral recall . .	0 to 5	6	7 8	9 - 10
	SPEED oral (seconds)	. . . .	67 or more	66 —— 51	50 or less
SECOND READER 2-2	VOCABULARY context	. . . .	5 or less	6 7 8	9 - 10
	isolation	. . . .	12 or less	13 —— 23	24 - 25
	ERRORS word recognition	8 or more	7 6 5	4 3 2	1 - 0
	total	8 or more	7 6	5 4 3	2 - 1 - 0
	COMPREHENSION oral recall . .	0 to 5	6	7 8	9 - 10
	SPEED oral (seconds)	. . . .	68 or more	67 —— 52	51 or less
	COMPREHENSION silent recall .	0 to 5	6	7 8	9 - 10
	total interpretation .	. . . .	0 1 2 3	4 5 6	7 - 8 - 9
	SPEED silent (seconds)		112 or more	111—— 65	64 or less
THIRD READER 3-1	VOCABULARY context	. . . .	5 or less	6 7 8	9 - 10
	isolation	. . . .	12 or less	13 —— 23	24 - 25
	ERRORS word recognition	8 or more	7 6 5	4 3 2	1 - 0
	total	8 or more	7 6 5	4 3	2 - 1 - 0
	COMPREHENSION oral recall . .	0 to 5	6	7 8	9 - 10
	SPEED oral (seconds)	. . . .	53 or more	52 —— 39	38 or less
THIRD READER 3-2	VOCABULARY context	. . . .	5 or less	6 7 8	9 - 10
	isolation	. . . .	12 or less	13 —— 23	24 - 25
	ERRORS word recognition	9 or more	8 7 6 5	4 3 2	1 - 0
	total	9 or more	8 7	6 5 4 3	2 - 1 - 0
	COMPREHENSION oral recall . .	0 to 5	6	7 8	9 - 10
	SPEED oral (seconds)	. . . .	61 or more	60 —— 41	40 or less
	COMPREHENSION silent recall . .	0 to 5	6	7 8	9 - 10
	total interpretation . .	. . . .	0 1 2 3	4 5 6	7 - 8 - 9
	SPEED silent (seconds)	. . . .	68 or more	67 —— 51	50 or less

2

(Printed in the U.S.A.)

General Scoring Sheet, continued	frustration	instructional		independent
		questionable	definite	independent
FOURTH VOCABULARY	. . . .	12 or less	13 —— 23	24 - 25
ERRORS word recognition	15 or more	14 — 8	7 6 5 4 3	2 - 1 - 0
total	15 or more	14 — 10	9 8 7 6 5	4 - 3 - 2 - 1 - 0
COMPREHENSION oral recall . .	0 to 5	6	7 8	9 - 10
silent recall . .	0 to 5	6	7 8	9 - 10
total interpretation . .	. . . .	0 1 2 3 4 5	6 7	8 - 9 - 10
SPEED oral (seconds)	. . . .	74 or more	73 —— 60	59 or less
silent (seconds)	. . . .	60 or more	59 —— 45	44 or less
FIFTH VOCABULARY	. . . .	12 or less	13 —— 23	24 - 25
ERRORS word recognition	15 or more	14 — 8	7 6 5 4 3	2 - 1 - 0
total	15 or more	14 — 10	9 8 7 6 5	4 - 3 - 2 - 1 - 0
COMPREHENSION oral recall . .	0 to 5	6	7 8	9 - 10
silent recall . .	0 to 5	6	7 8	9 - 10
total interpretation . .	. . . .	0 1 2 3 4 5	6 7	8 - 9 - 10
SPEED oral (seconds)	. . . .	74 or more	73 —— 60	59 or less
silent (seconds)	. . . .	53 or more	52 —— 45	44 or less
SIXTH VOCABULARY	. . . .	12 or less	13 —— 23	24 - 25
ERRORS word recognition	15 or more	14 — 8	7 6 5 4 3	2 - 1 - 0
total	15 or more	14 — 10	9 8 7 6 5	4 - 3 - 2 - 1 - 0
COMPREHENSION oral recall . .	0 to 5	6	7 8	9 - 10
silent recall . .	0 to 5	6	7 8	9 - 10
total interpretation . .	. . . .	0 1 2 3 4 5	6 7	8 - 9 - 10
SPEED oral (seconds)	. . . .	70 or more	69 —— 60	59 or less
silent (seconds)	. . . .	45 or more	44 —— 36	35 or less
SEVENTH VOCABULARY	. . . .	12 or less	13 —— 23	24 - 25
ERRORS word recognition	15 or more	14 — 8	7 6 5 4 3	2 - 1 - 0
total	15 or more	14 — 10	9 8 7 6 5	4 - 3 - 2 - 1 - 0
COMPREHENSION oral recall . .	0 to 5	6	7 8	9 - 10
silent recall . .	0 to 5	6	7 8	9 - 10
total interpretation . .	. . . .	0 1 2 3 4 5	6 7	8 - 9 - 10
SPEED oral (seconds)	. . . .	70 or more	69 —— 60	59 or less
silent (seconds)	. . . .	38 or more	37 —— 30	29 or less

COMPARATIVE STRENGTH CHART
(performance within the instructional range)

weak   ave.   strong

independent reading level . . . . ———

minimum instructional level . . . ———

maximum instructional level . . . ———

frustration level . . . . ———

word calling level (if any) . . . . ———

listening level . . . . ———

WORD RECOGNITION ————————————

context ————————————

isolation ————————————

ORAL READING ————————————

speed ————————————

comprehension ————————————

errors ————————————

SILENT READING ————————————

speed ————————————

comprehension ————————————

3

discourage the student, and yet difficult enough that he will make some errors with which the teacher can assist him. This continual teacher assistance or "instruction" would permit the student to continue to climb the reading skills hierarchy.

Research by Killgallon (1942) which was popularized by Betts (1946) suggested that there were three rather distinct levels of reading difficulty; these were characterized as independent, instructional, and frustrational (see Table 9-1). Although the Killgallon-Betts concepts have been widely adopted by reading methods authors over the last two decades, they have been questioned by many researchers (Hunt, 1969; Spache, 1969; Powell, 1968). Spache (1969) maintains that the standards are arbitrarily high and that teachers do not follow them. Powell (1968) discovered that first- and second-graders could attain a comprehension level of 70 percent with an average word recognition of 85 percent (some 10 percent less than the Betts-Killgallon criterion).

The controversy continues, for despite the wealth of commentary, none of the evidence pro or con is definitive. We simply have no detailed research that follows up reading at the various percentage possibilities to determine whether or not the pupils were achieving in optimum fashion. Because of other variables—interest, teaching strategies, and so on—it is unlikely that we will be able to reduce the process to numerical categories that will be applicable to every child. Since we must operate in the absence of empirical

Table 9-1 / Levels of reading difficulty

Level	Word recognition skill	Comprehension skill
Independent:		
Individual has almost no difficulty in pronouncing or understanding; needs no help.	99% of words pronounced correctly	90% of questions answered correctly
Instructional:		
Individual has enough difficulty to require instruction.	95% of words pronounced correctly	75% of questions answered correctly
Frustrational:		
Reader demonstrates various behaviors which impede reading success.	90% of words or less pronounced correctly	50% or less answered correctly

support, we suggest that teachers employ the criteria shown in Figure 9-3, which are adapted from Powell's research. They tend to reflect a liberalization that seems commensurate with observed reality.

These criteria are offered only as guidelines to the diagnostic reading teacher. As we have suggested earlier, error counting may not be as important as determining the reasons for the errors or "miscues" as Goodman (1965) describes them. Diagnostic reading teachers should keep the criteria in mind when making observations of reading behavior, but be flexible about moving the pupil up or down if his subsequent efforts show the original placement decision was inappropriate.

The technicalities of setting criteria for instructional level placement are important, but we must not lose our perspective: our goal is the most expedient means for discovering which book or books are appropriate for various individuals. Because this determination task is so different in the various grades, our testing jobs will vary sharply, as is apparent in the following illustrations:

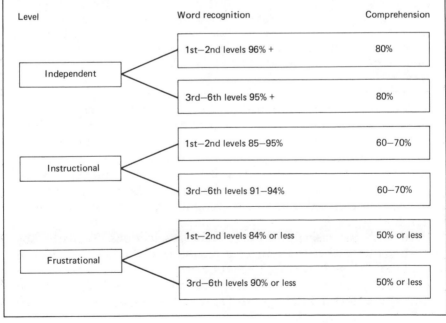

Figure 9-3 / Recommended criteria for determining the appropriateness of material. Adapted from W. R. Powell, "Reappraising the Criteria for Interpreting Informal Inventories," paper presented at the thirteenth annual convention of the International Reading Association, Boston, 1968.

Level	Word recognition	Comprehension
Independent	1st—2nd levels 96% +	80%
	3rd—6th levels 95% +	80%
Instructional	1st—2nd levels 85—95%	60—70%
	3rd—6th levels 91—94%	60—70%
Frustrational	1st—2nd levels 84% or less	50% or less
	3rd—6th levels 90% or less	50% or less

Mrs. Thomas, second grade

Mrs. Thomas meets her new group. Soon, the children are asked to take turns reading orally from Preprimer 3. She notes the oral performance of each child against the word recognition criterion for this level (85-95 percent instructional). After the first round, she has a rough idea of whether all the children can read this material. If she is doubtful about some, she can assign them another task (pending further determination), and go on to repeat the process as often as necessary in an attempt to measure word recognition facility.

Mrs. John, second grade

Mrs. John plans her class time so that she will have a few minutes with each child. In the conference, she begins by having the child read orally from Preprimer 3. This is followed by questions. Next, the child reads a similar selection silently and answers the questions at the end. These procedures are repeated with increasingly difficult materials until the teacher has a rough determination of the instructional level.

Mr. Bill, fifth grade

Mr. Bill hands each student a packet of stories with questions on the back of each. He tells the students to read each story silently and then turn to the back and answer the questions before proceeding to the next story. As the students finish, Mr. Bill notes the time elapsed. Later, he scores the answered questions and makes tentative decisions about which students can read at which levels (at which speeds).

Mr. Tom, sixth grade

Mr. Tom gives each pupil in his class a 250-word excerpt from one of the first stories in the geography text. Every fifth word is deleted from the selection, and he asks each student to fill in the deleted words as best he can. After the students are finished, Mr. Tom applies an answer key and criterion score to each pupil's work to determine whether or not the student can read the selection (and presumably the geography text) at an instructional level.

Although each teacher in these examples is doing very different things, it is evident that each is attempting to get at individual instructional levels. Mrs. Thomas is using only the dimension of word recognition in her group assessment technique, while Mrs. John is assessing each individual's silent and oral reading skill (word recognition and comprehension). Mr. Bill in the fifth grade is not so much concerned with word recognition as he is with comprehension, so he is determining the pupil's skill in answering questions with increasingly difficult reading selections. Similarly, the sixth-grade teacher is attempting to find out whether students can read their assigned geography text or not.

In the pages that follow, informal measures will be discussed under the broad headings of (1) word recognition techniques,

(2) comprehension techniques, and (3) combination techniques (which include varying combinations of word recognition, comprehension, and fluency).

Word recognition techniques

Since the task of turning code elements (graphemes) into their sound counterparts (phonemes) is a prominent part of the reading act, pupil skill in this task is often measured by tests of words in isolation and in context.

Words in isolation / For situations in which teachers want a quick estimate of a pupil's reading level, tests of isolated word recognition skill can be useful. Two tests for assessing a pupil's reading achievement via word-attack skill are described below. The Sight Word List, although the slower of the two, provides an extensive sampling of the basic sight words that comprise the majority of primary reading words. Of course, its value is limited to the measurement of primary reading skill. The second measure, the Queen's College Sample List, draws a few words representative of words at each grade level through the fifth grade. Individual teachers or groups in school systems may choose to make similar tests, using their own basal series for sampling purposes.

Determining reading achievement: sight word list

Step 1 / At a relaxed moment, sit down with the pupil and ask him to read the first list of words (usually cut away from the others and devoid of a grading label such as "preprimer"). If you prefer, place the words on individual cards. (The lists are those in Table 4-1, Dolch Basic Sight Words.)

Step 2 / As the student reads the words, the examiner marks the errors on his master list, as follows:

which	No mark is made if the word is correctly pronounced.
~~which~~	A line is drawn through words the student cannot make any attempt to pronounce within 10 seconds.
	A substituted word or word part is written above as indicated.

 If a student corrects a substitution within the 10-second time allotment, place a small *c* by the word to indicate *correction.* Such corrections are not normally counted as errors.

Step 3 / Since the prime purpose of this test is to determine reading achievement, testing should be stopped when the task is obviously too difficult. The test can be considered too difficult if a student misses thirteen or more words on any list.

Step 4 / Instructional levels can be approximated by the use of the following table of maximum allowable errors:

Preprimer	8 errors or less is instructional or better
Primer	10 errors or less is instructional or better
First reader	8 errors or less is instructional or better
Second reader	9 errors or less is instructional or better
Third reader	8 errors or less is instructional or better

Determining reading achievement: Queens College list*

Step 1 / At a relaxed moment, sit down with the pupil and ask him to read the first list (usually cut away from the others and without grading labels such as "preprimer"). The words may be placed on individual cards if you wish.

Preprimer	Primer	First reader	Second reader
am	all	another	clang
big	cake	cry	fruit
run	how	hopped	quick
dog	from	gate	teach
up	into	snow	sound
look	story	next	music
to	that	bunny	often
me	wanted	thought	straight
it	playing	well	dark
good	milk	running	cannot

Third reader	Fourth reader	Fifth reader
cheek	addition	accomplish
reason	blizzard	commotion
plain	compound	decorate
freeze	embrace	essential
knife	groove	marvelous
inch	introduce	grateful
moment	magic	population
president	nonsense	remarkable
shovel	permanent	suggestion
whale	scratch	territory

Step 2 / As the student reads the words, the examiner marks the errors on his master copy.

Step 3 / The list in which a student misses no more than two words indicates his instructional level. Three or more errors indicates likely frustration.

Words in context / Noting a pupil's word recognition facility in context provides the teacher with a better index of reading skill

*Albert J. Harris, *How To Increase Reading Ability*, 5th ed. (New York: McKay, 1970), p. 178. Used by permission of the publisher.

than does the observation of word recognition skill in isolation. This is because the more complete communication effect of connected material can offer the thinking reader much word recognition assistance (Goodman, 1965).

Word recognition errors / Although we have established criteria for making judgments about whether certain reading selections are independent, instructional, or frustrational (Figure 9-3), we have neglected to answer a basic question: *What are word recognition errors?* Like the debate about the percentages of the various reading levels, there is similar debate concerning what should be counted as word recognition errors. A pupil may be rated as instructional in a given book by one examiner and frustrational by another examiner. Acting rather arbitrarily on my own experiences, I wish to indicate two categorizations of oral word recognition errors—definite and indefinite.

Definite errors
Words told / The pupil pauses for 10 seconds or more without offering the word. In order to keep him moving, we tell him the word as we mark through it on our test copy (or text); for example:

The dog ~~which~~ came to the house . . .

Substitutions / When a student substitutes a word part, word, phrase, and so on, we circle the part that was missed and place the substitution above it; for example:

The dog ~~which~~ came to the house was my poodle.

Substitutions that do not sharply interfere with meaning are seldom counted as errors.

Omissions / Omitted word parts, words, phrases, sentences, and so on are circled and counted as single errors; for example:

The big dog sat on the (wide) road.   1 error

(He did not see the car coming at him.)   1 error

The driver honked his horn loud(ly.)   1 error

Indefinite errors
Insertions / Often good readers will insert words that correspond with their oral speaking patterns. Such insertions should not be counted unless they alter meaning significantly. It is useful to mark them so that you may determine later whether they affected meaning or not; for example:

Let's walk to the top ^of it^ and roll down.

Repetitions / Repetitions may be stalls for time while pupils are struggling with words ahead. They may also be attempts to obtain clarity from what they have already read. Because they may represent so many different things, we suggest that they not be counted unless they significantly interfere with the fluency and understanding of the reading. They should be marked so that you can make judgments of their interference; for example:

Bill and Jane are coming to the house on Saturday.
We want to get the bunkhouse ready for them.

Phrasing / Pupils who are overpracticed on isolated sight word cards tend to read in a word-by-word fashion in the early stages of reading instruction. Other students for other reasons fail to phrase material well. Because most children seem to improve phrasing with increasing word recognition and comprehension skill, we are reluctant to specify how inaccurate phrasing should be counted in an error count. We do feel it should be marked and noted so that efforts can be made to solve the underlying causes. Marking is usually done by placing vertical marks where undue pauses are noted; for example:

The man| got| in | the | wagon and| drove away.

For the teacher anxious to put the theory to work by actually testing students in connected reading, we offer the following explanation of the preparation, administration, and scoring of an informal test of connected word recognition skill.

Determining reading achievement: words in context

Step 1 / The stories to be tried by the student should come from texts you plan to use for his instruction. The specific stories chosen should (1) represent the first, middle, and end portions of each text; (2) start at a meaningful point where the student will not be confused by a lack of pertinent information; (3) be at least 100 words in length. Stories that are typed and gathered into an informal reading inventory should probably (1) have only one story on a given page, (2) have no indications of the grade level of the selection (on the student's copy), (3) have well-developed, literal comprehension questions that adequately sample the main points, and (4) be typed in such a way that line length, and so on conform closely to the texts from which the stories are taken. Stories that are to be read directly from the texts should be marked in advance with pencil slashes in order that the examiner may control the necessary length and prepare appropriate questions.

Step 2 / As the student reads the selection, the examiner should mark his copy of the test or text in the manner prescribed in the section on errors that follows. If the marking procedure is too distracting, the teacher might tape record the reading for subsequent analysis.

Step 3 / Count the number of definite word recognition errors in the selection, and then divide this number by the number of words in the selection; for example:

Case A: Jane makes 8 definite errors in a 100-word selection.

$$(1) \quad 100 \overline{)8.00} \atop \underline{8\ 00} \quad {\scriptstyle .08}$$

(2)   1.00 (or total of words)
      .08 (words missed)
      .92 (or 92% accuracy—word recognition)

Case B: Joey makes 12 errors in 135-word selection.

(1)   135 $\overline{)12.00}$
            .08
            10 80

(2)   1.00
      .08
      .92   (or 92% accuracy—word recognition)

Step 4 / Determine by the use of the following criteria and judgment the level of difficulty of the selection.

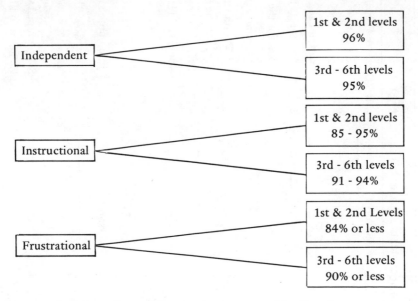

In order that the reader may more graphically view contextual word recognition assessment, examples of (1) a typed inventory and (2) a test taken directly from the text are illustrated in Table 9-2 and Figure 9-4. Table 9-2 shows Jane Smith's performance on a typed inventory prepared, scored, and judged by her teacher. The information on the right side of the table has been left blank so that you can: Compute the word recognition accuracy (percentage correct); record the computation (W.R.); and determine whether the reading level for each selection is independent, instructional, or frustrational. You can compare your judgments with those of the author by referring to the material at the end of the table.

Table 9-2 / Word recognition in context: a teacher-constructed test

A (Code for Preprimer 1) 38 words

Come, Rex
See me jump.
Jump, Rex, jump.

See Jane, Skip.
See Jane and Rex run.
Rex can play, Skip.
Play with Rex and Jane.
Come, Skip.
Come and play with (me).   *us*
See Rex Jump
Jump with Rex.

38) W.R. _____ Level _____

B (Code for Preprimer 2) 50 words

Jane ran for the ball.
She said, "Come here, Bill(y)."
I can not see the ball.
Look for it, Bill(y).
Look for the ball."
Ann came with the ball.
Bill(y) said, "Here comes Ann.
She ^got the ball for you.   *is*
Here she comes with it.
Come and play ball, Ann."

50) W.R. _____ Level _____

C (Code for Preprimer 3) 56 words

Th
"(Wh)ere is Skip?" asked Billy.
"Come out here, Skip.
You can do ~~many~~ tricks.
Do a trick for (the children).
They want you to get the flag.

"Jump up, Skip, jump up."
"Bow wow," said Skip.
"Bow wow, bow wow."
up
Skip jumped ^for the flag.
He got it in his ~~mouth~~   *all*
"Good Skip," said ^the children.

56) W.R. _____ Level _____

Teacher scoring and judgments of Jane's performance

A. $38\overline{)1.00}$ quotient $.02$

W.R.: 98%

Level: Independent

B. $50\overline{)1.00}$ quotient $.02$

W.R.: 98%

Level: Independent

Explanation:

"Billy" was counted as an error only *once* because the teacher did not correct the error. If it were corrected and subsequently made again, the maximum count would be two errors. Although one word can make a great deal of difference at times, this one did not. Insofar as we are measuring word recognition skill, there is no point in letting a single word or two count out of proportion. The insertion of 's in "She got the ball for you" does not critically alter meaning.

C. $56\overline{)4.00}$ quotient $.07$

W.R.: 93%

Level: Instructional

Explanation:

The following were counted as errors by the teacher:

"there" for "where"—substitution
"them" for "the children"—substitution
many, mouth—words told

The first substitution was definitely an error because the child did not realize it was a question. The second substitution was a good one and did not alter meaning much, so it could probably be ignored. The insertions of "up" and "all" were not counted as errors because they did not hamper meaning. The repetition (uncounted) indicated an effort to attach the unknown word *mouth*.

Figure 9-4 shows a portion of an informal text conducted directly in the pupil's reader. In the example, Mrs. Jones marked the errors made by Bill and Tom as they read orally. Note her markings and compute what you think were her judgments about the word recognition accuracy of these two boys (accuracy percentage, probable difficulty level).

From her samplings, Mrs. Jones concluded the following: "Read selection well. No significant errors. Word recognition problems do not appear obvious at this level." In the course of subsequent samplings, Mrs. Jones may find that Bill and Tom fluctuate in their fluency and word recognition. This is to be ex-

Figure 9-4 / Word recognition in context: testing directly from the text.

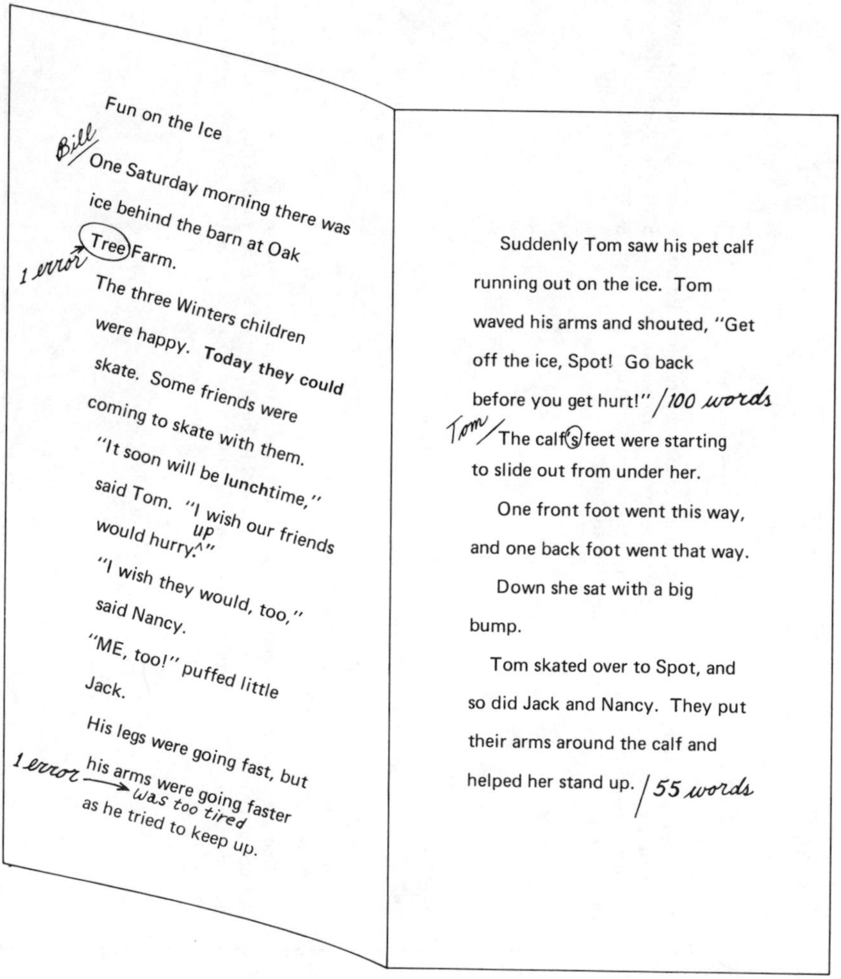

Fun on the Ice

Bill

One Saturday morning there was ice behind the barn at Oak

1 error (Tree) Farm.

The three Winters children were happy. Today they could skate. Some friends were coming to skate with them.

"It soon will be lunchtime," said Tom. "I wish our friends would hurry.^" up

"I wish they would, too," said Nancy.

"ME, too!" puffed little Jack.

His legs were going fast, but

1 error — his arms were going faster was too tired as he tried to keep up.

Suddenly Tom saw his pet calf running out on the ice. Tom waved his arms and shouted, "Get off the ice, Spot! Go back before you get hurt!" / 100 words

Tom The calf(s) feet were starting to slide out from under her.

One front foot went this way, and one back foot went that way.

Down she sat with a big bump.

Tom skated over to Spot, and so did Jack and Nancy. They put their arms around the calf and helped her stand up. / 55 words

pected. If, however, they consistently read with great ease and comprehend accordingly, she may wonder if the placement is really appropriate. The converse would be true if their performances were poor in this and subsequent samples. Then she would be concerned with getting the boys into reading materials that were less difficult.

Comprehension techniques

Without question, the most important determinant of a pupil's reading achievement is the extent to which he understands the various reading materials with which he works. Although indications of such understanding can be obtained from formal tests, they are of limited value for telling us whether the pupil can function in specific books and materials. For judgments of how well any pupil can actually understand, it is imperative to test his understanding of the materials in question. Pupil comprehension of given materials can be tested with (1) questioning procedures and (2) closure procedures.

Questioning / Questioning is the way most teachers make on-the-spot assessments of how well pupils understand. Probably the greatest number of assessments occur in oral questioning sessions with groups, although many checks are made with written questions. Both oral and silent questioning practices are potentially valuable as well as dangerous means of assessment. Oral questions allow teachers to ask a large number of questions in rapid-fire fashion, but there is always the possibility that few, if any, pupils will be thoroughly checked out on their understanding of a story. We have all seen situations in which:

A few students do most of the answering.

A few others will appear to offer good responses by relating experiences rather than providing tangible evidence.

A few will follow the discussion closely and be able to answer many logical possibility questions.

A few may miss their questions because of a miscommunication, even though other evidence might indicate understanding of the primary concepts.

It should be added, however, that despite the weaknesses, oral sessions are essential to beginning reading instruction and are useful at any point as opportunities for seeking elaboration as well as for providing the child with inadequate handwriting and spelling skills a means for demonstrating his understanding of written materials.

Silent questioning frequently demands writing skills beyond the capabilities of beginning readers. As soon as pupils can use this means, however, it is well for them to do so, because it provides a sampling technique that is much more likely to give the teacher an accurate assessment of individual pupil understanding. We recommend the use of silent questions as the primary determinant of achievement. In making judgments of pupil understanding of written materials, the following guidelines should be noted.

Guidelines for determining comprehension by oral and silent questioning

Guideline 1 / The determination of the comprehension level is essentially a measure of literal understanding. This means that the questions should be of the recognition, recall, and organization variety (although some ideas are more implicit than explicit and require extending skill).

Guideline 2 / The criterion of acceptable understanding should be predetermined. The reader will recall that earlier we accepted the 60 percent or better criterion. This criterion should apply to both multiple-question and organization situations in which the pupil may be asked to summarize, list the main points, and so on.

Guideline 3 / In concert with Guideline 2, it is important that the elements to which the criterion will be applied are predetermined. This simply means that the questions are carefully screened to see that they are representative of the major understandings involved in the reading material. If a tellback is involved, the elements that should be told back should be listed (preferably in sequence).

Guideline 4 / Question formulation can hold the key to the validity of your test. The greatest limitation to all testing lies in the formulation of the questions. Specific suggestions that can assist in the development of valid questions are the following:

Avoid the practice of going through the content and systematically writing out the questions (unless you plan to allow the students to answer in this fashion). Unless the assignment calls for a great amount of detail recall, you may create questions even you cannot answer.
Check your questions out in advance on others (preferably pupils with demonstrated understanding at the levels concerned). By doing this, you have a check on the content of your questions and whether or not they communicate.
Do not try to squeeze ten questions out of every testing situation. Some content lends itself to only a few questions (three or four), so seek to develop questions that get at important points. The ritual of making up ten questions when ten would require nitpicking is a common and dangerous practice.
Follow up on the questions that are missed by asking them orally. You frequently can determine whether the question is misleading, whether the student read something else into it, and so on. There are many interpretations we can never find unless we seek out the variant interpreters.

Guideline 5 / If comprehension testing is to be conducted via oral questioning, provision should be made for all students to register a response to each question. Each student should make a written response or a signal response (to be discussed in detail in Chapter 13) to each question. The question. can then be discussed by an individual pupil or pupils. The teacher can note signal responses instantly and get immediate feedback as to who is catching on to what. With the paper response, the teacher will not know who did not understand until after the session when he corrects the papers.

The preceding guidelines are applicable to all types of reading materials. Because children's reading is not limited to the basal reader, it is recommended that the teacher employ a systematic testing program in the various materials (news magazines, science texts, social studies texts, music books, spellers, and so on).

Closure procedures / A second means for determining comprehension by informal means is the closure or cloze test. This test works on the Gestalt principle of closure, which states that we effect closure when we see enough parts of a familiar entity. In reading, pupils demonstrate closure or understanding by inserting needed words that have been deleted from a story. Although the words may be deleted at random, this practice does not give us precise information on the pupil's restoration job; rather, deleted words should probably be every fifth or tenth word (Bormuth, 1967; Rankin and Culhane, 1969).

Steps for the preparation, administration, and scoring of a cloze test are given below. It should be pointed out that although cloze tasks are useful from the beginning of reading instruction, those such as the following (omitting every fifth word) prove to be rather difficult for students below a fourth-grade reading level.

Determining reading achievement by a fourth-grade-level cloze test
Preparation

Step 1 / Select a relatively free-standing selection of at least 275 words (55 cloze blanks) from the portion of the book you plan to use for instruction. (Free-standing means the beginning of a section, chapter—material that does nor depend too much on previous information).

Step 2 / Delete every fifth word.

Step 3 / Type up the cloze test, being sure to allow the same number of spaces for every deleted word. The spaces should be large enough for the students to write in the longest words.

Administering, scoring, and judging

Step 1 / Hand a test to each individual and ask him to write in the blank spaces the words he thinks should be there. Indicate that you realize the task is difficult and that it will probably be necessary for him to erase and change words as he works on the problem. Encourage the students to complete every blank. *Do not provide a time limit, as this is a power test.*

Step 2 / When the tests are completed, mark every word that is not exactly the same as the deleted word from the story. Total up the number of correct responses (unmarked) and place that score at the bottom of the paper.

Step 3 / Determine the difficulty level of each pupil's effort on the following scale (established by Rankin and Culhane, 1969):

Independent level—the student correctly replaces 61 percent or more of the deleted words. (Thirty-three words or more correct.)

Instructional level—the student correctly replaces 41 percent or more of the deleted words. (Twenty-two words or more correct.)

Frustrational level—the student correctly replaces 40 percent or less of the deleted words. (Less than twenty-two words correct.) *Note:* Bormuth (1967) recommends other percentage criteria for making such determinations.

Although the preceding testing may seem complex, it is actually rather easy from the standpoint of the examiner, as he has only to make a deleted word selection, administer it, and then compute the scores. The technique seems most appropriate for upper-grade teachers in assessing the readability of a multitude of instructional materials such as *My Weekly Reader* and content area texts (geography, science, English), as well as the assigned reading materials. In addition to the advantages of wide content sampling, cloze testing is rather simple in terms of administration and scoring. Among the disadvantages are the frustrating nature of the task (especially to children below fourth-grade level) and test score variation that appears more akin to topic content than vocabulary and sentence difficulty.

Combination techniques

It is generally desirable to combine certain word recognition and comprehension techniques. The major problem seems to be the determination of when to apply each technique. In this section, we will present material on which combinations (or single tests) are most appropriate for the following situations: Quick instructional identification (quickly making a tentative judgment about a pupil's instructional level), quick instructional verification (quickly verifying your initial tentative judgment), extensive instructional identification (making an extensive identification of a pupil's instructional level), and extensive instructional verification (making an extensive verification of a pupil's instructional level). Ideally, we should all make extensive identifications and verifications, but classroom realities make this difficult (as well as unnecessary) under most circumstances.

The reader will note that the dimension of fluency has been added to the word recognition and comprehension techniques. Obviously, fluency cannot stand alone as a technique for making decisions about instructional levels (even though we have suggested that oral fluency in the sense of intonational elements can signal comprehension). Fluency is most often measured in terms of oral and/or silent rate (see rate norms given in Chapter 6), and this needs to be combined with something else. Table 9-3 illustrates recommended achievement determination techniques for the tasks of instructional identification and verification. You will note that the suggested techniques vary in terms of grade level and intensity of assessment.

Preprimer through second reader / Although the administration of isolated word lists may be the quickest means, it rules out too much valuable context analysis skill to be highly recommended. For quick instructional identification, we suggest that the teacher allow each pupil in the group (small) to read a selection orally. This measure will reveal little about comprehension, but it will yield a most valuable estimate of placement that can be verified in a subsequent session in which questions are asked of each pupil after his oral reading.

Extensive identification allows the teacher to strike comparisons

Table 9-3 / Recommended achievement determination techniques: preprimer through grade 8 reading levels

Determination task	Word recognition		Comprehension		Reading fluency	
	Isolated	Context	Question	Cloze	Oral	Silent
PP 1^2						
Quick instr. ident.		x				
Quick instr. ver.		x	x			
Ext. instr. ident.	x	x	x		x	
Ext. instr. ver.		x	x		x	
2						
Quick instr. ident.		x				
Quick instr. ver.		x	x			
Ext. instr. ident.	x	x	x		x	
Ext. instr. ver.		x	x		x	
3						
Quick instr. ident.		x				
Quick instr. ver.		x	x			
Ext. instr. ident.	x	x	x		x←——→x	
Ext. instr. ver.		x	x		x←——→x	
4-8						
Quick instr. ident.			x			x
Quick instr. ver.			x			x
Ext. instr. ident.		x	x	x		x
Ext. instr. ver.		x	x	x		x

between isolated and connected word recognition as well as to get indications of comprehension and oral fluency. If time permits, such judgments can be valuable for assessing differences between pupil skills in isolated and connected reading. Extensive verification calls for the same measures, with the exception that the isolated word list is omitted because it is no longer useful.

Third reader / By the third reader level, a pupil should have a silent rate that is significantly higher than his oral rate in independent level reading. Thus, fluency testing is suggested. Other than noting the comparative oral and silent reading rates, the procedures remain the same as those suggested for the previous levels.

Fourth reader and above / By fourth reader level, we should not be greatly concerned about oral word recognition; rather, our primary concerns must be for comprehension and the rate at which it is accomplished silently. Therefore, we suggest that all determinations of instructional levels should employ both factors. An additional option for checking comprehension is the cloze test, which offers a useful means of group testing in a way other than questioning.

Summary

When a teacher suggests that it is necessary to discover where a pupil "is" in terms of reading achievement, he usually refers to the pupil's standing on a skills ladder; for example, reading at the third-grade reading level. Finding out where the student is involves both formal and informal tests. Formal reading tests range from the reading portions of comprehensive achievement tests to analytical skills tests. Informal means of testing for level involve word recognition tests (in isolation and context) and comprehension tests (by questioning and closure procedures).

Formal reading tests are useful for giving a teacher a view of student performance in comparison with a normative group, but they are very limited for determining whether or not a pupil can read a specific text or selection. Informal tests in the actual reading materials possess the greatest value for the teacher for making instructional decisions.

10 Reading potential

Behavioral objectives
1. Accurately explain the concept of *reading potential* and its importance to diagnostic instruction.
2. Describe the reading potential measurement techniques proposed by (a) Harris and (b) Bond and Tinker, their underlying rationales, and their limitations.
3. Determine pupil reading potential via the use of formal or informal tests of listening comprehension.

Due to a number of circumstances, some children do not develop word recognition skills compatible with their ability to understand language. As a result, their ability to comprehend printed materials is seriously limited. We therefore see an immediate discrepancy between reading achievement and reading potential (the achievement that might be anticipated if the student had good word recognition skills). Consider the case of Joe Brown, who has a reading potential of third grade and a reading achievement of first grade. Through means we will explain, we know Joe has the potential to read third-grade material. Yet his reading achievement is only first grade, or some two years below what "it should be." A greater insight into the importance of the concept of reading potential is gained from speculations about Joe and some of his third-grade classmates:

Name	Grade	Age	Achievement level
Joe B.	3	8	First reader
Bob	3	8	Third reader
Mary	3	8	Second reader
Sue	3	8	Primer

The list might suggest that Bob is the brightest boy in the group because he is the only one achieving at grade level and that Sue must be the worst. Both assumptions however, are quite likely to be erroneous. Reading potential does not necessarily correspond with grade level. Although we can expect most third-graders to have the capability to read third-grade readers effectively, we know that some will have either greater or lesser abilities than others. Some children in Joe's class should be reading at a second-grade level and some at a fourth- or fifth-grade level. Reading potential is a determination of an individual's ability to understand language material heard and not read. We might find that Bob has an understanding level of fourth reader via his listening skills, but a reading achievement level of third reader. The discrepancy shows that although he is reading at grade level, he is not reaching his potential. Conversely, it might be discovered that the reading achievement levels of Joe, Mary, and Sue reflect their understanding levels, so that their teacher might be satisfied with their achievement.

Without such determinations, it is difficult to know whether a child should be praised or pushed. As teachers, we feel badly if we discover that we have prodded and pushed a slow-learning Sue to the point of total frustration because of our lack of awareness of her understanding deficiencies. We feel very different emotion when we find that a high-potential pupil has not been stimulated to reach toward his potential, but has rather coasted through our class. Because of the impact of the Rosenthal and Jacobsen (1968) study in which pupil achievement seemed to be the result of high or low teacher expectations, the reader may be prone to shy away from efforts to determine reading potential for fear that such expectations will bias his teaching. Such fears are certainly well founded, but it should be realized that the determinations of reading potential are the results of teacher measurements, and not something contrived (as in the study cited) or the results of intelligence tests given under dubious circumstances. It seems imperative that we have some comparatively objective gauge of a pupil's potential, or we are left to make rough, intuitive guesses which will be as good or as bad as our intuitions.

The question of whether we should seek measures of reading potential is not really the problem. The problem is *how.* How can we effectively measure a child's potential? This question in turn must be broken down into two: How *do* we measure reading potential? How *should* we measure reading potential?

Although it is not empirically verified, I have a strong suspicion that we do measure potential by the scores we see on standardized group intelligence tests. That is, we set up a general expectation, such as "he's pretty sharp" or "he's average" or "he's pretty slow." Endless personal testimony indicates the dangers of such a practice. The dangers are so great, in fact, that many school districts have stopped using the tests. In addition to using test results in this way, some reading authorities have developed means for using them in more specific ways for reading potential prediction (we will discuss these in the section on "Reading Potential Formulas").

As for the question of how we *should* measure reading potential, I suggest with listening comprehension tests.

Reading potential formulas

There are numerous formulas for approximating a pupil's reading potential, but two have received the greatest attention. They are the Harris plan (1970) and the Bond and Tinker formula (1968).

The Harris plan

Harris indicates that "reading potential" is synonymous with "mental age" as determined by an individualized or a nonverbal group intelligence test (tests in which students are not penalized by their inability to read). "Mental age" is a normative mental age determined by a pupil's relative standing on an intelligence test; for example, pupils scoring in the normal IQ range of 90 to 110 are presumed to have the mental age of the average child in their age group. If we note the test results for Joe, Bob, Mary, and Sue on one such intelligence test, we might derive the following "reading potentials" using the Harris formula:

Name	Grade	Age	Instructional level	Reading potential*
Joe	3	8	1^2	4 (125 IQ)
Bob	3	8	3^1	3 (100 IQ)
Mary	3	8	2^1	2 (89 IQ)
Sue	3	8	P	3 (100 IQ)

*As based on the anticipated achievement levels of the various mental ages.

By utilizing mental age results as expectancy measures of reading, it appears that Bob and Mary are achieving where they should be, but that Joe and Sue are sharply below where they should be in accordance with their mental age (reading potential in this scheme).

Even though the Harris plan uses intelligence tests that do not require pupils to read, there is still cause for concern in the use of the mental age as a determinant of reading potential. Conceivably, bright youngsters without some of the educational experiences related to the nonverbal tasks sampled by the intelligence tests may go unrecognized.

The Bond and Tinker formula

Bond and Tinker add the dimension of school experience (the amount of reading instruction that might be anticipated) to the intelligence dimension for their assessment of reading potential:

$$\text{Reading expectancy} = \text{Years in school} \times \frac{\text{IQ}}{100} + 1.0.$$

With reading expectancies determined by this formula, the following results are noted for Joe, Bob, Mary, and Sue.

Name	Grade	Age	Instructional level	Reading potential	
Joe	3	8	1^2 (2.0 × 1.25 = 2.5) + 1.0 =	3.5	(4)*
Bob	3	8	3^1 (2.0 × 1.00 = 2.0) + 1.0 =	3.0	(3)
Mary	3	8	2^1 (2.0 × .89 = 1.7) + 1.0 =	2.7	(2)
Sue	3	8	P (2.0 × 1.00 = 2.0) + 1.0 =	3.0	(3)

*Reading potential as determined by Harris technique.

Although the Bond and Tinker formula produces more precise placements in terms of the student's potential (grade and portion of grade as opposed to only grade), there are disconcerting factors. Joe, the student with an IQ of 125, has a reading potential of only half a grade greater than that of Bob and Sue who have 100 IQs. The difference between Joe and Mary (89 IQ) is less than a year. The formula seems rather questionable when one applies it to children who depart significantly from the broad part of the intelligence curve.

Listening comprehension tests

Because of the many questions attending the use of reading potential formulas, scholars such as Durrell (1955), Spache (1963), and others have emphasized what appears to be a logical alternative—the listening comprehension test. It is based on the assumption that if a pupil can demonstrate a certain degree of understanding of material read to him, he can be expected to read such material once he has developed the word attack skills he lacks. Tests of listening comprehension have become synonymous with reading potential. Teachers interested in using the listening comprehension test as a means for determining reading potential have access to both formal measures with established norms and informal measures that have no such norms.

Formal listening comprehension tests

Formal listening comprehension tests frequently comprise one part of a larger testing battery. Illustrative of such test batteries are the following:

Durrell Listening-Reading Series (Harcourt Brace Jovanovich, 1969). / This test measures both listening and reading comprehension skill at the primary, intermediate, and advanced levels. Listening tests at the primary level test vocabulary and sentence listening. In the intermediate and advanced listening tests, the child's vocabulary and paragraph listening skills are checked. These tests can be administered to a group or class.

The Spache Diagnostic Reading Scales (California Test Bureau, 1963) / The reading potential portion of this test begins after the pupil reaches his independent level (highest level at which 60 percent comprehension is maintained according to Spache). When the comprehension falls below 60 percent, the teacher reads the selections to the pupil and asks the questions. The highest level at which the student can answer 60 percent of the questions is considered the reading potential. (Note that Spache's criterion of acceptable comprehension is lower than the 70 percent most frequently found).

McCracken Standard Reading Inventory (Klamath Printing Company, Klamath Falls, Ore., 1966) / After pupils reach the frustration level according to the test norms, the teacher is directed to a special set of paragraphs and questions in the examiner's manual. From these paragraphs, the teacher chooses the selection parallel in difficulty to the one in which the student reached frustration. The teacher reads the selection to the pupil and then asks him to answer the ten accompanying questions. If the pupil can successfully answer seven of the ten questions read to him, it is presumed that he understands the material well enough. The process of the teacher's reading and asking questions is repeated in increasingly difficult selections. The reading potential is said to be the highest level at which the pupil can answer seven of ten questions correctly.

Informal listening comprehension tests

In lieu of purchasing formal listening comprehension tests, teachers may construct their own by using increasingly difficult selections from materials such as the S.R.A. Reading Laboratories (Parker, 1961), basal reader pages, or other reading materials. Short selection materials such as the SRA stories provide the teacher with ready-made questions, although they may not be precisely what she wants.

The use of excerpts from basals for reading potential testing permits the teacher to obtain a measure of the pupil's potential to read the series materials in use at the school. It should be noted, however, that as the reading content becomes more mature and varied, the possibilities become such that a student may understand certain ones and fail to get the meanings of others because of his unique experience background. A one-shot test of reading potential therefore seems to possess slight validity in terms of predicting the pupil's potential to read the other stories in the volume.

Improper questions and questioning practices can negate the predictive value of teacher-made tests of reading potential. Consequently, the following guidelines should be noted when attempting listening comprehension sampling in groups:

Guideline 1 / Sessions should be brief so that the students can give their undivided attention to the task. It takes considerable time to read a selection to the pupils, ask the follow-up questions, and permit pupil response opportunities. Pupils should seldom be asked to listen and respond to more than two selections at a sitting in the early grades; nor should a teacher use such long, uninterrupted time segments for diagnosis.

Guideline 2 / When possible, pupils should be provided with simple answer sheets that expedite the response task. Multiple-choice responses can save the time frequently demanded by written responses.

Guideline 3 / Observe response actions carefully so as to note undue frustration with the task. If continued testing is frustrating, the session should be stopped and arrangements made for (1) individual checks of those pupils demonstrating distress (probably without written response modes) and (2) continuing group checks of those not demonstrating unusual behaviors.

Guideline 4 / Results should be checked at the completion of each session so as to determine continuance tasks. Not only does the teacher need to find out which children seem capable of listening and responding to more difficult selections, he needs to determine follow-up means to see whether or not some of the apparent drop-outs can understand when exposed to other selections. Often, an inability to respond may be triggered by situational variables other than listening comprehension—for example, the way the child feels, confusions with response modes, fixations upon certain distracting factors.

Guideline 5 / Tentative assessments of potential should be periodically rechecked.

While there is argument as to the precise amount of understanding necessary to say that a given material is at a child's understanding level, the 70 percent criterion of accuracy is widely accepted. Because this would seem to dictate the development of at least ten questions per selection, which is often difficult, we would suggest that the criterion of understanding should simply be *whether or not the student seems to understand the story for the most part.* Certainly, teachers make judgments of this sort with varying numbers of questions as well as with varying pupil "tell backs" of what happened. We prefer such intuitive judgments rather than those made in accordance with a rigid percentage figure.

Although it is not amenable to group testing, the individual pupil "tell back" of a story seems to be a useful means for assessing potential. The following table illustrates such a testing situation. Linda J. was found to be reading instructionally at the preprimer 2 level:

Checking reading potential by the tell-back technique

Teacher reads	Linda J. retells	Teacher evaluates
PP 3	Verbatim	No problems.
P	Verbatim	No problems.
1^2	Main elements, in sequence	Good understanding evident.
2^1	Main elements, not in sequence	Understanding is evident even though out of order.
2^2	Emphasizes one portion, adds little else	Understanding dubious—teacher asks pointed questions and student responds accurately. Understanding is evident with teacher stimulation.
3	Mentions a few details	Understanding dubious. Subsequent questioning verifies initial judgment.

Although the samples were brief, the teacher had definite evidence that Linda J. could understand well beyond her preprimer 2 reading level. Further checking should be done to verify the reading potential of 2^2 that was suggested by this checking session.

Perhaps the process of planning and carrying out reading potential assessments as illustrated by listening comprehension tests may seem too laborious and unnecessary to some teachers; they may argue that such a process is carried on informally each day in the classroom through group discussions of stories, assignments in content subjects, and so on. In many instances, this is very true; but there are certainly many other instances in which the samplings are extremely limited because of overly aggressive children, extremely timid children, and limited questioning practices.

Summary

Reading potential refers to the individual abilities of children to understand language. Children with word recognition problems often cannot read materials at their reading potential because of these problems. Measures of pupil reading potential contrasted with reading achievement level indicate the amount of discrepancy between the two elements and suggest to teachers whether the student is underachieving, overachieving, or achieving in accordance with his understanding ability. Reading potential seems to be roughly gauged by pupil intelligence test scores, although many educators have reservations about this practice. Similar reservations exist about the use of intelligence scores in techniques such as those of Harris and Bond and Tinker.

Listening comprehension tests, both formal and informal, appear to be the most useful means for assessing what pupils' understandings of reading materials are. Assuming that pupils could, with word recognition skills, read those materials they understand as a result of hearing appears to be a valid assumption. However, tests devised to measure such understanding may be invalid if great care is not given to such things as sample selection, question development, and judgment criteria.

11 Specific skills needs

Behavioral objectives
1. Describe what is meant by (a) the outlined program, (b) nonsystematic diagnosis, and (c) systematic diagnosis.
2. Describe the Reading Skills Checklist, Levels 1 through 4, and its use in determining (a) word recognition skills and (b) reading comprehension skills.
3. Describe the Reading Skills Checksheet and its use in the recording of word recognition and reading comprehension skills needs.
4. Apply suggested measurement techniques for determining specific skills needs in word recognition, comprehension, and fluency.

Means for diagnosing skills

Once a student's instructional level has been accurately determined (Chapter 9), the teacher needs to pinpoint the various skills needs that will permit growth. Three means for determining what skills will be taught to the student can be described in terms of (1) the outlined program, (2) nonsystematic diagnosis, and (3) systematic diagnosis.

Probably the most common means of diagnosing needs is the outlined program method, in which the teacher uses a set of materials with a built-in skills sequence. Because the skills are sequenced in accordance with the increasingly difficult story material, the teacher logically assumes that the students need to be taught the skills as outlined by the program. Thus, the diagnosis is built into the skills program. As we have indicated previously, it is impossible to anticipate the exact sequence, difficulty, and time required for individual students to acquire various skills, so there is no assurance that the sequence is appropriate or of sufficient duration unless other assessments are made.

Closely akin to the outlined program is the nonsystematic diagnosis. This is the data-collecting behavior of the teacher who listens and observes carefully to note the skills deficiencies of pupils. The diagnosis is nonsystematic because the teacher does not use specific tests, but rather informally notes the various kinds of errors that emerge in reading (notably oral reading and responses to comprehension questions). Usually, the teacher collects such data as the children perform in the outlined program.

Systematic diagnosis is the use of either formal or informal measures of specific reading skills. That is, the teacher systematically tests a student's sight word knowledge in isolation, his consonant blending skill, inferential question-answering abilities, and so on. Systematic diagnosis can be valuable, but it can also be a waste of time. Often, such tests are given to pupils who have skills needs not measured by them (some students do not have any of the skills being measured, while others may have all the skills). Systematic diagnosis should be employed only if it can reveal needed skills dimensions that can subsequently be attended to by the teacher. Extensive data collections alone are rather unimpressive.

In order to put the three means of determining skills in perspective, we suggest the following:

Step 1 / Find each child's instructional reading level.

Step 2 / Determine by nonsystematic diagnosis the kinds of reading skills that are lacking at this instructional level (by observing the student's oral and silent reading as well as his responses to comprehension questions).

Step 3 / If there are prominent deficiencies in a given skill area (such as beginning consonant sounds), utilize systematic diagnosis to determine specifically which elements can and cannot be attacked.

Formal or informal measures may be employed for the systematic diagnosis of reading skills. The reader who would like to study and use certain formal instruments might refer to *Reading Tests and Reviews* (Buros, 1968) for detailed evaluations and descriptions of the various reading tests; for brief discussions of a few tests, see Chapter 9 of this text. The emphasis in the remainder of this chapter will be on informal measures, for we conceive of the diagnostic reading teacher as an "on-the-spot-troubleshooter." The teacher's task is basically one of deriving quick but accurate skills measurements. Cumbersome diagnostic batteries (or even separate skills tests extracted from such batteries) are often unnecessary if the teacher understands the skills and possesses the necessary measurement techniques.

Sequences of reading skills objectives

In Part Two we discussed the three major skills areas of word recognition, reading comprehension, and fluency, but not their sequence. Although reading skills emerge in varied fashions in individual pupils, there is some value in understanding the sequences planned by the authors of basal series. If we do not have any conception of how to proceed to teach such skills, we can hardly be effective.

The Reading Skills Checklist

A useful aid for noting how the specific skills are patterned in a reading program is the scope and sequence chart, which is frequently prepared by publishers to indicate the specific skills goals of the program. In our experience, such charts are usually very large and difficult to handle. To combat the size problem and develop a more practical aid with which teachers could direct their reading skills program, I have developed an aid called the Reading Skills Checklist.* As you will see, the checklist consists of the various reading skills normally taught in the various series texts (preprimer, primer, first reader, and so on). Many teachers commented that the checklist was a good short course in terms of when and where the various skills were introduced. They began to use the checklist as a means for checking whether or not certain students possessed specific skills at a given level.

There was a serious problem, however, in the use of the Reading Skills Checklist that was initially developed. The sequence of skills in our checklist seldom matched the sequences in the various basal readers because we had deliberately created an "eclectic" checklist that could be used in many schools. As a result of our experiences, we wish to suggest the following: (1) The Reading Skills Checklist can be useful in any program, but its greatest value seems to be in an individualized reading program employing a variety of basal and nonbasal materials. (2) If you employ a single basal series, the Checklist can be most useful to you as a guide for constructing a checklist that parallels your series.

The Reading Skills Checklist, as shown in Figure 11-1, illustrates a means by which the teacher can (1) see where the children have been and where they are going on a reading skills continuum and (2) make determinations of individual skills needs. Although checklists might be organized along lines other than the conventional grade levels, the Reading Skills Checklist is so arranged because it approximates a sampling of the major basal series. One side of each checklist page contains the word recognition skills normally taught in such graded materials; the other side contains the reading comprehension skills I have developed. These do not necessarily parallel the specific labels of the various series. Fluency is not treated in the checklist and should be determined by the suggestions in the last part of this chapter.

---

*The checklist idea was also inspired by Walter B. Barbe's *Barbe Reading Skills Checklist* (Cuyahoga Falls, Ohio, 1960).

Figure 11-1 / The Reading Skills Checklist.

READING CHECKLIST   BY FRANK J. GUSZAK

Pupil Names	Blue		Salmon	Light Green	Yellow	Pink	Dark Green	Pupil Names
	R.R.	1	2	3	4	5	6	

Frank J. Guszak, Copyright 1971

READING READINESS

VISUAL DISCRIMINATION		AUDITORY DISCRIMINATION	OTHER ADJUSTMENT FACTORS
Ocular Motility/Directionality	**Form Perception**	Child reveals whether or not he can auditorially discriminate between specific phonemes in initial, medial, and final positions by saying "different" when tchr. pronounced word pairs are different.	Child appears rested and free from excessive fatigue.

Ocular Motility/Directionality	Form Perception	Auditory Discrimination	Other Adjustment Factors
Child can visually follow with both eyes working in unison: —an object moving from side to side in front of him (about two feet away) —an object moved out and in (about one to three feet in front of the child)	**Geometric Forms** Child can point to or mark a shape that is different, Child can match shapes in hand to those presented by the teacher (or some other person)	**Initial** bat pat cat fat rat rat rat hat sat mat nat mat dat wat jat lat chat shat stat slat spat scat plat flat	Child appears to have high energy level. Child appears attentive. Child appears free of disabling fears (of task, teacher, other children, etc.).
Child can draw well rounded, closed circles on paper or blackboard.	Child can color within the outline of a shape.	**Medial** bet bet bet bit bit bot bot but bate bite bite bote bote bute bate bete	Child responds positively to teacher oral directions. Child does not become easily disturbed over small setbacks.
Child can draw straight lines from dot-to-dot, progressing from left to right.	**Letters** Child can do the following: —match letters —match letter with one shown and removed —can point to letter named —can match upper and lower case letters	**Final** bat bap baf bas bam ban bab baf bav baf	Child seems enthusiastic about tasks.
Child can follow from left to right with finger.	Oo Ee Aa Ff Cc Nn Tt Jj Xx Zz Bb Dd Ll Kk Ss Uu Rr Vv Ii Qq Pp Gg Mm Ww Yy Hh		Child relates positively to peers, teachers, etc.
Child can follow line of print on experience chart visually as the teacher reads and points.	**Words** Child can identify words by drawing lines between words in phrase/sentence. e.g. that/big/brown/dog		Child can attempt tasks with minimal teacher attention.

VOCABULARY DEVELOPMENT

Shows he understands the following by:
a. following directions or answering questions which include the given word
b. using words in meaningful context

SPACE	TIME	NUMBER	VALUE	SIZE	COLOR	CONDITIONS	CAUSE AND EFFECT	OTHER
around	before/after	none/all	right/wrong	short/tall	black	hot/cold	if—then	push/pull
away	never/always	few/many	good/bad	short/long	white	wet/dry	because—of	start/stop
by	once/always	either/both	pretty/ugly	big/little	red	old/new	why	give/take
far/near	now/then	one		small/large	yellow	soft/hard	how	come/go
here/there	yesterday/today	two		narrow/wide	green	full/empty		like/dislike
in/out	today/tomorrow	three		thin/fat	blue			
off/on	never/soon	four			purple			
open/close	morning/night	five			orange			
to/from		six			brown			
up/down		seven						
front/back		eight						
front/middle		nine						
middle/back		ten						
top/bottom								
inside/outside								
first/last								
before/after								
high/low								
above/below								
under/above								

READING READINESS COMPREHENSION

Predicting/Extending	Locating Information	Remembering	Organizing	Evaluating Critically
Predicts convergent outcomes from: pictures picture and title title oral description story situations	Locating objects— Locating pictorial elements, i.e., biggest Follows verbal directions	Remembering simple sentence content	Retells: sentence sentence set paragraph story	Makes judgments about the desirability of a: character situation
Predicts divergent outcomes		Remembering the content of two or more simple sentences in sequence	Outlines orally the sequence of the story	Making judgments about whether stories are fictional or non-fictional by noting: reality fantasy exaggeration
Explain story character actions Explain gadget operations		Remembering paragraph content	Reorganizes a communication into a: cartoon picture picture sequence	
		Remembering story content		

1 WORD RECOGNITION

SIGHT WORDS

Pre-Primer 1 (PP1)

and	go	can
here	i	not
come	a	to
the	jump	cat
is	me	

Pre-Primer 2 (PP2)

down	three	make
up	little	run
in	big	see
ride	look	you
one	my	he
two	play	she

Pre-Primer 3 (PP3)

blue	it	am
red	said	to
green	we	who
find	that	are
for	what	do

PRIMER

all	he	so
am	into	soon
are	like	that
at	must	there
ate	new	they
black	no	this
brown	on	too
but	our	under
came	out	want
did	please	was
do	pretty	well
eat	ran	went
four	ride	what
get	saw	white
good	say	will
have	she	with
		yes

FIRST READER

after	has	over
again	her	put
an	him	round
any	his	some
as	how	stop
ask	just	take
by	know	thank
could	let	them
every	live	then
fly	may	think
from	of	walk
going	old	were
had	once	when
	open	

PHONIC ANALYSIS SKILLS

Consonants

Single

Initial	Final
cat	cat
dat	cad
jat	cam
sat	can
mat	cab
gat	cap
lat	
hat	
nat	
rat	
fat	
bat	
tat	
pat	

Blends, Digraphs

*that
*chat
spat
drat
blat
brat
*Digraph

Vowels

Single

- Short a — cat
- Short i — bit
- Short o — not
- Short e — net
- Short u — nut
- Silent e — at, ate

Phonograms

-at
-it
-ot
-et
-ut
-ate

STRUCTURAL ANALYSIS SKILLS

Roots, Compounds, Contractions

Finds parts in compound words, e.g. cannot

Pronounces contracted forms: isn't, I'm, I'll

Endings

Inflects endings: -s, -ed

-ing

Inflects possessives: 's, Jane's

Prefixes, Suffixes

Syllables

Can tell number of (vowel) sounds in various words:
Bill	1
Billy	2
Billyjo	3

Dictionary

Locates picture words in a picture dictionary or reference such as Richard Scarry, **Best Word Book Ever.**

Predicting/Extending	Locating Information	Remembering	Organizing	Evaluating Critically

Predicts convergent outcomes from:
  pictures
  picture and title
  title
  oral description
  story situations
 	
Predicts divergent outcomes
 	
Explain story character actions
Explain gadget operations
Generalizes from sets of information in story(ies) (Include task of identifying an unstated **main idea**).
	Locates specifics within written materials
	  phrase (s)
	  sentence (s)
	  paragraph (s)
	  page numbers
	  parts of a story (beginning, middle, end, etc.)
	
	Locating information with book parts
	  titles
	  stories
	  table of contents
	
	Locating information with reference aids
	  picture dictionaries
		Remembering simple sentence content
		
		Remembering the content of two or more simple sentences in sequence
		
		Remembering the factual content of complete and complex sentences and sentence sets
		
		Remembering paragraph content
		
		Remembering story content
			Retells:
			  sentence
			  sentence set
			  paragraph
			  story
			
			Outlines orally the sequence of the story
			
			Reorganizes a communication into a:
			  cartoon
			  picture
			  picture sequence
				Makes judgments about the desirability of a:
				  character
				  situation
				
				Makes judgments about the validity of a:
				  story
				  description
				  argument, etc.
				by making both **external** and **internal** comparison
				
				Making judgments about whether stories are fictional or non-fictional by noting:
				  reality
				  fantasy
				  exaggeration

1 COMPREHENSION

2 WORD RECOGNITION

SIGHT WORDS

Pronounces instantly in isolation and context

all	him	saw
am	his	say
an	if	sing
and	into	six
are	laugh	soon
at	let	ten
big	live	upon
blue	may	us
call	my	who
can	no	why
come	old	wish
do	on	your
down	one	about
funny	put	after
go	saw	always
good	said	around
he	she	ask
help	sit	because
here	stop	been
I	three	before
in	today	best
is	two	buy
it	was	does
jump	will	for
like	work	found
little	yes	full
look	yellow	gave
make	again	grow
me	ate	hold
out	but	how
play	cold	just
pretty	cat	keep
ran	fast	kind
red	first	much
ride	five	must
run	four	off
see	fly	once
so	give	only
the	goes	round
to	going	sleep
up	got	small
we	had	take
you	has	tell
as	hot	thank
away	its	that
be	long	they
black	made	this
brown	many	too
by	new	try
came	not	under
did	of	walk
eat	open	well
fall	please	were
find	or	white
for	our	with
get	pull	
going	read	
have		
her		

PHONIC ANALYSIS SKILLS

Pronounces phonemic counterparts of the following graphemes and blends with adjacent elements

CONSONANTS		VOWELS		
Single	**Blends, Digraphs**	**Single**	**Digraphs, Diphthongs**	**Phono-grams**
Review	Review	Review:	ea	-an
Initial	*th	Short	oo	-and
c	*ch	bat	ay	-at
d	sp	bet	ai	-ack
j	dr	bit	oa	-ap
s	*wh	not	ou	-ab
m	pr	but	oi	
k			oy	-et
g	Continue:	Review:	oe	-el
Final d	st	Silent		-eg
h	tr	rat	Unstable:	-ed
w	fr	rate	ei	
n	br		ie	-og
r	gr	Long (in		-ok
f	fl	open		-om
t	gl	syllable)		-on
b	cl	ba by		-ot
v	bl	be lief		
y	sl	bisect		-un
p	pl	going		-ut
Silent	*ph	Y as a		-ug
k-knight	sm	vowel		-us
w-know		baby		
b-bomb	*Digraph	cry		

PHONIC ATTACK PLAN

Blend the sound of the beginning consonant, consonant blend, or digraph with:
1. The **short vowel sound** of a single vowel in the middle of a word, e.g. blaf.
2. The **long vowel sound** when:
   —There is one vowel and e on the end (silent e), e.g. blafe.
   —There is one vowel and it is on the end (open syllable), e.g. bla.
   —There are two vowels together (blaif) excluding diphthongs & problem digraphs.

STRUCTURAL ANALYSIS SKILLS

Produces sounds characteristically associated with the following elements; blends with adjacent elements in words

Roots Compounds Contractions	**Endings**	**Prefixes Suffixes**	**Syllables**
Finds common root words, e.g. **faster** **jumping** **flyer** **biggest** **surprised** **nearly**	Inflects endings: -s -ed -ing	Reads prefixes un-untie re-replay	Every syllable has a sounded vowel.
Finds parts in new compounds, e.g. **apple tree** **farm house**	Notes comparisons, e.g. quick **quicker** thick **thickest**		Pupils use following generalization: When the first vowel sound in a word is followed by two consonants, the first syllable usually ends with the first of these, e.g. bul let pic ture
Pronounces new contracted forms, e.g. **we're** **it's** **can't** **won't**	Reads word that drops final e, e.g. ride **riding**		

Dictionary

Locates words in a picture dictionary

2 COMPREHENSION

Predicting/Extending	Locating Information	Remembering	Organizing	Evaluating Critically
Predicts convergent outcomes from: pictures picture and title title oral description story situations	Locates specifics within written materials phrase (s) sentence (s) paragraph (s) page numbers parts of a story (beginning, middle, end, etc.)	Remembering simple sentence content	Retells: sentence sentence set paragraph story	Makes judgments about the desirability of a: character situation
Predicts divertent outcomes	Locating information with book parts titles stories table of contents	Remembering the content of two or more simple sentences in sequence	Outlines orally the sequence of the story	Makes judgments about the validity of a: story description argument, etc. by making both **external** and **internal** comparison
Explain story character actions Explain gadget operations Generalizes from sets of information in story(ies) (Include task of identifying an unstated **main idea**).	Locating information with reference aids picture dictionaries maps (political) dictionaries	Remembering the factual content of complete and complex sentences and sentence sets	Reorganizes a communication into a: cartoon picture picture sequence	Making judgments about whether stories are fictional or non-fictional by noting: reality fantasy exaggeration
Restores omitted **words** in context		Remembering paragraph content		
Labels feelings of characters, i.e. sad—glad		Remembering story content		

3 WORD RECOGNITION

SIGHT WORDS	PHONIC ANALYSIS SKILLS						STRUCTURAL ANALYSIS SKILLS					Dictionary
Pronounces instantly in isolation and context the basic sight words in the previous list	Pronounces phonemic counterparts of the previously-listed graphemes, blending them with adjacent elements.						Produces sounds characteristically associated with the following elements and blends with adjacent elements in words.					Uses the dictionary pronunciation key to sound out unknown words:
	CONSONANTS		VOWELS			Phono-grams	Roots, Compounds, Contractions	Endings	Prefixes, Suffixes	Syllables		
	Single	Blends, Digraphs	Single	Digraphs, Diphthongs								

(Write in the few words that may cause some difficulty)

Sight words:
any, better, both, bring, carry, clean, could, done, don't, draw, drink, eight, every, hurt, know, light, myself, never, own, pick, right, seven, shall, show, their, them, there, these, think, those, together, use, very, want, warm, wash, went, what, when, where, which, would, write

CONSONANTS

Single — Initial: c, d, j, s, m, g, h, w Final: r, d b, c, t, k, z, y Final: n, r, x t, p

Blends, Digraphs — Initial: wh, th, ch, ph, sh, sp, dr, pr, tr, fr, br, gr Final: th fl, ng gl, cl, nd, bl, pl, ph, tw

VOWELS

Single — Short: a, e, i, o, u   Long: a, e, i, o, u   Silent e   Y as a Vowel

Digraphs, Diphthongs — Review: ea, oo, ay, ee, oy, ai, oa, ou, au, oi, oy   Review: ei, ie

Phonograms — -at, -et, -it, -ot, -ut, -ar, -er, -ir, -or, -ur, -ack, -all, -an, -ick, -ill, -ind, -et, -eat

PHONIC ATTACK PLAN

Blend the sound of the beginning consonant, consonant blend, or digraph with:

1. The **short** vowel sound of a single vowel in the middle of a word—blaf.

2. The **long** vowel sound when:
   —There is one vowel and e on the end. (silent e)—blafe
   —There is one vowel and it is on the end (open syllable)—bla
   —There are two vowels together (vowel digraph)—blaif *(Note exceptions)

3. Blend the above to the final consonant.

Roots, Compounds, Contractions
Finds common root words, e.g. **usually**
Finds parts in new compounds, e.g. **every thing**
Pronounces new contracted forms e.g. we're, it's, let's, she's, I've, they've, they'll, aren't, won't

Endings
Inflects endings: -s, -ed, -ing
Notes comparisons, e.g. tall, taller, tallest
Reads wds. that drop final e, rate, rating

Prefixes, Suffixes
un-, re-, be-, -ly, -less, -ness, -en, -ful, -ish

Syllables
Every syllable has a sounded vowel.

When the first vowel sound is followed by th, ch, sh, these combinations are not divided and go with the first or second syllable. e.g.: dishes, mother.

When the first vowel sound in a word is followed by two consonants, the first syllable usually ends with the first of these consonants: e.g.: bullet, picture.

When the first vowel sound is followed by a single consonant, that consonant usually begins the second syllable: e.g.: station.

When a prefix is added to a root word, the root word is usually accented: e.g.: inside.

In most two-syllable words (excepting prefixed ones), the first syllable is accented: e.g.: happy.

In inflected or derived forms of words the primary accent usually falls on or within the root word, e.g.: boxes, untie.

Dictionary
ā—hat, ā—age, â—care, ä—father, e—let, ē—equal, ėr—term, i—it, ī—ice, o—hot, ō—open, ô—order, oi—oil, ou—out, u—hut, ū—put, ü—rule, ū—use, ə represents: a in about, e in take, i in pencil, o in lemon, u in circus

Predicting/Extending	Locating Information	Remembering	Organizing	Evaluating Critically
Predicts convergent outcomes from: pictures picture and title title oral description story situations	Locates specifics within written materials phrase (s) sentence (s) paragraph (s) page numbers parts of a story (beginning, middle, end, etc.)	Remembering simple sentence content	Retells: sentence sentence set paragraph story	Makes judgments about the desirability of a: character situation
Predicts divergent outcomes	Locating information with book parts titles stories table of contents	Remembering the content of two or more simple sentences in sequence	Outlines orally the sequence of the story	Makes judgments about the validity of a: story description argument, etc. by making both **external** and **internal** comparison
Explain story character actions	Locating information with reference aids picture dictionaries maps (political) dictionaries encyclopedias atlases globes telephone books	Remembering the factual content of complete and complex sentences and sentence sets	Reorganizes a communication into a: cartoon picture picture sequence	Making judgments about whether stories are fictional or non-fictional by noting: reality fantasy exaggeration
Explain gadget operations Generalizes from sets of information in story(ies) (Include task of identifying an unstated **main idea**).		Remembering paragraph content		
Restores omitted words in context		Remembering story content		
Labels feelings of characters, i.e. sad—glad				
Explains why story characters hold certain viewpoints				

3 COMPREHENSION

4 WORD RECOGNITION

PHONIC ANALYSIS SKILLS

(Note the elements that have not been highly developed)

CONSONANTS

Single

Initial	Final
c	d
j	
s m	c
g g	
w	n
r	b
f	t
b	k
p	s
k	
z	
y	

Blends, Digraphs

Initial	Final
wh	th
th	ng
ch	nd
ph	ph
sh	ch
sp	sh
dr	
pr	
tr	
fr	
br	
gr	
fl	
gl	
cl	
sl	
pl	
tw	

VOWELS

Single

Short	**Long**
a	a
e	e
i	i
o	o
u	u
	Silent e
	Y as a vowel

Digraphs, Diphthongs

ea, oo, ay, ee, oy, ai, oa, ou, au, oi, oy, ei, ie

Phono-grams

-at, -et, -it, -ot, -ut, -ar, -er, -ir, -or, -ur, -ack, -all, -an, -ick, -ill, -ind

STRUCTURAL ANALYSIS SKILLS

(Note needs from prior lists)

Roots, Compounds, Contractions

Finds common root words instantly.

Finds parts in new compounds.

Pronounces new contracted wds.

Endings

Inflects endings.

Notes compar-isons.

Reads wds. that drop final e.

Prefixes, Suffixes

dis-, in-, mis-, anti-, non-, com-, con-, pre-, sub-, tri-, post-, de-, pro-

-ness, -ment, -able, -ish, -ant

Syllables

Every syllable has a sounded vowel.

When the first vowel sound in a word is followed by two consonants, the first syllable usually ends with the first of these consonants: e.g.: bullet, picture.

When the first vowel sound is followed by th, ch, sh, these combinations are not divided and go with the first or second syllable; e.g.: dishes, mother.

When the first vowel sound is followed by a single consonant, that consonant usually begins the second syllable; e.g.: station.

When a prefix is added to a root word, the root word is usually accented; e.g.: inside.

In most two-syllable words (excepting prefixed ones), the first syllable is accented; e.g.: happy.

In inflected or derived forms of words, the primary accent usually falls on or within the root word; e.g.: boxes, untie.

Two vowel letters together in the last syllables of a word may be a clue to an accented final syllable; e.g.: complain, conceal.

When there are two like consonant letters within a word, the syllable before the double consonants is usually accented; e.g.: beginner, letter.

DICTIONARY SKILLS

Correctly uses key:

a	hat, cap
ā	age, face
ã	care, air
ä	father, far
b	bad, rob
ch	child, much
d	did, red
e	let, best
ē	equal, elite
ėr	term, learn
f	fat, if
g	go, bag
h	he, how
i	it, pin
ī	ice
j	jam,
k	kind, seek
l	land, coal
m	me, am
n	no, in
ng	long, ring
o	hot, rock
ō	open, go
ô	order
oi	oil, voice
ou	house, out
p	paper, cup
r	run, try
s	say, yes
sh	she, rush
t	tell, it
ŧʜ	them, smooth
th	thin, both
u	cup, but
u̇	full, put
ü	rule, love
v	very, save
w	will, woman
y	young, yet
z	zero, breeze

Schwa ə

about, taken, pencil, lemon, circus

MULTI SKILL ATTACK PLAN (FOR UNKNOWN WORDS)

FIRST — Try your context clues by quickly rereading whatever segment (line, paragraph, etc.) is necessary to provide you with a clue. If you need more help, move to the next step.

SECOND — Look for the largest structure in the word (root, syllable, etc.):
If you find a possible root word, work out the adjoining affixes, etc.
If you don't find the root word, attempt to make visual breaks by noting large syllables. Apply the attached syllable rules to them.

THIRD — Using your context again, try various pronunciations of the most likely word or syllable sounds. If nothing happens, try other sounds.

FOURTH — Skip the word and continue on if it doesn't seem crucial to the meaning and doesn't appear often.

FIFTH — If it seems important, check its pronunciation in your dictionary.

Predicting/Extending	Locating Information	Remembering	Organizing	Evaluating Critically
Predicts convergent outcomes from: 　pictures 　picture and title 　title 　oral description 　story situations Predicts divergent outcomes Explain story character actions Explain gadget operations Generalizes from sets of information in story(ies) (Include task of identifying an unstated **main idea**). Restores omitted words in context Labels feelings of characters, i.e. sad—glad Explains why story characters hold certain viewpoints	Locates specifics within written materials 　phrase(s) 　sentence(s) 　paragraph(s) 　page numbers 　parts of a story (beginning, middle, end, etc.) Locating information with book parts 　titles 　stories 　table of contents Locating information with reference aids 　picture dictionaries 　maps (political) 　dictionaries 　encyclopedias 　atlases 　globes 　telephone books 　newspapers	Remembering simple sentence content Remembering the content of two or more simple sentences in sequence Remembering the factual content of complete and complex sentences and sentence sets Remembering paragraph content Remembering story content	Retells: 　sentence 　sentence set 　paragraph 　story Outlines orally the sequence of the story Reorganizes a communication into a: 　cartoon 　picture 　picture sequence	Makes judgments about the desirability of a: 　character 　situation Makes judgments about the validity of a: 　story 　description 　argument, etc. by making both **external** and **internal** comparison Making judgments about whether stories are fictional or non-fictional by noting: 　reality 　fantasy 　exaggeration Making judgments about whether the author is trying to amuse, bias, etc. the reader. Detects in reading materials the following propaganda techniques: 　—bad names, e.g. wallflower 　—glad names, e.g. superstar

4 COMPREHENSION

STRUCTURAL ANALYSIS SKILLS

Produces sounds characteristically associated with the following elements and blends with adjacent elements in words

Roots, Compounds, Contractions	Endings	Prefixes and Meanings	Suffixes and Meanings	Syllables
Finds root words instantly, e.g. **arrangements**	Inflects endings: -s, -ed, -ing	**Not** dis disappear, in invalid, un untrue, ir irregular, il illegal, non nonsense	**Like** -ish foolish	When the first vowel sound is followed by th, ch, sh, these combinations are not divided and go with the first or second syllable; e.g.: dishes, mother.
Locates parts in new compounds instantly, e.g. **stand off**	Notes comparisons, e.g. dull, duller, dullest	**Against** anti antiwar	**One Who** -ent resident	When the first vowel sound is followed by a single consonant, that consonant usually begins the second syllable; e.g.: station.
Pronounces new contracted forms instantly, e.g. **hadn't**	Reads words that drop final e, style, styling	**For** pro pro-war	**State Of** -ance ignorance arrogance	When a prefix is added to a root word, the root word is usually accented; e.g.: inside.
		Before pre pretest		In most two-syllable words (excepting prefixed ones), the first syllable is accented; e.g.: happy.
		After post postwar		In inflected or derived forms of words, the primary accent usually falls on or within the root word; e.g.: boxes, untie.
				Two vowel letters together in the last syllables of a word may be a clue to an accented final syllable; e.g.: complain, conceal.
				When there are two like consonant letters within a word, the syllable before the double consonants is usually accented; e.g.: beginner, letter.

MULTI SKILL ATTACK PLAN (FOR UNKNOWN WORDS)

FIRST Try your context clues by quickly rereading whatever segment (line, paragraph, etc.) is necessary to provide you with a clue. If you need more help, move to the next step.

SECOND Look for the largest structure in the word such as: root word, prefix, large syllable.
If you find a possible root word, work out the adjoining affixes, endings, etc.
If you don't find the root word, attempt to make visual breaks by noting large syllables. Apply the attached syllable rules to them.

THIRD Using your context again, try various pronunciations of the most likely word or syllable sounds. If nothing happens, try other sounds.

FOURTH Skip the word and continue on if it doesn't seem crucial to the meaning and doesn't appear often.

FIFTH If it seems important, check its pronunciation in your dictionary.

DICTIONARY SKILLS

Pupils sound words with:

a	hat, cap
ā	age, face
ã	care, air
ä	father, far
b	bad, rob
ch	child, much
d	did, red
e	let, best
ē	equal, elite
ėr	term, learn
f	fat, if
g	go, bag
h	he, how
i	it, pin
ī	ice
j	jam
k	kind
l	land, coal
m	me, am
n	no, in
ng	long, ring
o	hot, rock
ō	open, go
ò	order
oi	oil, voice
ou	house, out
p	paper, cup
r	run, try
s	say, yes
sh	she, rush
t	tell, it
ŧħ	them, smooth
TH	thin, both
u	cup, but
ù	full, put
ü	rule, love
ū	use, music
v	very, save
w	will, woman
y	young, yet
z	zero, breeze

Schwa ə
about
taken
pencil
lemon
circus

5 WORD RECOGNITION

5 COMPREHENSION

Predicting/Extending	Locating Information	Remembering	Organizing	Evaluating Critically
Predicts convergent outcomes from: pictures picture and title title oral description story situations	Locates specifics within written materials phrase (s) sentence (s) paragraph (s) page numbers parts of a story (beginning, middle, end, etc.)	Remembering simple sentence content Remembering the content of two or more simple sentences in sequence	Retells: sentence sentence set paragraph story	Makes judgments about the desirability of a: character situation Makes judgments about the validity of a:
Predicts divertent outcomes	Locating information with book parts titles stories table of contents	Remembering the factual content of complete and complex sentences and sentence sets	Outlines orally the sequence of the story	story description argument, etc. by making both **external** and **internal** comparison
Explain story character actions		Remembering paragraph content	Reorganizes a communication into a: cartoon picture picture sequence	Making judgments about whether stories are fictional or non-fictional by noting:
Explain gadget operations	Locating information with reference aids picture dictionaries dictionaries encyclopedias atlases globes telephone books newspapers classified ads bus schedules	Remembering story content		reality fantasy exaggeration
Generalizes from sets of information in story(ies) (Include task of identifying an unstated **main idea**).				Making judgments about whether the author is trying to amuse, bias, etc. the reader.
Restores omitted words in context				Detects in reading materials the following propaganda techniques:
Labels feelings of characters, i.e. sad—glad				—bad names, e.g. wallflower —glad names, e.g. superstar —transfer, e.g. the "all American boy" —testimonial —band wagon technique —card stacking
Explains why story characters hold certain viewpoints				

6 WORD RECOGNITION

SPECIALIZED READING VOCABULARY

Mathematics and Science	Social Science	Roots, Compounds, & Contractions
number (cardinal, ordinal)	scale	Instantly recognizes root words and added parts
numeral	legend	
set (equivalent, matched like, unlike)	meridians	
	parallels	
	longitude	
minuend	latitude	Instantly pronounces or mentally responds to compounded elements
subtrahend	terrain	
difference	political	
	poles	
muliplicand		Instantly responds to contracted forms
× **multiplier**	ancient	
product	medieval	
quotient	modern	
divisor) dividend		
	ethnology	
hypothesis	linguistics	
data		
validity		
reliability		
input		
output		
feedback		
matrix		
solid—liquid		
one-dimensional		
two-dimensional		
three-dimensional		
circular		
triangular		
rectangular		
ellipsoid		
sphereoid		
conduction		
convenction		
radiation		

STRUCTURAL ANALYSIS SKILLS

Prefixes and Meanings

Prefix	Meaning	Example
dis	(not)	disappear
in		invalid
un		untrue
ir		irrelevant
il		illegal
non		non-count
anti	(against)	anti-war
pro	(for)	pro-war
pre	before	pre-test
post	after	post-test
super	above	superman
sub	below	suborbital
uni	one	unicycle
bi	two	bicycle
tri	three	tricycle
re	again	replace
semi	partly	semi-dressed
trans	across	trans-Atlantic
mini	small	mini-skirt
micro	very small	micro-skirt

Suffixes and Meanings

Suffix	Meaning	Example
ish	like	foolish
ent	one who	resident
able	capable of being	capable
ible		edible
ance	state of being	arrogance
ence		violence

SILENT READING PURPOSES	NEEDED READING SKILLS CLUSTERS	RATE STRATEGIES
GENERAL PURPOSES APPLICABLE TO VARIOUS CONTENTS		
Locating specific information in reading materials: reference materials non-reference materials	Locating	Scanning (Searching through materials for specifics, 400 w/p/m and up)
Remembering specific content for testing, telling, etc.	Locating, remembering, organizing	SQ3R (Survey, Question, Read, Recite, Review)
Preparing oral and written reports	Locating, organizing, remembering	Scanning (SQ3R) Skimming Slow re-reading
Preparing evaluations of materials	Locating, predicting, evaluating	Scanning. Skimming Slow re-reading
Following written directions and instructions	Locating, remembering, organizing	Scanning Skimming Slow re-reading
Enjoyment or recreation	(Varying combinations of above, depends upon whether it is newspaper, novel, etc.)	(Varies from skimming or scanning to very slow)
PURPOSES APPLICABLE TO SPECIFIC CONTENTS		
Science	Locating information in classification patterns, reading diagrams, charts	Relatively slow (depending upon reader's background)
Social Science	Locating information in graphs, globes, time lines, tables, etc. Locating and withdrawing info, from periodicals of various sorts	
Mathematics	Reading to solve problems (Organize-Locate-Solve) Reading problem equations, number lines,	

6 COMPREHENSION

The Reading Checksheet

While the Reading Skills Checklist is most useful as a scope and sequence chart as well as a means for checking progress, we discovered that the teacher needed some systematic way to keep up with the results of his teaching and checking. The result, called the Reading Checksheet, was essentially a blank page that carried the same skills labels as the checklist, as well as specific information about the child's (1) reading potential, (2) word recognition level, and (3) comprehension level. (The Reading Checklist and Reading Checksheet are available from Educational Program Development, P.O. Box 4231, Austin, Texas, 78765.) With the aid of a loose-leaf notebook, the teacher could keep each child's Reading Checksheet and subsequently use it for guiding his skills growth. Specific details about the use of these instruments will be discussed later. In the checksheet illustrated in Figure 11-3, we note Billy Jones' reading potential (or reading expectancy), his word recognition level, and his comprehension level (the latter two refer to instructional levels). Skills needs for Billy are indicated by the elements that have been written in by the teacher as a result of his diagnosis (nonsystematic and/or systematic). The teacher has a useful profile of Billy's specific needs.

Determining needed reading skills

The following discussions concern systematic determinations of reading skills sequences in certain reading levels. Rather than using a level-by-level format, we will discuss the reading skills under the subcategories of the major skills dimensions of word recognition, reading comprehension, and fluency. Included in the word recognition section are context skills, sight words, phonic skills, structural analysis skills, and dictionary skills. The reading comprehension section contains locating, remembering, organizing, predicting outcomes/extending ideas, and evaluating critically. Fluency includes both oral and silent fluency.

Determining needed skills: word recognition
Context skills

As indicated in Chapters 4 and 5, context analysis skills are critically important to reading development because they are the bridges between the written message and the child's understanding of that message. An illustration in Chapter 4 indicated how all vowels could be omitted from a story and blanks inserted in their places. Your reading of that selection indicated the power of context, for you probably read it without great difficulty. Another illustration of the power of context skills is seen in a research

Figure 11-2 / The Reading Checksheet.

SIGHT WORDS	PHONIC ANALYSIS SKILLS				STRUCTURAL ANALYSIS SKILLS				
	CONSONANTS		VOWELS						Dictionary
	Single	Blends, Digraphs	Single	Digraphs, Diphthongs	Phono-grams	Roots, Compounds, Contractions	Endings	Prefixes, Suffixes	Syllables	

Reading Expectancy	RR	PP1	PP2	PP3	P	1^2	2^1	2^2	3^1	3^2	4	5	6	7	8
Word Recog. Level	RR	PP1	PP2	PP3	P	1^2	2^1	2^2	3^1	3^2	4	5	6	7	8
Comprehension Level	RR	PP1	PP2	PP3	P	2^1	2^1	2^2	3^1	3^2	4	5	6	7	8

Pupil's Name _____

WORD RECOGNITION CHECKSHEET

Figure 11-2 / (Continued).

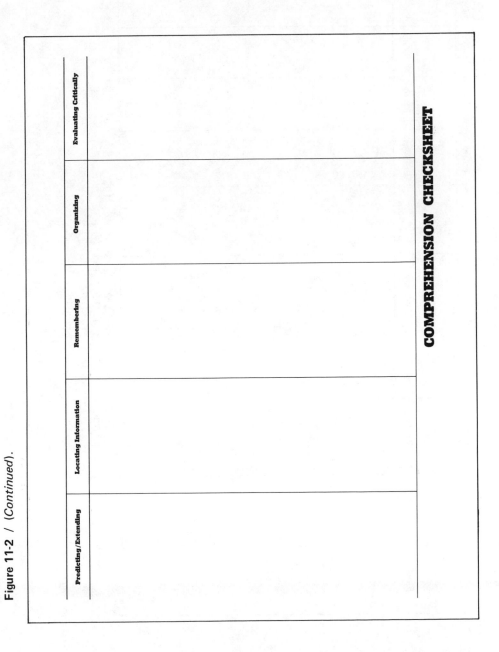

COMPREHENSION CHECKSHEET

Predicting/Extending	Locating Information	Remembering	Organizing	Evaluating Critically

Figure 11-3 / Billy Jones' reading potential, word recognition level, and comprehension level.

Sight Words	Phonic Analysis Skills					Structural Analysis Skills					Dictionary
	Consonants		Vowels			Roots, Compounds, Contractions	Endings	Prefixes Suffixes	Syllables		
	Single	Blends, Digraphs	Single	Digraphs, Diphthongs	Phonograms						
black +	c–	ch–			–an	something	wants				
blue +	g–	th–			–ab	hen/house	Sally's				
enough		bl–			–am		Pete's				
{there	–h	st–			–at						
{where	–b	pr–			–ad						
please	–m	tr–									
know	–t	fr–									
pretty	–d	dr–									
they		br–									
yellow		gr–	–d–								
{then			–e–ı								
{when			–ı–ı								
duck											
your											

WORD RECOGNITION											
Billy Jones											
pupil name											
	Rd. Expectancy	PP1	PP2	PP3	P	1²	2¹	2²	3¹	3²	4	5	6
	Wd. Recog. Lev.	PP1	PP2	PP3	ⓟ	1²	②	2²	3¹	3²	4	5	6
	Comprehension	PP1	PP2	PP3	ⓟ	1²	2¹	2²	3¹	3²	4	5	6

Figure 11-3 (*Continued*)

COMPREHENSION

Billy Jones
/pupil name

Predicting/Extending	Locating Information	Remembering	Organizing	Evaluating Critically
Predict different story endings Restore omitted words State main idea of story	Use table of contents Locate specific sentences Locate animal words in picture dictionary		Outline orally sequence of story	Judge whether story is real or imaginary.

study by Goodman (1965). Goodman asked first-, second-, and third-graders to read lists of words in isolation. After marking the errors (and not correcting them), Goodman had the children read stories containing the same words. The results, shown in Table 11-1, provide dramatic evidence of the power of context. Because evidence exists that reading should be taught as a meaning-getting process from its inception, teachers must begin assessing or determining the child's anticipatory or context skills from the onset of the readiness program. Here are some specific suggestions:

Situations	Strategies for determination
Teacher reading to the children.	Stop and condition the pupils to continue by inserting the needed word, phrase, or sentence.
Pupil who is reading orally stops.	Although you have probably found that he cannot use context adequately (that is, providing that the context gives the necessary cues), it is useful to employ the following strategies: Wait for about 15 seconds to see if he will attempt the word, go back, and so on. If he does not, ask him to back up on the sentence or sentences and see if he can decipher the word.
Pupil who is reading substitutes totally incorrect word (a word that does not make sense) and continues reading.	Again, you more than likely have an indication that the child perceives of reading as "word calling" when he reads "He got on his *house* and galloped away." Such a serious problem must be met on the spot with such wedges as "Try that again," "I'm not sure I understand that," or a call for a repeat of what the child read.
Pupil who is reading substitutes with a good replacement and keeps going.	This indicates that he is using context clues beautifully and that your concerns may be with other word recognition skills at *another* time.
Pupil who is reading repeats several times, in order to preserve the ongoing meaning.	Such repetitions are healthy behaviors of a good context user. If the repetitions are constant, however, the material may be frustrational.

Table 11-1 / Average numbers of words missed by first-, second-, third-graders on list and in actual story context

Grade	Average missed in list	Average missed in context	Ratio
1	9.5	3.4	2.8:1
2	20.0	5.1	3.9:1
3	18.8	3.4	5.5:1

Source: K. Goodman, "A Linguistic Study of Cues and Miscues in Reading," *Elementary English*, 42 (1965), 639-643.

Although I feel that some of the most valuable determinations of context analysis can be made in oral reading situations because of the unique opportunity to observe the products of the child's thought processes, I also think silent reading tasks are important. Cloze testing (discussed in Chapter 5) is a valuable aid. The following variants of cloze testing should aid pupils in utilizing context:

Context analysis task: select the correct element
The teacher explains that the child is to select the correct word from the three given and draw a line from it to the blank where it fits.

1. I _____ the ball.
   eat   see   look

2. Bobo _____ for the ball.
   look   looks

Context analysis task: write in the correct element
The teacher uses the same task as above, except that the student has to write in the word.

Context analysis task: paste in the correct element
The teacher employs the same task as above, except that closure is effected by the pupil's pasting the correct word into a space.

Most basal programs have workbook and duplicator pages that provide such activities and tests of skills. These items should not be ignored by the teacher interested in developing a pupil's sensitivity to meanings. As is the case with so many things, the relevancy of the task is the crucial concern. Fill-in-the-blank exercises have received blanket criticism that sometimes obscures the usefulness of valuable closure tasks which elicit and develop reading skills. No one wants to force the facile reader to perform such tasks, but we surely can see possibilities for the pupil who fails to use the context for attacking unknown words.

Sight words

From the preceding chapters, the following generalizations concerning the value of sight words in a reading program should be noted:

Generalization 1 / Sight word recognition is normally the first word recognition technique introduced by most basal programs (although context clues are usually included to some extent).

Generalization 2 / Sight words are so named because the ability to read or call such words is usually based on the pupil's memory skill in recognizing the configuration and/or distinctive features of the word (first letters, ascending or descending letters).

Generalization 3 / Sight words include (*a*) words that have tangible referents, such as *girl, dog, green*; and (*b*) words that have intangible referents, such as *the, when, have*.

Generalization 4 / The 220 Dolch Sight Words, which consist primarily of intangible referent words, constitute an important base for reading because of their frequent occurrence.

Generalization 5 / Because of a lack of tangible referents and a high number of phonic explanations, there is much merit in teaching the Dolch words as elements that can be instantly recognized in contextual situations. Presumably, this provides the reader with a core vocabulary as well as the means (base words) for generating the sounds of other words.

Generalization 6 / Because sight words are necessary for achievement, it is possible to make fairly accurate estimates of reading achievement on the basis of sight word knowledge (Chapter 9).

A common means for determining a pupil's skill in sight word retention is holding up sight word cards (usually from the basal series packet) to determine whether individual students have learned the various words—for example, *Dick, Jane, Sally, Puff, look, jump*. Although most sight-word-oriented basals recommend the teaching of the vocabulary in natural phrase patterns (if some of the first pages of the preprimer can be called natural phrase patterns), the practice of teaching such words in advance, in isolation, appears common. Whether such instruction results in word-by-word readers is not as easy to determine as some would suggest, but it certainly seems to deprive the young reader of the valuable linguistic cues of seeing the various words as parts of larger meaning contexts.

Beyond calling the names of words on cards, pupil knowledge of sight words is commonly tested through group oral reading sessions in which each pupil reads a segment of the story. As we have seen by the comparisons of word-calling proficiency in iso-lation and in context (Goodman, 1965), the latter means (oral reading in context) appears to shed more light on the pupil's functional sight word recognition skills.

The following suggestions concern the testing of sight word knowledge in the various levels of development (as equated with the normal basal divisions of increasing difficulty—preprimer 1, preprimer 2, preprimer 3, primer, first reader, and so on).

Preprimer 1 and 2

1. Emphasis should be placed upon reading whole sentences. As students read sentences orally, their recognition problems should be noted for special attention.
2. Special practice with sentence cards, sentences on board, and so on should be provided for pupils experiencing word difficulties.
3. After such sentence practice, separate phrase or word cards should be used. When such phrase or word cards are used for testing, it is important that these cards:

   Stimulate as precisely as possible the type style of the book so as to avoid confusing the child with variant configurations.

   Do not bear markings or other tell-tale differences that might attract the attention of the child and result in his learning the wrong stimulus; for example, "dog" is the card with the bent corner.

   Be of similar size so that they can be fitted into phrase or sentence frames for contextual testing:

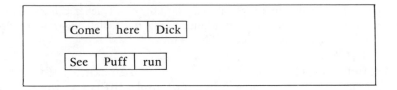

   Be cued so that they can be used as self-teaching and self-testing devices through the use of picture referents and sound referents (illustrated in Chapter 13).

Preprimer 3

The same elements as above are used, with the addition of built-in textual devices for checking group attainment via wide-scale measurement tasks. Al-though the teacher should be aware of each pupil's sight words needs and should be working to meet them, it is sometimes necessary for some teachers to test a total reading group at once. Tests for such situations are often available in the basal program, usually in an accompanying workbook. Essentially, the tests call for the pupils to select and circle a word called out by the teacher from a group of words:

Teacher direction / I'm going to say a word that's in the first box (points to the box on her copy of test). You find that word and draw a circle around it. (Pause for response before subsequently continuing through test).

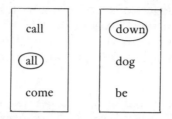

Primer
The same type of testing as suggested above can be carried out with the vocabulary of any program. Significant attention should be given to the high-frequency words (Dolch) that occur in the vocabulary. By the end of the primer, it is common for the children to have encountered at least a hundred of the basic sight words.

First reader
Forty to fifty more new words are usually added to the growing list of sight words (Dolch) by the completion of the first grade. These words, coupled with the emerging phonic and structural analysis skills, are supposed to enable the pupil to read over 300 words by the end of the first grade (many more if one counts words that can be generated from consonants and phonograms or if the pupil has exceptional inductive substitution skill).

Second reader and above
If a pupil is struggling in a second reader or above, a teacher can get a valuable estimate of the problem by administering the Dolch Sight Word Test (Chapter 5) either in single-word or phrase form.

Profiling the results of informal sight word testing / By jotting down sight words that cause individual pupils difficulty, the teacher can subsequently provide more practice in the troublesome elements. Illustrative of such notes are the sight words written down for Billy Jones' Checksheet and shown in Figure 11-4.

Phonic skills
The phonic skill determinations included here concern consonant, vowel, and phonogram elements. Suggestions are made concerning individual and group means of testing.

Informal tests: consonants / These tests are designed to determine whether or not the student can successfully blend the sounds of consonants with word elements. They presume a knowledge of auditory and visual discrimination. For descriptions of the means of testing whether or not pupils can perform such auditory and visual tasks, refer to Chapter 8.

Consonants: initial

Individual testing	Group testing

Teacher shows the child a known sight word; for example, *cat, can.* The child says the word. The teacher then writes the word *bat* or *ban* below the stimulus word and the child is asked to pronounce it. In similar fashion, the teacher solicits substitution tasks with each of the consonants:

cat	fat
bat	mat
lat	dat
hat	sat
gat	jat
tat	pat
rat	kat
wat	yat

Teacher gives each pupil a sheet such as the following and then directs them: "Listen carefully. I will read a word and you are to draw a circle around the word I read in each line. Look at the first line and circle *bag*."

bag	1.	dag	pag	bag
cuff	2.	cuff	fuff	luff
lime	3.	time	lime	kime
back	4.	hack	tack	dack
gate	5.	fate	gate	hate
tail	6.	sail	fail	tail
rack	7.	rack	pack	back
wake	8.	wake	vake	lake
fate	9.	gate	fate	rate
mail	10.	mail	sail	nail
date	11.	bate	date	pate
sack	12.	sack	back	rack
jack	13.	kack	jack	lack
pail	14.	rail	bail	pail
kite	15.	bite	fite	kite
yell	16.	yell	bell	tell
bail	17.	sail	mail	hail

Figure 11-4 / Billy Jones' checksheet—sight word needs.

Sight Words	Phonic Analysis Skills				
	Consonants		Vowels		
	Single	Blends, Digraphs	Single	Digraphs, Diphthongs	Ph
black blue enough {there {where please know pretty they yellow {then {when duck					

Rd. Expect. PP1 PP2 PP3 P
W. R. Level PP1 PP2 PP3 (P)
Comp. Level PP1 PP2 PP3 (P)

Billy Jones
WORD RECOGNITION

Consonants: final, single

Individual testing	Group testing

| The teacher task is the same as the preceding task except that consonant substitution is at the end rather than the beginning.* | The teacher task of reading a cue word is the same. Now the teacher asks pupils to mark the word that ends like each word read aloud. |

cat   (stimulus word)
cac
cag
caf
cam
cad
cas
caj
cap
cak
can

cac	1. cad	cac	cag
cag	2. cag	cac	can
caf	3. cak	caf	cat
cam	4. can	cam	cad
cad	5. can	cam	cad
cas	6. cac	cas	caf
caj	7. cag	caj	caf
cap	8. cap	caf	cab
cak	9. cag	cas	cak
can	10. can	cam	cad

*Words such as *cal, car, caw* are omitted because of the variant vowel forms.

Consonants: initial, blends, digraphs

Individual testing	Group testing

| The testing task is the same consonant substitution task as employed with the initial, single consonants. Substitution now involves the blends and digraphs. (Level I of the Reading Skills Checklist contains a list of common blends.) | The testing task remains the same as the group task described for initial, single consonants. A student marking page must be developed to contain the elements the teacher wishes to test. |

cat   (stimulus word)
brat
blat
spat
grat

brat	1. bart	brat	blat
blat	2. brat	plat	blat
spat	3. spat	taps	sbat
grat	4. gnat	grat	gart

Consonants: final, blends, digraphs

Individual testing	Group testing

| Consonant substitution is effected at the end of the word. | Pupils are asked to mark the word pronounced by the teacher. |

plan   (Stimulus word)
pland
plang
plath

pland	1. plan	pland	plank
plang	2. plang	plan	planc
plath	3. plak	plat	plath

Informal tests: vowel elements / Vowel-element testing concerns single vowels, adjacent vowel pairs, and phonograms. Included under single vowels are long and short vowels, and *r, l, w* controlled vowels. Adjacent vowel pairs concern vowel digraphs and diphthongs. Phonograms are word elements containing both vowel and consonant elements to which an initial consonant element can be added, for example, *chick.*

Vowel elements: single / The determination as to whether a single vowel is long, short, varied (*r, l, w* controlled), or silent (silent *e* rule) is largely described by the following generalizations:

Closed syllable generalization / When a word or a syllable contains a single vowel and ends in a consonant, the vowel is usually short; for example, *at, bit, let.*

Open syllable generalization / When a word or a syllable contains only one vowel and ends with that vowel, the vowel is usually long; for example, *he, go, define.*

Silent *e* generalization / In words or syllables with two vowels, one of which is final *e,* the *e* is usually silent and the first vowel is long; for example, *fine.*

R, l, w generalization / When a word or syllable contains a single vowel followed by *r, l,* or *w,* the vowel usually has a sound that is neither long or short; for example, *bar, all, awful.*

The individual and group testing techniques will be keyed to the above generalizations.

Vowels: closed syllables generalization

Individual testing	Group testing
The teacher determines by vowel substitution whether the child can identify the vowel sounds. Child pronounces each word.	Teacher gives each student an unmarked copy of the following and asks him to circle the words she calls out (left-hand column).

bat	(stimulus word)	bat
bet		bet
bit		bit
bot		bot
but		but

1. bat	bet	bit	bot	but
2. bat	bet	bit	bot	but
3. bat	bet	bit	bot	but
4. bat	bet	bit	bot	but
5. bat	bet	bit	bot	but

Vowels: open syllables generalization

Individual testing	Group testing
Teacher determines by vowel substitution whether or not the pupil can pronounce these syllables:	Teacher gives each student an unmarked copy of the following and asks him to circle the elements called out.

Individual testing	Group testing

pla						
ple	pla	1. pla	ple	pli	plo	plu
pli	ple	2. pla	ple	pli	plo	plu
plo	pli	3. pla	ple	pli	plo	plu
plu	plo	4. pla	ple	pli	plo	plu
	plu	5. pla	ple	pli	plo	plu

Vowels: silent e generalization

Individual testing	Group testing
Teacher simply checks pupil skill in reading random applications of rule.	Teacher gives each student an unmarked copy and asks him to circle the element read in each line.

rafe	rafe	1. raf	rife	rafe	rufe
tife	tife	2. tif	tafe	tife	tufe
hefe	hefe	3. here	hefe	hef	hufe
kote	kote	4. kote	kot	kake	kufe
bute	bute	5. bute	but	bate	bote

Vowels: r, l, w generalization

Individual testing	Group testing
As recommended in Chapter 5, these elements are taught through phonograms and/or key words (*car, her, bird, fur, corn, all, saw*). Testing checks pupil skill in applying these sounds to unknown words, often of the nonsense variety.	Teacher gives each student an unmarked copy of the following and asks him to circle the elements called out.

r: char	char	1. chare	char	chur
ber	ber	2. bere	bar	ber
chir	chir	3. chir	chire	chor
thur	thur	4. thure	thur	thor
forn	forn	5. furn	forn	farn
l: chall	chall	6. chull	chall	chale
lalt	lalt	7. lalt	lilt	lult
w: taw	taw	8. tow	taw	tuw
fraw	fraw	9. fraw	fruw	frow

Vowels: adjacent / Numerous studies of the performance of adjacent vowel pairs have caused us to be more aware of the shortcomings of the old two-vowel generalization, "When two vowels go walking, the first one does the talking (is long), and the second is usually silent." As we saw in Chapter 5, the generalization might be more accurate if it were phrased this way: "When two vowels go walking, the first vowel is usually long and the second silent, unless the two vowels are *ei* and *ie*, or a diphthong (Burmeister, 1968).

With the abundance of adjacent vowel situations in most materials, pupils have ample opportunities to test the two-vowel generalization. The construction of specific tests of nonsense words does not appear wise because of the large number of sounds attached to the various vowel pairs. The use of the attack plan generalization in combination with context clues provides the young reader with a useful set of attack tools.

Vowels: phonograms / In Chapter 4, the potential values of teaching pupils common phonograms that indicate long and short vowel situations, *r* controlled elements, and others were outlined. Although the teacher may choose whichever phonograms she thinks are most valuable, the subsequent follow-up in terms of practice often proves difficult without special materials. For this reason, there is merit in considering one of the commercially produced programs as a supplement. Materials such as the Fries Merrill Linguistic Readers (1966) and Goldberg and Rasmussen's S.R.A. Basic Reading Series (1965) provide rather extensive review of the patterns introduced and might serve as testing or teaching devices. For lists of common phonograms, see Chapter 5 and the Reading Skills Checklist, Levels I and II, as well as the skills charts of basal series.

Profiling the results of informal phonic skills testing / Simple notations about individual pupil's phonic skills needs can serve as aids to the teacher in planning for both group and individual instruction. If we again look at the case of Billy Jones and his reading skills needs, we see in Figure 11-5 the phonic skills needs added to the previously listed sight word needs.

Structural analysis skills

Determining pupil skills in identifying the basic types of word structures can be done through both observation of oral reading behaviors and written test situations for individuals or groups.

Observation of the omission of structural elements appears to be the most usable determination technique. Every first-grade teacher's ear is attuned to hear whether Billy puts the *-s* on the word *look* after he has been taught this structure. Similarly, the teacher's ears perk up when she notes an approaching situation in which the student will have to add the inflectional *-ed*. In much the same fashion, all teachers need to be aware of the increasing number of structural elements that contribute to the increasing difficulty of texts.

Implicit in the idea of structural analysis is the pupil's instant identification of such language structures as root words, affixes, endings, and syllables without an intervening letter-by-letter sounding process. Although the most valuable determination of pupil structural analysis skill will be based on on-the-spot observation, teachers may wish to explore needs in this area systematically. The following informal assessment techniques may be used.

Root words

Individual testing	Group testing
Teacher places words containing root words on the board and asks the child to (a) circle the root word, (b) cover up all but the root word, (c) erase all but the root word. (See sample words at right.)	Teacher gives each student an unmarked copy of the following and asks him to circle the root words called out (which are in their reading vocabularies).

1. (play)ful   5. smallest
2. (run)ning   6. happening
3. jumped   7. gladly
4. catcher

Figure 11-5 / Billy Jones' checksheet—phonic analysis skills needs.

Sight words	Phonic analysis skills				
	Consonants		Vowels		
	Single	Blends, Digraphs	Single	Digraphs, Diphthongs	Phon
black	c-	ch-		-a	
blue	g-	th-		-e	
enough		bl-		-i	
there	-h	st-			
where	-j				
please	-n	-ck			
know	-m	-st			
pretty					
they					
yellow					
then					
when					
duck					
your					

	Rd. Expect.	PP1	PP2	PP3	P	1² (2¹)
	W.R. Level	PP1	PP2	PP3	(P)	1² 2¹
Billy Jones	Comp. Level	PP1	PP2	PP3	(P)	1² 2¹

WORD RECOGNITION

Compounds

Individual testing	Group testing
Teacher writes words containing two words on the board and asks the child to (a) divide the two words, (b) cover each word while pronouncing the other word. (See sample words at right.)	Teacher gives each student an unmarked copy of the following and asks him to draw a line between the two words making up the word.

1. hen\|house   4. himself
2. chicken\|pen   5. everyone
3. something   6. another

Contractions

Individual testing	Group testing
Teacher writes contractions on the board and asks the student to correctly pronounce the word and give its equivalent. isn't—is not I've—I have	Teacher gives each student an unmarked copy of the following and asks him to circle the word in each line that is the equivalent of the word read.

don't	1. donut	do not	won't
isn't	2. is not	is it	into
she's	3. she is	she'll	sheep
he'd	4. he would	he did	hid

Endings (inflectional)

Individual testing	Group testing
Teacher asks pupil to read words and underline or circle endings. jumped catches playing runs	Teacher gives each student an unmarked copy of the following and asks him to circle the word pronounced.

jump	1. jumped	jumping	jump
runs	2. run	runs	rans

Prefixes

Individual testing	Group testing
Teacher asks pupil to read words and underline or circle prefixes. undress misfire rerun incorrect	Teacher gives each student an unmarked copy of the following and asks him to circle the word pronounced and underline the prefix.

rerun	1. re(run)	rayon	runner
untie	2. tieup	untie	unity

Suffixes

Individual testing	Group testing
Teacher asks pupil to read words and underline or circle the suffix.	Teacher gives each student an unmarked copy of the following and asks him to circle the word pronounced and underline the suffix.

foolish
beautiful
backward

foolish	1. foolish	fool	foulie
fanciful	2. fanciful	fantsy	phantasy
sixteen	3. sixtine	sixteen	sixty

Syllabication / In Chapter 4, the following four steps were given as means to divide and sound multisyllabic words:

Step 1 / Auditory discrimination of syllable units.

Step 2 / Visual discrimination of the structural units that make up the sound units heard.

Step 3 / Application of phonic generalizations to the sounds that can be expected of vowels in open and closed syllables.

Step 4 / Application of the visual division generalizations.

Auditory discrimination of syllable units, the first step, should begin in the readiness phases of reading instruction as teachers sensitize children to the separate sounds they hear in words—for example, in their own names: Jim-my, Sal-ly, E-liz-a-beth. Pupils are then shown the written referents for the sounds or syllables (Step 2), and the concept of syllables is expanded to the point where the pupil knows syllables auditorily and visually. The third step in the process involves the basic phonic understandings of what to expect in the way of a vowel sound when the vowel is in different patterns with consonants—open syllable, closed syllable, silent -e syllable. Such knowledge is utilized in the attack of both single and multisyllabic words. (These generalizations were discussed in preceding sections on phonics.)

Syllabication is the process of breaking down a word visually into its basic components for the purpose of applying the phonic attack skills that will result in accurate pronunciation. It is this visual breaking of unfamiliar parts that is the most difficult thing to teach systematically. For pupils who intuitively recognize common syllable patterns because of previous learning, the syllabication process is an inductive operation that does not require any systematic application of rules; for others, the rules must be learned and applied until the process of syllabication becomes automatic. These rules and the informal means for testing them are discussed below.

Generalization 1 / When the first vowel sound in a word is followed by two consonants, the first syllable usually ends with the first of these consonants; for example, bul/let, ac/tion. *Exception:* When the first vowel sound is followed by two consonants which are digraphs (*ch, th*) or blends (*bl, st*), these combinations are not divided and go with the first or second syllable.

Individual testing	Group testing
Teacher asks the child to read the elements aloud and note their syllabic breaks. (The teacher also has the opportunity to observe the phonic generalizations applied.)	Teacher gives words to pupils on prepared sheets and asks them to mark where words should be divided.
	achag
achag	bacfure
bacfure	chaffet
chaffet	bathet
bathet	

Generalization 2 / When the first vowel sound is followed by a single consonant, that consonant usually begins the second syllable; for example, sta/tion.

Individual testing	Group testing
Teacher asks child to read the elements aloud (as above).	Teacher gives words to pupils on prepared sheet (as above) and asks them to mark syllable divisions
setin	
himut	setin
nefut	himut
	nefut

Generalization 3 / Prefixes and suffixes are generally separate syllables; for example, mis/trust.

Individual testing	Group testing
Teacher asks child to read the elements aloud (as above).	Teacher gives words to pupils on prepared sheet (as above) and asks them to mark syllable divisions.
regurg	
prechack	regurg
indebile	prechack
raction	indebile
agerful	raction
	agerful

Generalization 4 / The endings -ble, -cle, -dle, -gle, -kle, -ple, -tle, -zle usually make up the final syllable; for example, ap/ple.

Individual testing	Group testing
Teacher asks child to read the elements aloud (as above).	Teacher gives words to pupils for marking (as above).
regurgible	regurgible
fractible	fractible
origitle	origitle
lazzle	lazzle

Profiling the results of informal structural analysis tests / The prominent structural elements Billy Jones is encountering in his primer-level reading include endings, compounds, contractions, and possessives. Figure 11-6 shows teacher estimates of his problems with these units.

Dictionary skills

Dictionary skills begin to develop in the readiness and preprimer portions of the reading program as children use picture clues to

Figure 11-6 / Billy Jones' checksheet—structural analysis

Sight Words	Phonic Analysis Skills					Structural	
	Consonants		Vowels			Roots, Compounds, Contract.	Endings
	Single	Blends, Digraphs	Single	Digraphs, Diphthongs	Phono.		
black	c_	ch-	-d			something	wants
blue	g-	th-	-e			her/house	
enough		bl-	-i				Sallys
there	-h	st-					Petes
where	-j						
please	-n	-ch				don't	
know	-m	-st					
pretty							
they							
yellow							
then							
when							
duck							
your							

Rd. Expect. PP1 PP2 PP3 P 1² ②¹ 2² 3¹
W.R. Level   PP1 PP2 PP3 Ⓟ 1² 2¹ 2² 3¹
Comp. Level PP1 PP2 PP3 Ⓟ 1² 2¹ 2² 3¹

Billy Jones
WORD RECOGNITION

identify words with visual referents. From such a beginning, the pupil moves on to the use of the first letter of an unknown word matched with the word's picture counterpart. Progressing further up the skills ladder, the student learns to use the pronunciation key of his glossary or dictionary for the sounding out of unknown words.

Picture dictionary

Individual testing	Group testing
Ask pupil to find and point to word for apple (use picture as key). Ask pupil to tell the following by locating picture clue from spelling. Johnny eats an *orange*. Tommy plays with his *dog*.	(Same as individual techniques.) Ask pupils to draw what Johnny found: 1. orange 2. dog 3. chair

Pronunciation key

Individual testing	Group testing
Give pupil the spelling of an unknown word and ask him to find and say its pronunciation.	Give pupils the spellings of some unknown words and ask them to write phonetic respellings. Give pupils the spellings of some unknown words and three phonetic spellings for each. Ask them to find and circle the correct respellings.

Determining needed reading skills: comprehension

Assessment in this area is concerned with how well individuals can perform the following reading tasks: locating information, remembering, organizing, predicting outcomes and extending ideas, and evaluating critically.

Locating information

The arbitrary nature of classifying certain skills as word recognition and others as comprehension is evident when we deal with dictionary use, which falls into both categories. This is because the student has to be able to use the so-called comprehension skill of location (via initial letters) to arrive at the point at which he sees the unknown word—for example, *Aardvark*. Only after he has found the unknown word in the dictionary can he apply the word recognition skills of (1) using the diacritical markings to pronounce the word or (2) using the phonetic respelling to pronounce the word.

Observation must be the primary means of assessment in this

dimension of comprehension, as well as in the others. The teacher sets the task—for example, "Locate the page number of the story 'We Go To Fun Park,'" and then watches to see which students locate the page number as well as how the various students go about it. Such observation is systematic and is followed up by some special assistance where needed. It is my opinion that the best means of assessment is the kind of observation just described, but some teachers may wish to use other forms of measurement, such as those in the table below.

Task	Assessment activity
Locating specifics within written materials	
Locating specific phrases	Read a phrase from the story to the children and ask them to mark it lightly with a pencil.
Locating specific sentences	Use same type of activity as above; give pupils Ditto copies of the story and directions such as, "Put two lines under the sentence that tells where the boys went."
Locating specific paragraphs	Ask the pupils to put a given number of check marks by a certain paragraph; for example, "Put one check mark in the left margin by the paragraph that tells where the story was taking place. Put two checks by the paragraph that tells what the boys found."
Locating specific page numbers	Give pupils two or three paper clips, and ask them to locate and clip certain pages by number or pages that provide specific answers to questions.
Locating specific parts of a story or chapter	Give pupils two or three paper clips and ask them to clip such things as the setting, introduction, or summary.
Locating information with book parts	
Locating story or chapter titles	Read two or three titles to the children and ask them to find the titles, pencil mark them, and paper clip the pages on which the titles are located.
Locating stories	Same activity as above.
Locating Preface	Ask the children to paper clip the first page of the preface.

Task	Assessment activity
Locating Introduction	Same activity as above.
Locating and using the Contents	Ask the children to use contents to locate two or three story titles read to them and mark or clip them.
Locating publishing information (publisher, copyright date)	Ask the children to list the publishers and the copyright dates of some of their school texts.
Locating lists of illustrations	Ask the children to mark with paper clip.
Locating specific chapters	Ask the children to paper clip specific chapters.
Locating and using indexes	Ask the children to write down the page numbers of information you specify.
Locating and using bibliographies	Ask the children to follow specific textual references to the bibliography, and then note such things as publication date and publisher.
Locating and using footnotes	Same as above.
Locating glossaries	Ask children to locate and clip.
Locating appendix	Ask children to locate and clip.

Locating information with reference aids

Locating with picture dictionaries	Ask the children to locate by picture or spelling specific entries and paper clip them.
Locating with word dictionaries	Ask the children to locate specific words and list the page numbers on which they are found.
Locating specific information with word dictionaries	Ask the children to write the meanings of specific words.
Locating specific information with encyclopedias	Same as above.
Locating specific information with atlases	Ask the pupils to locate specific areas and paper clip them.
Locating specific information with maps	Ask pupils to locate specific places on individual maps and make a pointer with masking tape.
Locating specific information with globes (earth, lunar)	Tape pointer markers with masking tape.
Locating specific information with telephone books	Because the telephone book is useful for finding a great deal of information, assessment activities can involve writing the page numbers or actual phone numbers of individuals, indicating the

Task	Assessment activity
	number of pizza parlors, and so on.
Locating specific information in newspapers, using index	See index skills.
Locating specific information in newspaper parts	A teacher can jot down notes on specific elements to be found in a given edition and ask the children to locate them and write them down.
Locating specific information in magazines	Same as above.
Locating specific information in timetables	Activities center around locating specific information needed.

Remembering

Children must remember the unfolding events of a story; if they do not, they may be like the child who simply attaches names to the various word configurations. Probably the most common assessment of memory is the oral teacher question asked in the reading group. Because of the rapidity with which a teacher can phrase a question and receive a response, it lends itself well to both broad and quick samplings. Despite its ease of use, however, there are several limiting factors:

1. Too often oral questions tend to focus on unimportant details.
2. Overuse of minute detail questions can program students into very narrow thinking patterns; for example, the student misses the general theme while looking for the colors of the three balloons.
3. Teachers tend to get answers from only a few students and consequently receive deceptive feedback about the understanding of the whole group.

To combat these problems, we offer the following recommendations on memory questioning:

Details / Avoid picking apart stories for minute detail questions. Later in the reading program you will be concerned with details, but initially you want students to remember the basic action or story line.

Coverage / In group questioning situations, make conscious efforts to direct appropriate memory questions to individuals in need of such questions. Maintain some kind of crude tally to be sure you are getting broad coverage and not maintaining a dialogue with one child. Permit students to have adequate opportunities for response. Often, incorrect judgments are made because students' response opportunities are short-circuited.

Variety / Occasionally, plan multiple-choice questions in advance. Give the students blocks containing three different colors that can be keyed to the three answer possibilities; for example:

Where were Bill and Jack going?
If they were going to the fair, show *red:*
If they were going to the show, show *green:*
If they were going to the store, show *blue:*

Organizing

In the organization process the student must, through oral or manipulative means, demonstrate his understanding of reading materials. If a student can accurately tell back a story he has read, we can assume he has literally understood its sequence. Similarly, a student may tell us the same thing by putting in order a scrambled set of events, such as a pictorial sequence.

The measurement of student understanding by the retelling process requires little explanation beyond the directives indicated in the Reading Skills Checklist (see Figure 11-1). Since this aspect of reading comprehension is frequently neglected because of the amount of time required, here are some quick group assessment techniques.

Picture arrangement / The students are given several pictures which, when properly arranged on a larger piece of paper, will indicate the correct sequence of story events.

Numeration / With either pictures, phrases, or sentences, the students are asked to number these elements in terms of story sequence.

Dramatization / Under careful teacher control, students do an impromptu dramatization of selective bits that reveal an understanding of the sequence.

Visualization / Students attempt to visualize certain stories in a single picture that captures pertinent elements or in a comic strip. The teacher should plan this carefully.

Predicting outcomes and extending ideas

Too much prediction is based on the idea of asking students to anticipate what will happen on the next page. They generally know rather precisely what is going to happen because of early explorations, listening to other groups, and so on. Thus, we would suggest other possibilities in line with the skills breakdown of this category.

Task	Assessment activity
Predicting convergent outcomes	Convergent thinking suggests the type of thinking that leads to the most likely contingencies.

Task	Assessment activity
	Teachers should push for convergent thinking on the part of young readers that leads to alternatives other than those in the story and related to children's own experiences.
Predicting divergent outcomes	Our society puts a high premium on *some* forms of divergent thinking; for example, clever TV commercials. Because of the value of such mental exercise, certain questions should elicit student responses of this type.
Explaining why story characters hold certain viewpoints or ideas	Such explanation is critical if children are to be conditioned to discern individual motivations. Questioning must draw on both convergent and divergent dimensions. Role playing sometimes provides the teacher with insight as to how the student can read the role (and consequently achieve this behavior).
Generalizing from sets of information in a story or stories (identifying main ideas)	In most beginning reading stories, the main ideas are rather ill-defined, since the emphasis is on the repetition of certain words. Soon, however, ideas go beyond such simple bits as "Sally wants to play ball, but Dick doesn't want her to" to more complicated elements; for example, maybe Dick has a basic dislike for girls conditioned by unpleasant mother figure experiences. To work in this area requires that the teacher be aware of the main ideas himself and that he learn to question carefully so as to find out whether students are obtaining generalizations that go beyond literally following the words.
Labeling feelings of characters	The perennial smiles of characters in some of the beginning readers often mask the actual feelings real children would have. Thus, teachers need to see whether

Task	Assessment activity
	children relate in such a way as to see likely emotional implications.

Evaluating critically

The previous topic actually blends into the task called evaluating critically, because before one can evaluate intelligently, he has to make some comparisons with other sources. Essentially, the student compares on the basis of external criteria (information of a similar nature found elsewhere) and internal criteria (the internal logic within a communication). The following assessment suggestions are offered:

Task	Assessment activity
Making judgments about the desirability of a character situation	Beyond asking the child to make such judgments, it is critical that we seek the reason for his position. Initially, the student may make a very simple emotional response, but such behavior gives way to more reasoned thought under the careful questioning of a perceptive teacher.
Making judgments about the validity of a story, description, or argument by making comparisons with other sources of information	In initial reading, the sources for outside information are generally the children's own experiences, along with some vicarious ones obtained from such sources as television. These sources should be tapped frequently by teacher questions, both in terms of assessment and instruction.
Making judgments about the validity of a story, description, or argument by making comparisons within as to internal consistency, logic, and so on	"Do the actions of Jack in this story seem consistent with his earlier actions?" might be such a question. Subtle shifts of, for example, character attitudes should be noted by the teacher and tested.
Making judgments about whether stories are fictional or non-fictional by noting reality, fantasy, exaggeration	This is a variant of the task above, in which the student is directed to look for plausibility.
Making judgments about whether the author is trying to entertain, amuse	Most initial reading stories are not amenable to such analysis;

Task	Assessment activity
bias	questions should be used sparingly.

Profiling the results of informal comprehension skills testing / Just as in the case of word recognition, Billy's teacher should have a well-developed working profile of his strengths and weaknesses in the varied reading comprehension tasks. These are shown in Figure 11-7.

Determining needed reading skills: fluency

Initially, teachers use oral reading fluency as a check on the pupil's rapidly increasing sight vocabulary and word attack skills. As these word attack skills become automatic, the teacher's attention shifts to the student's skill in silent reading tasks. Thus attention is focused on how well the student performs the comprehension tasks, as well as how quickly. Conceivably, the teacher should provide fluency checks such as those shown in Table 11-2. The techniques for determining oral and/or silent fluency skill are given below.

Oral fluency

Step 1 / Count and mark off the words in your copy of the reader in units of 25.

Figure 11-7 / Billy Jones' checksheet—comprehension.

COMPREHENSION Billy Jones pupil name				
Predicting/ Extending	Locating Information	Remembering	Organizing	Evaluating Critically
Predict different story ending Restore omitted words State main idea of story	Use table of contents Locate specific sentences Locate animal words in picture dictionary		Outline orally sequence of story	Judge whether story is real or imaginary.

Table 11-2 / Suggested fluency checks

Material, Level	Oral fluency*	Silent fluency*
First Reader	50 (minimum)	50-60 (minimum)
Second Reader	70 (minimum)	70-80 (minimum)
Easy supplementary reading	80 (minimum)	80 (minimum)
Third Reader	90 (minimum)	110 (minimum)
Easy supplementary reading	100 (minimum)	120 (minimum)
Fourth Reader	120 (minimum)	140 (minimum)
Easy supplementary reading	(no check)	160
Content subject materials	†	100-200 (depending upon specific purposes)
Fifth Reader		
Content subject materials	†	100-300 (depending upon specific purposes)
Recreational		130-180

*Words per minute.
†Only occasional checks to determine any major difficulties. Almost total emphasis on silent fluency.

Step 2 / At a convenient time, ask each student to read orally for a period of time (1 or 2 minutes).

Step 3 / Mark how far the student progressed in the given time and then quickly add up the 25-word units plus any fraction; for example:

Joe read 1 minute:　25
　　　　　　　　　　25
　　　　　　　　　　25
　　　　　　　　　　 5
　　　　　　　　　　──
　　　　　　　　　　80 words per minute

Silent fluency

Step 1 / Use the same procedures as above, except that you ask the child to read silently.

Step 2 / At the end of a minute or two minutes, stop him and determine how many words he has read.

Step 3 / Because his rate must have a comprehension base, ask him to tell you back what he has read. In this way (or through questions), you can make an estimate of the comprehension that accompanied the rate.

Summary

Three different means for determining pupil reading needs are the outlined program, nonsystematic diagnosis, and systematic diagnosis. In the outlined program, reading needs are anticipated, whereas in the nonsystematic and systematic diagnostic methods, the teacher determines each pupil's skills needs. Nonsystematic determinations are made primarily through observation situations; systematic measurements involve explicit testing. The various systems are not independent and may be used in combination.

The Reading Skills Checklist represents a sequence of reading skills as they are most frequently taught in the various graded programs. With the aid of this instrument or one constructed to match a given program, the teacher can note skills needs in a nonsystematic or systematic fashion. The Checklist represents the skills curriculum; the Reading Skills Checksheet is the form for maintaining an informal account of each pupil's specific needs. Skills needs noted on the Checksheet include both word recognition and comprehension factors. Fluency notes may be added, as well as information pertinent to the child's instructional reading level and reading potential.

four
What the diagnostic reading teacher prescribes

Assuming that our diagnostic reading teacher knows the various reading skills and can make accurate determinations about pupil possession of such skills, he has arrived at the point of prescribing instruction that will develop new behaviors.

Over the past decade there has been controversy over the concept of behavioral objectives. Chapter 12, "Using Behavioral Objectives," seems to be the appropriate keynote to the prescription process. Once the teacher has determined the desired reading behaviors, his task is one of determining the most expedient means for getting the pupils to perform them. For such a determination, he must assess the potential effect of his direct teaching actions, as well as the potential effect of indirect actions by the pupil.

Chapter 13, "Direct Teacher Actions," spells out specific strategies that can be employed by teachers to assist pupils in more effective word recognition, comprehension, and fluency.

Chapter 14, "Pupil-managed Learning Experiences," emphasizes the means and materials by which teachers assist students in the process of assuming greater responsibility for their own skills instruction.

12 Using behavioral objectives

Behavioral objectives
1. List the reasons in support of the development of behavioral objectives.
2. List and describe the following parts of a behavioral objective: (*a*) statement of behavior, (*b*) when behavior will be exhibited, (*c*) criterion of success.
3. Rewrite three nonbehavioral objectives into behavioral form.
4. List the behavioral components that should characterize reading contracts at various reading levels.
5. List the reasons in support of the development of certain tasks that cannot be readily written into the behavioral objective format.

Behavioral objectives, or statements describing the behaviors to be performed by the learner as a result of the activity, have been used in this text from Chapter 4 on. Just preceding this paragraph, you read a list of specific behaviors you are to perform as a result of reading this chapter. In the event that you have doubts about the value of such formulations, let us take a closer look at the issues involved.

Why behavioral objectives?
Teaching may be viewed from one of two vantage points. The most frequent vantage point is that of what I, as a teacher, will do; the second is that of what the student will do. When the instructional focus is on what the teacher will do, assumptions are made about what the student will learn in the process. Often, the results of subsequent tests and observations are disappointing—we realize the students did not really get what we wanted them to get. But what did we really want them to learn? We may not be completely sure because we have not spelled out precisely what they should know or do. Conversely, when teaching is viewed from the standpoint of what the student should be able to do at the end of a given lesson or period of time, the focus is on the tasks of (1)

determining the most expedient means for him to learn the elements and (2) determining the most expedient means to find out whether he learned them or not. Perhaps the following table will help to clarify the differences between looking at the teaching act and at the learning act.

Typical objective	Probable meaning	Criticism
Will read orally	Will strengthen skill, show weak areas	Although reading orally may strengthen reading skill, it may weaken it if the student reads with great difficulty or no difficulty.
Will read a certain number of pages silently	Will be able to answer questions about reading	Reading silently gives no direction to the student other than not to make noise; it fails completely to detail silent comprehension or fluency skills.
Phonics—beginning consonants	Will be able to attach specific sounds to consonants in reading	No direction as to how the student will attack, what letters, and so on.
Develop reading readiness	Will be somehow more ready to read by virtue of the task	Does not explain in any way how readiness will be aided.

It should be evident that such objectives are almost meaningless to anyone except possibly the teacher. We can argue, though, that if the teacher knows what they mean, they can be useful. But to what extent does the teacher attach clearer, deeper meanings than those listed? Obviously, we do not know, but much of the current approach to reading seems to be based on the assumption that if we provide activities for oral reading, silent reading, phonics, readiness, and so on, the behaviors of reading will automatically develop. Undoubtedly they often do, much like the ways in which we learn to speak. Unfortunately, however, they sometimes do not, and then the teacher is at a loss as to what to do.

If the teacher works from a specific behavioral orientation (with or without behavioral objectives statements), he will note the behavioral breakdowns and set up appropriate objectives for individuals. Let us take the typical behavioral objectives cited above and indicate how they might be made more descriptive of specific learning outcomes.

Typical objectives	Possible behavioral objectives
Will read orally	Will read orally, making 6 or less errors per 100 running words. (*Note:* We now have a criterion of whether or not the student is reading the material at an *instructional* level.) or Will read orally, making the vocal inflections signaled by commas, periods, and question marks. (*Note:* We now have a measure of oral fluency that can indicate whether or not all these skills have been developed.) or Will read orally, pausing to repeat leadup phrases to difficult words and subsequently attacking the difficult words by the contextual clues. (*Note:* This specific objective might be used for a child with limited word attack who needs to tune in more to context clues.) or Will read orally, maintaining a rate of 60 words per minute. (*Note:* This gives us a fluency measure for a first-grade reader by which we can determine his relative mastery of the task.)
Will read a certain number of pages silently	Will read these pages silently and answer 6 memory questions accurately. (*Note:* We have some measure of his understanding of the pages.) or Will read these pages in 6 minutes or less (for an average of 110 words per minute or better). (*Note:* We have a measure of minimum acceptable rate for a fourth-grade-level reader.) or Will read these pages silently, averaging 120 words per minute or better and will correctly sequence 7 major ideas from the story.
Phonics—beginning consonants	Will correctly blend the following single consonants with the phonogram -*at*: *b, c, d, f, g, h, l, m, n, p, r, s, t, v.* (*Note:* This indicates that the student can probably attack these initial consonants with a short *a* situation.) or Will correctly substitute all the consonants (except *x*) in the initial and final positions in the word *cat.* (*Note:* This indicates whether the pupil can make consonant substitutions in the initial and final positions.)
Develop reading readiness	Will follow with his hand the left-to-right sequence on an experience chart as the story is read by the teacher.

Typical objectives	Possible behavioral objectives
	or
	Will correctly match like capital letters, small letters.
	or
	Will correctly match small letters with their capital-letter equivalents.
	or
	Will circle when asked the words in a brief sentence (demonstrating knowledge of word element).

These are but a few of the multitude of specific behavioral objectives that could be used to illustrate the possibilities inherent in the typical objectives, but they should suffice. Although it can certainly be argued that few teachers have time to do this type of written analysis, there seems to be little argument against analytic thinking or planning for a great portion of the reading program.

Why behavioral objectives? We think the answer is evident.

Components of the behavioral objective

A behavioral objective consists of (1) a statement of specific behavior, (2) a statement of when the behavior will be exhibited, and (3) a criterion of success.

A statement of specific behavior

Basic to the behavioral objective is a statement of what the learner will be doing. The portions of the objectives given above now shown in italics are the behavioral statements; for example:

Will read orally, making 6 or less errors per 100 running words.
Will read orally, making the vocal inflections signaled by commas, periods, and question marks.
Will read orally, pausing to repeat leadup phrases to difficult words and subsequently attacking the difficult words by the contextual clues.

As you can see, great differences in specificity can exist. It even seems possible to carry the specificity so far that the teacher cannot evaluate all the behaviors. An example of such an extreme would be the following statement about oral reading:

Will read orally, making 6 or less errors per 100 words in a prose style, 375-word sample of 25-point typeface, correctly aspirating the suprasegmentals signaled by the punctuation and contextual clues, and averaging 65 words per minute within nondialogue paragraphs and 60 words per minute in dialogue paragraphs.

A statement of when the behavior will be exhibited

As you have already noted, some statements indicate that the behaviors will take place while doing a task (such as oral reading) and others, after the task (such as the objectives at the beginning of this chapter). Terminal behavior is the term used to describe the end behaviors that will continue to exist after the learning sequence is completed. Thus, the objectives at the beginning of each chapter concern terminal behaviors that will be recalled and performed at later dates. Nit-picking over the temporal nature of the statement is of little value. Insofar as reading skills are concerned, we assume that we want to develop terminal behaviors, whether or not we make this completely clear in our statements.

Criterion of success

Mager (1962) indicates that behavioral objectives should include a criterion (or criteria) of success. In other words, the idea of "reading orally, making 6 errors or less per 100 running words" contains the criterion of "6 errors or less." If the student makes 10 errors, he is obviously short of our criterion. If he makes 3 errors, his performance is deemed satisfactory in light of the criterion.

It does not always seem realistic to put a criterion of success on the behavioral objective in reading. Perhaps the following illustrations will show why (in each, the criterion of success is shown in italics).

1. Student will correctly substitute all the consonants (except *x*) one at a time for the consonant *c* in cat *7 out of 10 times.*
2. Student will read stories from the Level IV Reading Lab, *answering 90 percent of the questions at the end correctly, 50 percent of the time.*

We are hardly interested in whether a student is accurate in consonant substitution 70 percent of the time, and so on. Some of these criteria are not realistic as we view the terminal behaviors, so they are of little value to us.

Restating nonbehavioral objectives

Quickly indicate how you would rewrite the nonbehavioral objectives in the list below. After you have written your responses at the right, read further to determine how your objectives agree with mine. Other alternatives are of course available.

1. Will read for expression
2. Will read for comprehension
3. Will read rapidly
4. Will know new words

1. Will apply correct intonations in oral reading
2. Will correctly answer 7 of 10 fact questions after reading story
3. Will read silently at a rate of (insert normative figure) words per minute
4. Will instantly pronounce new words (sight recognition)

   or

4. Will instantly sound and pronounce new words (attack)

   or

4. Will be able to give example of use of new word (if to "know new words" means to understand their meanings)

Types of behavioral components (PP 1-grade 8)

Behavioral objectives for many children will vary sharply in accordance with their place in the reading skills sequence—PP 1, 2, 3, and their specific needs within a skills level. It is therefore difficult to say categorically that every pupil needs to spend so many minutes on sight words, phonic skills, oral reading, question answering, and so on, but it is important to remember that pupils need to be developing in certain ways on the following fronts:

Oral reading	Heavy initial emphasis tapering off to greatly reduced emphasis by the end of second grade.
Silent reading	From reduced emphasis initially to almost total emphasis from second grade on.
Word attack	From heavy initial emphasis to less emphasis as terminal behaviors are developed. Emphasis will vary sharply in accordance with type of program—for example, look-say, synthetic phonics.
Fluency	From very slow to very rapid, in accordance with task, background of pupil, and so on.
Comprehension	Heavy emphasis throughout, but increasing sophistication with advancing levels within basic skills types.

The Reading Skills Checklist provides a guide to the various types of skills, but it is the teacher who must systematically sample the growth of the various skills and direct the emphasis. As greater sensitivity to the various skills develops, the teacher will be able to determine the relative emphasis.

A place for nonbehavioral objectives

We would be in an untenable position if we did not recognize the many reading goals that are developed completely apart from behavioral objectives. Many children learn to read well through other means, such as modeling the behaviors of another, intuitively deriving study aids, and so on. In other words, the ways of learning are certainly beyond the descriptive capability we currently possess. For this reason, we all provide certain "learning activities" that we feel sure do some terrific things. We sense these results even though we are often at a loss to describe them or how they happened.

Because these good things happen, it behooves us to provide for them as well as for behavioral concerns. They might be activities such as the following:

Pupil matching / Pupils can share thoughts, ideas, readings. We can define many of the behaviors necessary for developing English as a second oral language, but we can do little that compares with the simple pairing off of a non-English speaker with an English speaker.

Sharing sessions / Such sessions, when centered on books and ideas, can open up all kinds of behavioral paths we cannot begin to anticipate. Sharing sessions initiated with a single question can produce many high-level thinking (reading) skills.

Story telling / Story reading or telling by parents, teachers, and other children contains numerous behavioral change agents. No person seems too old to listen to a story read or told.

Summary

Behavioral objectives, or statements describing the behaviors that are to be performed by the learner, focus teacher attention on the end results of the instruction, rather than on aimless teaching activities. Teaching activities are meaningful when they expedite the economical development of pupil reading skills.

The most prominent parts of the behavioral objective include (1) a statement of specific behavior, (2) a statement of when the behavior will be exhibited, and (3) a criterion of success (indicating the measure of whether or not the behavior is satisfactorily performed).

The determination of the types of reading behaviors or skills is contingent upon each child's place in the reading skills sequence and his specific needs within that skills level. From initial emphasis on word recognition techniques (behaviors) and oral reading behaviors, the behavioral emphasis shifts to various silent reading skills.

Although objectives are essential for guiding the development of specific reading behaviors, it is evident that many students achieve them as the result of certain exposures that are beyond simple descriptions. Because of this, it is useful to plan learning activities that possess development powers which are not easily defined, such as story telling, sharing sessions, and interaction groups.

13 Direct teacher actions

Behavioral objectives
1. Contrast the goals, goals determination means, and direct teacher actions of basal and diagnostic reading instruction.
2. Describe the elements of a typical basal story unit and cite specific strengths and/or weaknesses of the various elements.
3. Describe direct teacher actions for developing pupil skills in word recognition, comprehension, and fluency.

Excepting affective outcomes, direct teacher actions have value only if there is some change in the pupil as a result of those actions. As we have seen in the previous chapter, such changes can be measured more accurately if they are stated in behavioral terms such as the following: The pupil will instantly and accurately blend all the single consonants with the phonograms *-an, -en, -in, -on,* and *-un.* Several teaching alternatives might be used to develop the aforementioned behavior, but certain teacher actions seem to be more efficient than others. It is these actions on which we will concentrate in this chapter.

The unique characteristics of diagnostic reading instruction
There is some danger that the discussion of teacher actions related to specific skills may present a fragmentary viewpoint of reading instruction. To avoid such an impression, remember that the large objective of diagnostic reading instruction is the development of an individual who "reads widely and critically in such a way as to solve his problems in a reasoned manner, to entertain himself and others, and to gain a deep appreciation of the joys and hardships of living." Consequently, separate skills instruction must contribute to the larger goal in a meaningful way.

Diagnostic reading instruction departs significantly from the dominant teacher "prescription process" of many of the basal series, in which individual needs are disregarded. The major differences appear to be goals, goal determination means, and direct teacher actions, as illustrated in Table 13-1. Basal authors rarely intend that their materials should be viewed simply as tasks to be completed and try to build in a variety of check tests and other means for focusing teacher attention on the skills goals of reading. Nevertheless, because of the dominant practice that equates book level to grade level, the coverage or completion of a given book often becomes the goal.

Because we all like to have things packaged in convenient, orderly arrangements, basal authors and publishers respond by compiling skills and learning activities in "story units." Further structure is imposed by the establishment of specific steps that can be carried out within each story unit. Although they are labeled in ways unique to the various series, the steps usually include the following: building backgrounds, introducing new words, guided reading, rereading, and extending or developing skills.

As illustrated in Table 13-1, diagnostic reading instruction differs from the basal instruction described here because the former is keyed to specific individual reading skills needs. The balance of this chapter presents direct teacher actions that are useful for developing word recognition, comprehension, and fluency skills. Conceivably, these teacher actions could be effected under some of the previously discussed basal lesson components.

Word recognition

Word recognition per se makes a poor behavioral objective because we really cannot tell anything about the silent recognition process

---

Table 13-1 / Differences in reading goals, goal determination means, and direct teacher actions, basal and diagnostic reading instruction

Reading goals	Goal determination means	Direct teacher actions
Basal:		
Task completion, e.g., lessons	Lessons followed in order on assumption that needs of children are same as those in lesson	Implementation of this teaching format: building background, introducing vocabulary, guided reading, rereading, extending skills
Diagnostic:		
Specific skills in word recognition, comprehension, fluency	Determination of individual skills needs (Chapters 8, 9, 10, 11)	Teaching strategies that elicit skills

in the brain unless we (1) hear individuals call the familiar referents of words or (2) hear some verbal evidence of understanding (or see written evidence). Because the first element is more commonly associated with what we mean when we talk about word recognition skill, we should probably label this area "word calling." Thus, as a rather broad objective, we might have the following:

When presented with printed words in isolation or in context, the student will vocally produce the sounds that are commonly associated with the printed symbols (allowing for slight changes that might be employed by nonstandard English dialect speakers).

This is a bit precise, but we are saying that our large goal for word recognition will be that "pupils say the words that are presented to them in print." With such an objective in mind, we must ask: "What direct teaching acts will effectively aid children to say all kinds of words (of varying length and construction) when they see them?"

A listing of the word recognition skills of context analysis, sight words, phonic analysis, structural analysis, and dictionary analysis does not answer the question, but it is a convenient organizing device for exploring the most productive direct teacher actions for developing each skill type.

Context analysis

Context analysis skill will not enable a child to pronounce every word he sees. Nevertheless, it is a skill that, when well developed, can permit a child to correctly call words in context that he would not be likely to call out of context.

Teacher-directed reading experiences that are designed to encourage the child to use cues apart from the word itself (such as pictures, the remainder of the sentence) seem capable of producing analysis strategies. Such teacher-directed activities include guidance in closure exercises and in oral reading sessions.

Teacher guidance in closure exercises is a program of conscious moves on the part of teachers to:

Have the children insert omitted words in oral sentences.
   She put milk and _____ in her cereal.
Erase certain words from language experience stories and have the children supply the missing words.
   We went to the bakery in a big _____
   We had some _____ to eat.
   Next month we are _____ to the fire station.
Put sentences and paragraphs on the board or on exercise pages that require pupils to effect closure.

Guidance in oral reading is an important behavior because it gives the teacher an opportunity to assist a pupil in seeking context clues. As we pointed out previously, teachers who supply unknown words instantly may be conditioning pupils not to use context analysis strategies. Conversely, if the teacher assistance is too slow or not directed toward contextual analysis use, the pupil may lose the thought line of the story. Because of the crucial importance of teacher direction of beginning oral reading, we offer the following strategies:

Situation	Teacher strategy
Child waits to be told unknown words	Wait a minute and see if this will suggest to the child that you expect him to attempt the word. If a favorable response is not obtained (and it probably will not be if he has no notion of what to do), ask him to go back a line and see if the preceding sentence and the words around it suggest the word. If things still do not go too well, try several oral rereadings until he makes a good guess.
Child reads on by inserting a word that has no meaning in the sentence context	A few children can do this and still obtain a meaning, but most cannot. The teacher's job is to get the pupil to focus on what he is saying (in a sentence sense). By inserting a "please try that again" or a "did that sound right to you?" it is possible to get the child's attention focused. Subsequent efforts should be planned so that these students can practice reading certain selections with key words covered or omitted. They must make the closures.
Child keeps reading by inserting good substitutions	*Remain silent.* Also try to keep other individuals from breaking the thought line. Although silent, you can note characteristic sight word, phonetic, or other deviations that can be checked out of context.
Child keeps repeating (self-correcting) in order to preserve ongoing meaning	Repetitions are frequently healthy elements of basic understanding. It is usually not too difficult to see whether the repetition is a stall or a legitimate effort at meaning. When repetitions become constant, it is likely that the student may be reading materials that are too demanding for his other word recognition skills.

Sight words

These are the words initially taught in most basals as whole units. They are used as the skeleton of the reading program because they occur frequently, contain many sound-to-symbol relationships that would be difficult to construct synthetically, and offer a means for subsequently attacking similar words.

A determination of the most expedient means of teaching such words is extremely difficult because of the absence of definitive research. Most of the research we have (Vernon, 1966) seems to be focused on the teaching of sight words as separate units, which in turn leads to research on the effectiveness of various stimuli and prompting techniques (Duell, 1968). Some directions are certainly evident for the perception of isolated words, but little is offered concerning the effects of teaching such words in larger contextual situations. Adding to the confusion is what appears to be a major gap between the intended and the actual teaching of sight vocabulary in the basal series. After the introduction of the story characters (and their picture referents), most basal authors direct teachers to induct children into sight reading via the oral reading of phrase and sentence units. Modeling the teacher, the children read the pages in unison and supposedly obtain the visual impressions of the words involved. Subsequently, the children are led into a series of opportunities to read the words in a pocket chart, workbook, on a blackboard, and so on.

Despite such direction, my observation indicates that many teachers systematically drill the pupils on sight word cards, usually in advance of reading them in whole phrases or sentences. Often, the teacher's objective is for the pupil to know all or most of the words in the first preprimer before he begins to read it. Certainly, such practices are at variance with the recommended use of the materials. As a result of this discrepancy, it is difficult to make generalizations about the relative effectiveness of the contextual approach (as advocated by the basal authors) and the isolated approach (as practiced by many teachers). My own position is that pupils might learn the sight words more quickly as the result of linguistic cues accruing from the connected reading experiences. The use of the isolated approach might result in sentence memorizers or, at least, children who do not know the words. There is another theory that the best results might be obtained if children were inducted into reading as much as possible by the contextual approach and then given practice on isolated words as a subsequent step. We favor such a combination because it seems to possess the strengths of both positions.

Because reading involves considerably more than making the right sounds for the right words, we strongly favor the language-experience approach described in Chapter 8 as a prelude to both the contextual reading of the preprimers and the subsequent practice on isolated sight words. Before children begin basal-type materials, they should be well oriented in such conventions as:

Reading from left to right
Satisfactorily making the return visual sweep
Noting the beginnings and endings of phrase and sentence units
Noting word elements by the spacings between them

When children begin the basal stories (after rich experiences in constructing and reading language-experience stories), we would suggest the following approaches, or sight word teaching strategies, to teaching sight reading (see Figures 13-1, 13-2, 13-3, 13-4, 13-5, 13-6, 13-7). Additional suggestions for rapid, average, and slow visual learners follow.

Rapid visual learners

Step 1 / The students should be encouraged to study the pictures, the number of words, and so on and then to anticipate what is being said.

Step 2 / The teacher should then encourage the children to follow the words closely as he reads them. The intent is twofold: The children are determining whether their anticipations were correct while reading with the teacher.

Step 3 / The teacher should clearly model the reading again, with the children following visually.

Step 4 / The teacher should invite the children to read with her as all read the story in unison. Difficult phrases can be repeated several times.

Step 5 / Individual volunteers can read sentences while the others follow visually.

Step 6 / From sentence reading, the teacher moves to the word unit and frames individual words with her hands. Pupils say the words framed.

Average visual learners

After completing the previous steps, also do the following:

Step 7 / Assist pupils to focus on distinguishing characteristics of words, such as: length and configuration, initial letter(s), and ascending letter features.

Step 8 / Utilize picture referents for such words as names of characters, things, and colors. Draw attention to associating some feature of the word with some feature of the referent; for example:

Slow visual learners

After completing the previous steps, also do the following:

Step 9 / Utilize sentence, phrase, and individual word cards for practice. Emphasize the larger elements, but give attention to single word elements as well. Where possible encourage the pupil to put a single word card on the corresponding word in a phrase or sentence (reading both units orally).

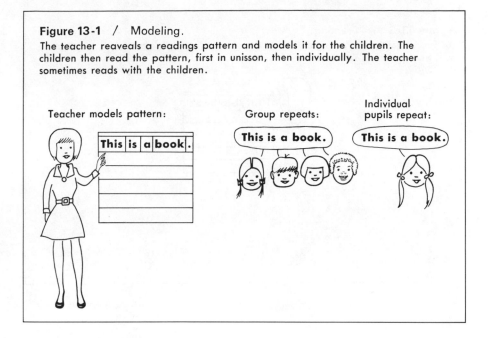

Figure 13-1 / Modeling.

The teacher reaveals a readings pattern and models it for the children. The children then read the pattern, first in unisson, then individually. The teacher sometimes reads with the children.

Teacher models pattern:

This is a book.

Group repeats:

This is a book.

Individual pupils repeat:

This is a book.

Figure 13-2 / Substituting.

After sentence and vocabulary have been modeled in context, the teacher will make substitutions and ask the group or the individual child to read the substitution.

That is a book.

That is a book.

That is a book.

This

Reprinted with the permission of the Southwest Educational Development Laboratory, Austin, Texas.

Figure 13-3 / Framing.
To focus attention on a single word in the sentence or phrase modeled, the teacher will frame a single word with her hands.

Figure 13-4 / Matching.
To focus attention on a single word in the sentence or phrase modeled, the teacher will have groups or individuals first read the whole sentence and then a word matching part of the sentence.

Figure 13-5 / Dialoging.

To increase pupil involvement in the reading and composing process, the teacher will structure dialogues for which the pupils use small pocket charts and word cards to ask and answer questions.

Figure 13-6 / Closing.

To maximize pupil's skill in using context clues, the teacher will omit words in various sentences. She will ask pupils to supply the missing word.

Figure 13-7 / Composing.
The teacher asks the children to use words in various types of compositions. It is akin to dialoguing, except that the nature of the composition tasks is not limited to dialogue situations.

Step 10 / Employ prompting tasks in which the children point to a word that represents a real object; for example:

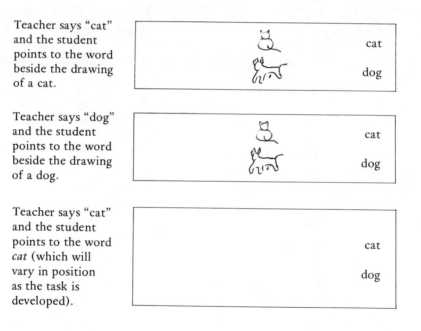

Teacher says "cat" and the student points to the word beside the drawing of a cat.

cat

dog

Teacher says "dog" and the student points to the word beside the drawing of a dog.

cat

dog

Teacher says "cat" and the student points to the word *cat* (which will vary in position as the task is developed).

cat

dog

Step 11 / Employ arrangements of words, such as three-letter words, four-letter words, five-letter words; words that begin with the same letter.

Step 12 / Have pupils pronounce the words with you as they simultaneously trace the letters on word cards with sandpaper letters. Repeat several times each day. (This activity should be teacher-directed so that incorrect responses are not fixed.)

Phonic analysis

Diagnostic reading teachers must perform teaching acts that assist the child to sound out unknown words independently by associating specific sounds with specific letters or letter groups. The success of the teacher actions must be measured in terms of subsequent pupil skill in attacking words phonetically.

We have learned that phonics is not a single system of teaching sound-to-symbol relationships, but rather a term used to describe nearly all organized efforts to teach such relationships. Because teaching actions will be determined by the type of phonics program adopted (or accepted by the teacher), it seems imperative to illustrate some of the prime methodological differences. These are shown in Figure 13-8.

The terms *inductive* and *deductive* are appropriate descriptors of phonics instruction because they describe very different means by which phonic skill can be developed. *Inductive* learning is based on psychological theory that holds that the most lasting and usable generalizations are those individuals discover for themselves. *Deductive* learning is based on an opposite set of beliefs that much learning is facilitated by giving the learner the generalizations and requiring him to practice them. When these concepts are applied to phonics instruction, it is evident that inductive phonics instruction would be designed to aid the learner in forming his own generalizations about what letters represent what sounds, whereas deductive phonics instruction would supply the generalizations and have the pupils put them to work immediately on unknown words.

In considering this dichotomy, we should note that there are wide variations between the polar positions on inductive and deductive instruction. The laissez-faire extreme of inductive phonics

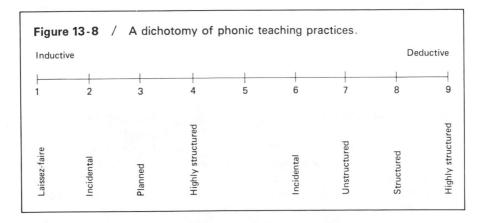

Figure 13-8 / A dichotomy of phonic teaching practices.

is that no teacher directions are given on sound-to-symbol relationships and that as a result of sentence and word reading, pupils effect their own generalizations. In the incidental teaching of inductive phonics, the teacher plays a role by occasionally asking the pupils to generalize about the likeness of sounds—for example, "In what way are the words *Bill* and *Bob* alike?" Planned inductive phonics is the structuring of reading materials in such a way that teachers can use specific lessons to aid pupils in generalizing about specific sound-to-symbol relationships. Highly structured and planned inductive phonics instruction vary only in the degree of structure written into the teacher's program. In the highly structured programs, the elements of the generalization process are detailed (so detailed, in fact, that the generalization process requires little on the part of the student other than reacting to the familiar pattern).

Deductive phonics at the highly structured extreme provides for teacher-directed instruction that is explicit about the sound-to-symbol relationships. Although deductive refers to the way in which the pupil learns and uses phonics, we usually think of synthetic phonic programs as the extreme example of deductive teaching, because in such programs the pupils are usually taught to construct or synthesize words by:

Initially learning to give the sounds of the vowels
Learning the sounds of the consonant elements
Blending the consonants with the vowel elements to form syllables
    and subsequently words

Two of these synthetic phonic programs are Words in Color (Gattengo, 1969) and The Writing Road to Reading (Spalding, 1962).

As we move toward the middle of the scale from the extreme deductive position, we see a decreasing emphasis on structure to the point where unstructured and incidental teacher acts are employed. The unstructured actions are practices in which teachers generalize about sound-to-symbol relationships in an unplanned fashion. Presumably, the students are to remember the generalizations given by the teacher and apply them. Incidental deductive teaching includes the same types of actions, but on an even less frequent basis.

Although many parents and teachers are impatient with reading people for failing to take strong stands on methods of phonics instruction, it should be evident that the decisions are far beyond simple, definitive positions. Because so many factors are involved, I have spelled out my position in detail below. I have been necessarily vague on some points in order to present a coherent, encompassing argument.

Point 1 / Some children need a laissez-faire phonics program. Generally, these pupils make up but a small portion of the school population. They have little or no need for phonics instruction because many of them have developed their own systems and have unusual word-learning capabilities. Such children enter school with reading skill or develop reading at a rapid pace in initial connected reading experiences (language-experience or preprimer).

Point 2 / Some children need only incidental inductive assistance for phonics learning. Such children are somewhat less skilled than the group described above. However, because they are above average in their understanding and visual memory skills, they require only incidental guides to the process of generalizing sounds from symbols. The teacher's task in phonics instruction is one of teaching the process which can subsequently be applied inductively by the pupil; for example, the teacher guides the child to generalize beginning single and double consonant sounds through incidental work with only a few consonant elements.

Point 3 / Most children (average) need to be systematically guided toward discovering the sound properties of the following elements: initial single consonants; final single consonants; initial blends and digraphs, final blends and digraphs; prominent short vowel patterns (CVC), prominent long vowel patterns (CVC-*e*), *r, l,* and *w* controlled vowels; adjacent vowel pairs.

Point 4 / Slower-learning children need to be systematically guided toward the preceding discoveries via more highly structured programs of phonics that have corresponding connected reading materials which provide much practice of the patterns being learned (and subsequent reinforcement of those learned). Because of the greater need for reinforcement, we recommend the use of both teacher- and commercially prepared materials utilizing the so-called alphabetic principle developed by Bloomfield (1941). Commercial materials developed on this principle include the Merrill Linguistic Readers (Fries et al., 1966), Let's Read (Bloomfield and Barnhart, 1961), and the Basic Reading Series (Rasmussen and Goldberg, 1964). Although we recommend these materials for use with slower children, they should be supplements to more meaningful books that employ realistic language and situations. Used alone, the so-called linguistic readers may destroy reading as a meaning-getting process. When used as supplements, they often contribute phonic attack to the other reading situations.

Point 5 / Learners who do not respond in accordance with their reading potential to initial reading instruction in the preceding phonic programs should be given highly structured deductive phonics instruction. Certainly, the decision to drop a program requires a great deal of thought, but the diagnostic reading teacher should have the ability to make it on the basis of a thorough knowledge of specific skills and varied learning materials. With such knowledge, he can drastically alter a program that appears to be going nowhere.

Point 6 / Unstructured and incidental deductive phonics instruction appears to be of little value. If the countless wasted hours of random prompting by teachers could be regained and put into the efforts recommended above, we would see tangible returns in increased pupil skills. I discourage *incidental* deductive phonics so strongly because it provides only a clue to guessing the word and does not draw upon symbol-to-sound relationships.

Basic to operating inductive programs is a thorough understanding of the nature of teacher actions in developing the word attack behaviors emphasized in Chapter 5: auditory discrimination of the elements, visual discrimination in which the grapheme (letter) and phoneme (sound) are associated, blending tasks in which one element is blended with another, and contextual application, in which the pupil actually uses the skill in contextual reading.

Auditory discrimination / Practice sensitizes pupils to the task of listening for a given sound within a word. Initial concerns are listening for beginning, ending, and rhyming sounds. The teacher's role is illustrated in the following example:

Teacher / Listen carefully; the names of three boys in our room are alike in some way that you can hear. Listen as I say the names of the boys and raise your hand if you can tell me how they sound alike.

Bobby   Billy   Burt

In this fashion, the students are led to identify the sound that we associate with the letter *b*, although no mention of this relationship is sought by the teacher at this point. The teacher would then seek to build on the sound association by (*a*) asking the children to say other words that began like the boys' names, (*b*) having the children find and cut pictures of things that begin with common sounds, (*c*) checking the students' skill in separating words with different beginnings. Practice in discriminating the different sounds may proceed through a number of prominent beginning consonant sounds, or attention may be focused upon the symbol (in this instance *b*) that represents the sound.

Visual discrimination / In the context of this discussion, it is the pupils' association of the grapheme (letter) with its phoneme (sound). The student is led to recognize that the sound that begins *Bobby, Billy,* and *Burt* is represented by the letter *b*. Such realizations are often difficult, so it is wise to let the pupils offer generalizations and avoid the temptation to tell them. After the auditory discrimination task described above, the words *Bobby, Billy,* and *Burt* would be given to the children visually to see if they note the common letter *b* that was paired with the common beginning sound; for example:

Teacher / Yes, all the words have the same sound at the beginning. In what way do all the words look alike? (Pupils look and note the common beginning.)

Blending / This is the ability to take known phonic elements and blend them together in accordance with their sound properties; for example:

ch-i-ck	str-a-p	gr-a-ph
ch-ick	str-ap	gra-ph

Because of their high frequency in beginning reading words, consonants are often taught first. It seems desirable for initial consonants to be blended to a known phonogram (such as -*an*) while visual discrimination is occurring. Thus, the pupil would avoid the tendency to articulate a consonant-vowel combination that does not exist—for example, when the student says "buh" for "b." Specific recommendations for blending tasks and their sequence are offered below:

Step 1 / Initial single consonants should be emphasized first. This emphasis should involve consonant substitution on a CVC word; for example:

*c*at	*f*at
*b*at	*m*at
*d*at	*n*at

With such an emphasis, pupils should not articulate isolated consonant sounds.

Step 2 / Short vowels, although not singled out for attention, are introduced before long vowels through the use of the CVC-type words above.

Step 3 / Final single consonants are emphasized after the initial single consonants are mastered (in terms of blending and contextual application). The emphasis is the same as in Step 1; consonant substitution is employed.

ca*t*	ca*f*
ca*b*	ca*m*
ca*d*	ca*n*

Step 4 / Short vowels are introduced through patterns in which children can substitute for initial and final single consonants and medial vowels; for example:

*b*at	*b*et	*b*it	*b*ut	*n*ot
cat	met	hit	nut	lot
mat	let	nit	hut	hot
can		bin	bug	nog
cam		din	lug	mob

Step 5 / Consonant blends and digraphs may precede or follow the short vowel patterns introduced in Step 4. These elements are treated in the same way that the initial and final single consonants were treated; that is, blended with phonograms in consonant substitution.

cat   brat
stat   chat
slat

Step 6 / The first attention to long vowel sounds is given to the silent *e* situations by contrasting CVC words and CVC-*e* words; for example:

rat   rate
bit   bite
cut   cute
rot   rote

Step 7 / Adjacent vowel pairs are taught as vowel digraphs with specific diphthong and erratic exceptions noted (see Chapter 4).

Step 8 / *R, l,* and *w* controlled vowels are taught through the phonograms that most commonly carry them, rather than through rules about *r, l,* or *w* affecting certain sound changes.

bar   pal   saw
her   bell   few
fir
for
fur   bull

Contextual application / This is the payoff for phonics instruction because the student applies his attack skills to the quick unlocking of unknown words. In Chapter 4 we presented the phonic attack plan. Such a plan represents a capsule summary of what a pupil should be able to do as a result of his teacher-directed learning experiences in the phonics program. Through inductive processes, the student should be able to complete the following steps:

Step 1 / Blend the sound of the beginning consonant, blend, or digraph with:

1. The short vowel sound of the letter in the middle—for example, *blaf.*
2. The long vowel sound when:
   A. There is a vowel-consonant-*e* ending (CVC-*e*)—for example, *blafe.*
   B. There is one vowel and it is on the end of a word or syllable—for example, *be, no, go.*
   C. There are two vowels side by side (except in the case of diphthongs and *ie, ei* combinations).

Step 2 / Blend the consonant and vowel elements into a whole word or syllable. If he does not know the word, he tries an alternate vowel sound.

Step 3 / If he still does not know the word, he checks its pronunciation in the dictionary or glossary (provided he has an understanding of the marking systems).

Structural analysis

Structural analysis is the set of skills by which readers isolate structural units in words and then blend these units with the other word parts. Well-developed skills in this area allow rapid and efficient word recognition. The primary structural units, as described earlier, are root words, compounds, contractions, endings, affixes, and syllables.

Root words, endings, and affixes / Since discussions of endings and affixes are somewhat limited without the presence of root or base words, the categories are combined here. Contrast is the important concern in helping children to note root words and their endings and affixes. The contrasts must be effected initially, between the root words and endings such as -s and -ed, which appear early in the first grade. Contrast can be accomplished in several ways, but most common are what we shall call (1) the before-and-after contrast and (2) the stand-out contrast. In the before-and-after contrast, we highlight the addition of endings by using lists such as these:

Before	cat	boat	jump	look	help
After	cats	boats	jumping	looked	helped

The stand-out contrast highlights the ending visually by such devices as printing the endings in another color, underlining them, or circling them. The same contrast procedures are applicable to prefixes and suffixes. Again, the attempt is to present the structural element in such a way that it is learned and recognized instantly as a unit.

Compounds / Compound words appear to be some of the more easily learned words because of their length and unique configuration. Extensive practice seldom seems called for if the student knows the elements that make up the compound. If he does not, then the primary task is to develop the sight words or attack mechanisms necessary to attack the words in question. After most beginning readers see that we can "stick some words together," they have little difficulty in noting such instances as *policemen, henhouse, something,* or *another.*

Contractions / Contractions seldom pose much mystery to children, who use them in daily speech. Generally, they learn most contractions as sight words, which is logical because of the lack of system with regard to which letters are omitted; for example:

don't	do not	(middle letter of second word omitted)
he's	he is	(first letter of second word omitted)
he'd	he had	(first two letters of second word omitted)

Contractions have to be attacked as whole units because phonic analysis may create problems with words such as *don't* (the child says "dontuh").

Syllables / The steps involved in teaching syllabication are these:

Step 1 / Auditory discrimination of syllable units. Pupils are sensitized through listening to the distinct number of vowel sounds that they hear in a word; for example, ge-og-ra-phy (4).

Step 2 / Visual discrimination of the structural units that make up the sound units heard. The students go beyond the auditory syllable counting and visually pair up the structures with the sounds they make; for example, ge-og-ra-phy.

Step 3 / Application of phonic generalizations to the sounds that can be expected of vowels in open and closed syllables.

A. When there is one vowel in a word or syllable and the vowel comes at the end, it usually has a long sound; for example, va/ca/tion.
B. When there is one vowel in a word or syllable and the vowel does not come at the end, it usually has a short sound; for example, bot/tle.

Step 4 / Application of the following visual division generalizations:

A. When the first vowel sound in a word is followed by two consonants, the first syllable usually ends with the first of these consonants—for example, bul/let, pic/ture. *Exception:* When the first vowel sound is followed by *th, ch, sh,* and other normal consonant combinations, these combinations are not divided and go with the first or second syllables—for example, moth/er.
B. When the first vowel sound is followed by a single consonant, that consonant usually begins the second syllable—for example, sta/tion.
C. Prefixes and suffixes are generally separate syllables—for example, dis/trust, sugges/tion.
D. The endings *-ble, -cle, -dle, -gle, -kle, -ple, -tle, -zle* make up the final syllable usually—for example, ap/ple.

Although not listed, accent or the degree of stress on a syllable has an important bearing on where a word is divided and ultimately sounded. In a multisyllabic word, the syllable that receives the greatest stress is said to receive the "primary accent." Other syllables may receive either "secondary accent" or no accent at all.

Reading comprehension

Previously, we described reading comprehension skills as thinking skills that are applied prior to, during, and after the visual scanning task by which written language is converted into associated meanings. From the very first page, we have stressed the theme of this book—that we are not doing an adequate job of developing these skills. Proposals for a solution have focused on such concerns as building better backgrounds through preschool child-development programs, developing more individualized learning situations, teaching more effective word recognition skills (normally phonics), improving or replacing basals, using more effective means of motivation, providing more reading practice, and improving teaching. With the exception of the first suggestion, all these factors seem to come under the direct influence of the teacher. If we accept the notion that our teaching is not producing the desired results, we must study what we are and are not doing. In the material that follows, we will survey the current status of comprehension instruction and then note specific strategies for the development of comprehension skills.

Current teacher actions for comprehension development

Both teachers and texts are charged with the responsibility for bringing about desired behavioral outcomes. The determination of what the role of each should be, however, becomes a problem because we really do not know how much power is built into the textual comprehension program. The observation that many teachers depart from it (especially in oral questioning) suggests some teacher skepticism. Perhaps the confusing nature of the comprehension classifications befuddles the best-intentioned individuals.

In seeking strategies for comprehension development, it seems sensible to look at the comprehension development strategies of the texts as well as the ways in which these strategies appear to be implemented. Although reading comprehension skill is by no means limited to the reading period, its initial development seems to be concentrated there (content reading tasks in areas such as science and social studies are initially limited because of the pupil's limited word recognition skills). Consequently, teacher actions for developing comprehension center around the following segments of the basal reader format: building backgrounds, guided reading, and extending skills.

Building backgrounds / Most series have an initial segment that involves the teacher in the process of getting the children "ready" to read a given story. Although a number of concerns enter this phase of instruction, the primary emphasis is one of laying the "understanding foundation" for what is going to be read. Since background building is directly related to the backgrounds of the individual pupils, it is very difficult to expect a teacher to follow the text suggestions exactly. These sections can be omitted in certain circumstances, while in others the teacher must extend their scope. The teacher must be an astute observer of potential pitfalls for his students in the understanding of the language of the upcoming selection (syntax, concepts, vocabulary, metaphor, prose style, related experiences, and so on). Clever questioning can determine in advance the problems to be averted.

Guided reading / In guided reading or purpose setting, the teacher provides the purpose for reading a given segment of a story; for example, "Read the first line and tell what happened to Jane." This strategy of questioning seems logical; if you want pupils to find specifics, you have to tell them what they are looking for. In reading, if we expect pupils to do such things as distinguish the important from the unimportant, we must give them guidance.

We hope that the guidance will transfer and that pupils will subsequently be able to guide themselves to the proper reading strategy in accordance with the task; for example:

Task or purpose	Reading strategy
Do well on a factual examination in a social studies text.	1. Survey the material quickly to identify and remember the main topics. 2. Think about what is already known in topic areas. 3. Read selectively to find out things that are unknown. 4. Read entire selection to fill in facts related to main topics. 5. Review main topics and attempt to recall supporting facts; look up the facts to test memory.
Find the population of Somalia in a geography text.	1. Locate Somalia in index. 2. Turn to pages in text about Somalia. 3. Scout headings to find most likely location of population information.

These are rather specific types of purposes. In initial reading instruction, teacher questions are usually designed to guide the children to such things as the major ideas of a communication, the sequence of these major ideas, and so on. It is hoped that such questioning will lead students to intuitively pick out the major elements and not get sidetracked by unimportant details.

To assist teachers in the guidance process, textbooks frequently contain purpose questions. At the outset of instruction, there seems to be nearly a question per line. As the students progress, the questions decrease in number in proportion to the increase in ideas and words. In a study of teacher questions in the reading circle (Guszak, 1967), I counted the number of purpose questions and found the following surprising ratios: Second-grade teachers asked 3.3 setting-purpose questions per story, whereas fourth-grade teachers asked 6.3 such purpose questions per story. We would have anticipated that second-grade teachers would ask a greater number of setting-purpose questions and that they would ask more questions than fourth-grade teachers. Because the sample was small, the results may have little meaning, but they certainly suggest the value of looking into the purpose-setting nature of the basal reading group.

The value of asking questions in advance of reading seems open to criticism. Research, most of which was done at the high school and college level (except for one study at the fourth-grade level), suggests that such questions tend to condition too-selective and consequently incomplete reading (Frase, 1967, 1968; Rothkopf, 1966; Goudey, 1969). That is, children who read without specific purposes perform better in terms of comprehending the total selection. While the research seems valid, several interpretations are possible. The results may refer to a specific kind of comprehension (detailed) and therefore have little bearing on purposes such as locating major ideas. It is also difficult to generalize the results to beginning reading, where prereading questioning may actually lead to better detailed comprehension than no such questioning.

Extending skills / The comprehension tasks in the workbooks that accompany basal readers usually contain what are commonly referred to as extending skills. The comprehension skills are presumably of the same nature as those involved in guided reading, but in workbook form. Such skills practice materials vary greatly in quality and quantity, and their effect on development seems to be largely unknown. The increasing number of supplemental comprehension programs (see Chapter 14) seems to at least suggest some apprehension concerning the effectiveness of both the guided reading and extending skills portions of the basal reading programs.

This is a capsule description of the teacher's direct role in developing comprehension according to structured basal programs. Since it is apparent that such formats are not being followed precisely, let us take a closer look at what we have observed teachers actually doing.

Observation 1 / Teachers do most of the talking, nearly all the questioning, and most of the verbal evaluating of pupil responses (Aschner et al., 1965; Bellack and Davitz, 1963; Guszak, 1967; McDonald and Zaret, 1967). Such domination precludes a great deal of student thinking. Chall comments that "the first grade teacher following the teacher's manual talks more than the pupils read. Her questions and directions tend to take the child's attention away from the text, rather than help him focus and concentrate on it" (Chall, 1967, p. 260).

Observation 2 / About two-thirds of teacher comprehension questions seek remembering outcomes (Aschner et al., 1965; Guszak, 1967; McDonald and Zaret, 1967, and others). My own research further suggests that the remembering outcomes are most often concerned with minute facts.

Observation 3 / Students anticipate the nature of comprehension questions rather well, as most are answered correctly on the first try (Guszak, 1968). In my study, 90 percent of the literal comprehension questions were answered instantly. Added to this is the strong possibility that a few students do most of the answering.

Observation 4 / Inferential types of questions (predicting/extending) constitute less than 15 percent of teacher questions (Aschner et al., 1965; Guszak, 1968; McDonald and Zaret, 1967).

Observation 5 / Evaluative types of questions make up approximately 15 percent of teachers' questions. My research indicates that evaluative questions most often ask only whether the children like or dislike something.

Observation 6 / Organization questions are seldom asked. Less than one-half of one percent of the questions classified in our study of the questions of certain second-, fourth-, and sixth-grade teachers called for organizing skill behaviors. From such findings it is easy to make inferences about pupil failings in summarizing, outlining, and so on.

This is not an indictment of teachers; it represents a set of observations based on what is admittedly limited research. Nevertheless, the information seems suggestive of actions that can and should be taken. We do need more research, but there is no reason to wait passively for definitive results. We can, as Spache (1963) wisely suggests, focus on the observed outcomes of the mental behavior. If we clearly describe the behavioral outcomes that seem to be important for reading instruction, we can logically test various means for obtaining them.

In Chapter 6, we described reading comprehension purposes, grouped them into a coherent structure, and indicated means for measuring their presence or absence in terms of pupil achievement. At this point, we turn our attention to some of the teacher actions that can stimulate the development of locating, remembering, organizing, predicting/extending, and evaluating behaviors.

Strategies for developing comprehension skills

Contrary to some viewpoints, predicting/extending skills are not the luxury items of the comprehension program, but rather a giant chunk of the foundation. This is so because reading is, to a great extent, a guessing game. We do "try to tell a book by its cover," anticipate a news item by the headline, envision the movie by its ad, and so on. The better informed we are, the better we guess. If the author of a book is well known and its subject familiar, we may be able to predict its contents rather well.

Because reading comprehension skill is so firmly grounded in the kinds of experiences that children have had, the first set of strategies concerns the use of predicting/extending skill in the first phase of the formal reading program—the readiness period. After this, we turn to beginning and subsequent reading.

Readiness program / Reading readiness begins soon after birth as the child develops the various potentials that subsequently allow him to manage oral and written language. The behaviors that follow can be developed in both the preschool and in-school years.

Behavior	Recommended strategy
Predicting/extending	
Predicting convergent outcomes from pictures	Pictures from various sources—children's books, comics, readiness texts—can indicate the beginnings of a possible happening; for example, two cars are going to collide. Seek pupil predictions of the likely consequences. When possible, structure situations so that after the predictions are gathered, the children can find out what did happen. This can be accomplished by showing the next picture, reading on in the book, or actually demonstrating certain inevitable consequences.
Predicting convergent outcomes from pictures, titles, oral descriptions	Essentially the same process as above. The important teacher role is one of withholding judgment and serving as an agent to get as many ideas as possible. When the ideas are in, the teacher can quickly summarize them before finding out what happened.
Predicting divergent outcomes	Some things are likely but not inevitable, so seek out incidents that could turn out in a number of ways and ask for the different kinds of things that could happen.
Explaining story character actions	"Why do you think that old wolf did that?" Characters react as they do for specific reasons. Children need to suppose. The suppositions should be offered freely, and they will be if the teacher keeps the atmosphere open with warm reception of all ideas, especially the bizarre.
Explaining gadget operations	Seek animated or illustrated explanations of how something works. Although young children like to ask how something works, they also like to speculate themselves, if encouraged. Even though the explanations may not be very clear, the process of attempting it forces analytical thinking that will, in time, pay off.

Behavior	Recommended strategy
Restoring omitted words, phrases	Stop in the middle of a line in which the next word is contextually cued by the others—for example, "The hunter dropped his _____ and ran." Seek to condition the child or children to make an immediate oral insert so that you can continue on without undue interruption in the story. This should be treated as a game, and no pressure should be exerted.

Locating information

Locating specific things	Although these are not strictly reading behaviors, it is useful for pupils and children to respond to oral directions to point to the yellow bird, for example. This is also a way for the parent or teacher to assess concept-vocabulary development (see Chapter 8).

Remembering

Remembering simple sentence, paragraph, story content	Stories that are continued from time to time should be brought up to date by the students' remembering what has happened. Similarly, questions can be asked at opportune points in the text; for example, when some earlier happening becomes important at the place you find yourself—he had only three wishes and he had already used up two.

Organizing

Retelling orally a sentence, sentence set, paragraph, story	This is about the same behavior as above except that the student has to manage a larger content, which inevitably involves some sequencing, omission of small detail, and so on. Such organization may take place in media other than language—through pictures, cartoons.
Outlining the sequence orally	The teacher emphasizes the sequencing task; for example, "Now tell me what he did first, then . . ."
Reorganizing communication into a logical sequence of happening, cartoon, picture	The teacher initially models tasks such as putting cartoon frames in a sequence of happening or making a simple line-drawing cartoon that translates the happening.

Evaluating critically

Making judgments about the desirability of a character, situation	The not so simple "Why?" inserted by the teacher into the pause following a pupil judgment can stimulate thinking. If a character is not liked, why is he not liked? Why does he seem mean?

Behavior	Recommended strategy
Making judgments about the validity of a story description or argument by making comparisons with other sources of information (external)	The teacher seeks to have the pupil compare and contrast the story description or whatever with his own referents and see whether or not it seems reasonable. Because children's referents may be limited, they tend to make superficial judgments that need to be probed by gentle questioning.
Making judgments about the validity of a story description, and so on by using internal comparisons	Logical reasoning techniques as suggested by Wolf et al. (1967) are useful to a limited extent in the readiness phase. The students should be sensitized to note internal contradictions—for example, the different names given to the same dog in different parts of the story.

Beginning reading / All the elements discussed above with regard to readiness are continued in the beginning reading program as parts of sharing sessions centering around the materials read by the teacher or the pupils. Comprehension continues to be developed through the teacher's reading of stories, newspaper articles, cards, letters to children. The discussions of these things will involve all the thinking skills that can subsequently be applied to reading. Although the practice of reading to schoolchildren has long been an approved activity, it has been given a new boost in the study by Cohen (1968) in which socially and culturally disadvantaged second-graders were read to each day from fifty selected books. Presumably as a result of being read to, the experimental group (about half the total sample of 580 children) showed significantly greater gains in vocabulary, word knowledge, and reading comprehension than the control group.

Some students and adults pick up books and proceed to dutifully read the title, the first paragraph, first page, second page, and so on without mentally projecting what the selection is going to reveal. At the end, they are often at a loss if they are asked to explain what they have been reading. Their failure seems to be largely explained by the absence of prediction or expectation. Because comprehension is affected by our initial expectations, it is crucial to condition readers in the various means of predicting the content of a selection in advance of detailed reading. In observing the behaviors of some of the widely publicized speed readers who demonstrate the values to be obtained from enrolling in such a program (for a substantial fee) we can see some of the anticipation tactics in evidence; for example,

1. They note the title.
2. They quickly scan the description on the dust jacket.

3. They preview the Contents page.
4. They carefully scan the chapters, headings, and unusual features.

After this preview, such readers systematically flip through the pages and complete certain materials very rapidly. Actually, if we might use an analogy, these readers have literally "cased the place." Guiding the "casing process" was their anticipation of what they could expect to find, determined by their experience background. By adjusting their ideas in the light of their preview findings, these readers had a strong idea of the contents, so their systematic reading was basically a scan to fill in a well-developed mental outline of the book.

Stauffer (1969) devotes most of his text to teacher strategies for causing pupils to anticipate the contents of a selection by the obvious clues. Called "Directed-Reading-Thinking-Activity" (D-R-T-A), this plan requires the pupils to perform tasks such as the following at the beginning of a given story selection:

1. Speculate verbally as to what the story will be about, using only its title.
2. Check the verbal speculations or predictions by studying the pictures.
3. Narrow the speculations in light of the picture information and speculate further.
4. Read a page at a time to verify speculations or develop new ones, and continue on through the story.

Because this type of prediction activity is so vital to reading at all levels, its primary emphasis in beginning reading is obvious. Here are some strategies.

Behavior	Recommended strategy
Predicting/extending	
Predicting convergent outcomes from pictures, titles, oral descriptions	The distinction between the teacher's role in this area and that of the "guided reading" structured in most basal programs is important. In the prediction strategy, the teacher places the burden of thinking on the student; the student must predict before verifying. In the guided reading strategy, the child's thinking is restricted to the task of verifying the teacher-made prediction. The prediction strategy follows the normal thinking behaviors of children: They identify with the

Behavior	Recommended strategy
	action unfolding pictorially and turn the pages to see if things work out as expected. The teacher seeks predictions that go beyond the information provided in the pictures.
Predicting divergent outcomes	Divergent outcomes are important because they represent the unexpected and the novel. Most of our emphasis in terms of comprehension strategy will be on convergence, but we must seek divergent predictions whenever they might demonstrate unexpected but valuable solutions to problems. Many stories illustrate the logical solution that can be reached convergently. Often it is easy to accept that solution and ignore the value of divergent ideas.
Explaining story character actions	See the readiness phase.
Explaining gadget operations	See the readiness phase.
Restoring omitted words	Some activities are suggested under the readiness phase, and specific suggestions for other teaching activities can be found in the Context Analysis section of this chapter.

Locating information

Behavior	Recommended strategy
Locating specifics within written materials:	Locating tasks require pupils to use the various protocols of our written communication to respond to a request ("Find the sentence that tells the cost"), make a request ("Which part of the story is best?"), identify specific segments, and so on.
page numbers	Pupils are initially guided to the placement of the page numbers by going through numbered pages (so that they note number order and page correspondence).
parts of a story	The generalized concepts of "first" and "last" are used in discussions from the outset. More discrete breakdowns are subsequently introduced.
sentences, paragraphs, phrases	Teachers simply direct pupils to the mechanical indicators of sentences (periods, question marks, exclamation marks) and paragraphs (indentation). Phrases are identified as sentence parts that do not appear to be fully developed.
Locating information with book parts: titles, stories	Pupils are systematically asked to locate a specific title in a listing of several titles. Similarly, they are asked to use printing

Behavior	Recommended strategy
	protocols and reading skills to locate a specific story among other stories.
Contents pages	In the first text containing a contents page, pupils should be guided to the practice of using this aid for locating stories read or to be read. A contents page is usually found in one or more of the preprimers. When this location skill is established at the outset of reading instruction, pupils are able to save much of the time wasted in hunting for stories.
Locating information with reference aids (picture dictionaries)	See the discussion in Chapter 5.

Remembering

Remembering simple sentence content, remembering the content of two or more simple sentences in sequence, remembering the factual content of complex sentences and complex sentence sets	Remembering is important behavior because it is basic to further understanding. Children must be assisted to remember those things that must be retained for further comprehension, for their value for one's well-being, and so on. Teacher prompts or questions for remembering should serve to resurrect important elements. In the process of prediction and verification, most pupils should be involved to the extent that they need not be bothered with after-the-fact remembering questions unless such questions have a bearing on upcoming events.

Organizing

Retelling a sentence, sentence set, paragraph, story orally	Broader in nature than most remembering tasks, organizing behaviors should be solicited in cases where a pupil is asked to "bring us up to date," "retell what happened to them at the well," and so on. The student is thus made to perform the task of sequencing, paring down, and delivering a résumé.
Outlining orally or in writing the sequence of sentence sets, paragraph sets, a story	In addition to retelling, pupils can list events, arrange teacher-prepared event slips, and so on.
Reorganizing the communication into a logical sequence via pictures, cartoons, graphic designs, formulas	See Chapters 5 and 11.

Behavior	Recommended strategy
Evaluating critically	
Making judgments	See the readiness phase.

Subsequent reading / By this phase of reading, pupils' reading purposes have become varied to the extent that they must be able to locate and use information in a number of sources, remember increasing amounts of factual material, organize involved communications, and evaluate many forms of printed media. It is difficult to put a specific grade level on such behaviors because they are largely conditioned by the pupil and the program. In some programs, alert second-graders may be doing involved study types of reading. The adage that children learn to read in the primary grades and read to learn in the intermediate grades certainly does not apply to all. Most of the skills mentioned previously will be carried over into subsequent reading, with the addition of the following:

Behavior	Recommended strategy
Predicting/extending	
Generalizing from sets of information in a story or stories (identifying main ideas)	In Chapter 6 we indicated that main ideas are often derived through generalizing. Thus, students need to be questioned closely in such a manner that they derive the generalization or main idea—for example, recognizing the behaviors that indicate Boo Radley's loneliness in *To Kill a Mockingbird*. The prime danger to pupil development in this area is the tendency to do the thinking for the child. Sometimes it is better not to finish off an unexplained dilemma by supplying the element. If the dilemma is left unanswered, pupils may later develop closure.
Labeling feelings of characters	Skillful questioning can guide pupils to infer feelings from specific actions or statements of the characters.
Locating information	
Locating information with book parts: Preface	Prefaces provide readers with insights into the author's purpose for writing, specific goals, and so on. Students should be asked to locate the types of books that contain prefaces and to indicate the kinds of

Behavior	Recommended strategy
	information contained in such elements.
Introduction	Same as above.
Publishing informa-tion (publisher, copyright date)	Information such as copyright dates, number of printings, and so on can provide readers with indexes of possible authority (newness, popularity) that might be applied to evaluating the material. Sensitivity to such information can be developed by questioning while the appropriate reading tasks are underway.

Remembering

Remembering salient points as well as facts	Remembering tasks become staggering from the intermediate grades on through the higher levels. Over thirty years ago, Dolch (1939) found up to fifty facts for each page of fifth- and sixth-grade science texts. Such intensive content in combination with extensive reading assignments contributes to deteriorating eye movement patterns and a concomitant comprehension loss, according to Carmichael and Dearborn (1947). Their research suggests that questions should be (1) inserted at crucial intervals in content reading and (2) interposed at different points in long reading tasks.

Evaluating critically

Making judgments about whether stories are fictional or nonfictional by noting reality, fantasy, exaggeration	Pupils are asked to cite specific story elements that suggest these qualities.
Making judgments about whether the author is trying to entertain, amuse, bias	Guidance in determining types of discourse provides a basis for pupils to collect evidence to support judgments. Newspaper and magazine materials that can be marked to emphasize such elements provide valuable source materials.

Fluency

"What can you do with a person who reads so slowly?" is a frequent question. The person who reads so slowly may be a six-year-old reading a preprimer orally, a sixth-grader reading his geography text silently, or a lecherous old man digesting the contents of *Myra Breckenridge*. Before we can answer in terms of what should be done to increase any individual's rate or fluency, we must know (1) how slowly he reads and (2) what he comprehends as a result of this reading. If his rate and comprehension are not sharply different from the norms for his grade or age level (Chapter 11), maybe he is not reading "so slowly." If, however, comprehension or rate are greatly below the norms, we need to know the following specifics:

Point 1 / *Who* is this reader? Age, grade, reading skills (word recognition, comprehension), reading potential, background of understanding for what he is reading, and so on.

Point 2 / *What* is he reading? The difficulty level of the materials (in terms of word attack skills, conceptual background, and so on).

Point 3 / *Why* is he reading? Because he wants to, his teacher wants him to, his mother demands it, he needs to find something of immediate value, and so on.

Point 4 / *When* is he reading? At a time when he normally plays, sleeps, eats?

Point 5 / *Where* is he reading? In the middle of the playground, in front of an exciting television program, in an unusually quiet place?

Although the when and where variables are important, we can often assist pupils in developing concentration to the extent that they can screen out many normal distractions. Most of our concern is centered on the who, what, and why and their interaction, because pupil reading skills, the nature of their reading materials, and their reasons for reading play the prominent roles in fluency. If word recognition skills are not instant, the reader will be unduly detained. If the concepts of the materials are not meshing with those of the pupil, he must slow down in order to attempt to understand. Of course, purpose regulates rate with skillful readers who know when to speed up or slow down and who also determine whether they want to remember detail or only salient points. Because a discussion of the means for improving fluency would mean repeating all the previous material describing the skills that affect it, the following statements will focus on a few additional strategies for assisting fluency development.

Initial reading fluency
Beginning readers do not have to read like this:

Oh (pause) Joan (longer pause)
Look (pause) at (pause) me (longer pause)
Look (pause) at (pause) him (longer pause)

Although great differences will exist between the most and least fluent readers, no one should read as if he were reading word lists. This pattern results from a misplaced emphasis on the reading of isolated words rather than whole sentences like those contained in the following language-experience story:

The Goodyear blimp
Tommy said, "We went to see the Goodyear blimp."
Billy said, "It was at the airport near the Longhorn Club."
Mary said, "We got to touch it."
Mike said, "Yes, and they said it was going to Houston."
Sandy said, "It's called the *America*."

For the specifics of teaching children to read whole units, such as stories and teacher-modeled reading, refer back to the Sight Word section of this chapter.

The onset of silent fluency

Oral reading is the necessary parallel of speech and consequently the logical means for initial reading. As soon as pupils show skill in word recognition, comprehension, and oral fluency, increasing emphasis should be placed on the use of silent reading for the checking of predictions generated about a page, story, and so on. This emphasis must necessarily be given at different times because pupils develop so differently, but it seems that most first-graders should be spending as much time in the latter half of the year reading silently as they spend reading orally. From the second grade on, depending upon the student's composite of skills, silent reading must definitely be the most-practiced skill so that visual processing will not be held to the speed of speaking skill. As we saw in Chapter 7, we should anticipate a tremendous upsurge in the differences between oral and silent reading by the third grade.

In the program suggested here, students will be provided with increased opportunities for reading many pleasurable materials rather than being tied to the often snail-like pace of basal instruction in which relatively few pages are read in the first and second grades. The practice of the reading act in appropriate (independent or instructional) materials has more bearing on subsequent fluency than any direct instructional activity by the teacher.

Speed reading

With the increasing complexity of living, we find ourselves in constant need of reading materials efficiently so as to correctly fill out our income tax, stay abreast of company newsletters, read church publications, and keep up with newspapers. Intermediate-grade pupils also often find themselves faced with extensive reading demands. Primarily in response to the problems of young people of high school age and above, educators and commercial entrepreneurs have been developing so-called speed reading courses designed to assist individuals to read more efficiently. Essentially, such courses are doing little more than what we should be doing in classrooms with pupils who have well-developed word attack and comprehension skills; that is, with or without machines (such as EDL's Control Reader), these students should be guided to:

Note the pictures, chapter headings, subheadings, and so on to get some notion of what is coming (predicting/extending)

Attend selectively to the task before them by meeting timed deadlines (which we can do effectively)

Locate organizers (such as chapter titles, headings in a chapter, and so on) in such a way as to obtain specific information rapidly (locating information)

Summary

Diagnostic reading instruction calls for direct teacher actions which differ sharply from those of the teacher of basal readers. Instead of focusing upon the completion of lessons, the diagnostic teacher seeks to determine the individual needs and plan accordingly for these diverse needs.

Pupil skills needs in word recognition, comprehension, and fluency necessitate specific types of direct teacher actions. Illustrative actions are detailed for the teacher in this chapter.

14 Pupil-managed learning experiences

Behavorial objectives
1. Describe the component parts and operation of the suggested structure for organizing pupil-managed learning experiences.
2. Describe learning activities and specific materials that might be profitably used in pupil-managed learning experiences in word recognition, comprehension, and fluency.

A wise man once remarked that the primary task of teaching was "to enable the child to teach himself." Although we frequently give lip-service to this goal, we seem reluctant to pursue it actively. To be a diagnostic teacher, one must realize that prescriptions for a large number of children cannot be closely directed, nor should they necessarily be if children are to become self-directed learners. Most children, even some of the most handicapped, are capable of directing their own learning experiences if they are given appropriate guidance at the proper time. Included in this chapter are suggestions concerning (1) the structure for organizing pupil-managed learning experiences and (2) useful learning activities and materials.

A structure for organizing pupil-managed learning

Reading skills will not emerge as the result of saying "go read"; they are the outcome of some kind of careful planning. The structure suggested here emerges from the determination instruments employed in the preceding chapters, specifically the Reading Skills Checklist and the Reading Checksheet. It is based on the following beliefs:

1. Pupils should be given specific knowledge about their skills mastered.
2. Pupils should be active participants in the process of establishing reading skills goals.
3. Pupils should be participants in the evaluation of their specific goal attainments.

4. Pupils should have decision-making powers over the selection of alternate ways of attaining specific skills.

Included in the structure are the Reading Packet, the autotutorial, and the evaluative conference. Each of these elements will be discussed in the pages that follow.

The reading packet

A plain manila folder serves as the container for the following pupil packet materials: a Reading Skills Checklist, the pupil's Reading Checksheet, pupil contract forms, and sample pupil papers. By means of such a packet, pupil and teacher maintain a continuous dialogue about reading skills growth. A Reading Skills Checklist geared to the child's instructional level is used as a sort of short-term curriculum guide (or possibly a long-term guide, depending on his abilities and successes).

Billy Jones, our model in Chapter 11, read at the primer level, so his checklist would reflect the anticipated skills of the primer program around which his reading activities would be centered (see Figure 14-1). Although the meanings of the various skills involved in the checklist might be vague to Billy, he would be guided to an increased understanding of his specific attainments in such skills as sight words, initial consonants, and endings. In time, his knowledge of his growth on the many skills fronts would become more apparent. A Reading Checksheet serves as the companion to the checklist so that Billy's short-term goals can be mapped out and periodically evaluated. The checklist could be used directly for this, but it seems better to assist Billy to see the numerous parts more clearly through his own checksheet (see Figure 14-2). Noted on Billy's checksheet are the elements that appear to give him most difficulty as well as many of his accomplishments so that he has a feeling of satisfaction. Such elements are also valuable for rechecking. Checksheets such as this provide pupils with (1) specific knowledge of accomplishments, (2) opportunities to project future goals, (3) checkpoints for evaluating progress.

Pupil contract forms are written contracts in which pupils agree to meet specific goals by completing specific tasks. Contracts parallel the checklist and checksheet in organization and provide the pupil with specific learning experiences for mastering short-term goals (seldom longer than a week). The formulation of the contract, in terms of its skills content, learning procedures, evaluation procedures, and teacher follow-up, are set by teacher and pupil. The teacher at first will play the major role

Figure 14-1.

1 WORD RECOGNITION

SIGHT WORDS	PHONIC ANALYSIS SKILLS — CONSONANTS: Single	CONSONANTS: Blends, Digraphs	VOWELS: Single	VOWELS: Digraphs, Diphthongs	Phonograms	STRUCTURAL ANALYSIS: Roots, Compounds, Contractions	Endings	Prefixes, Suffixes	Syllables	Dictionary
Pre-Primer 1 (PP1) and, here, come, the, is go, can a, not jump, to me, cat										Locates picture words in a picture dictionary or reference such as Richard Scarry, **Best Word Book Ever.**
Pre-Primer 2 (PP2) down, up, in, ride, one, two three, little, big, look, my, play make, run, see, you, he, she	Initial cat dat				-at		Inflects endings: -s -ed		Can tell number of (vowel) sounds in various words: Bill 1 Billy 2 Billyjo 3	
Pre-Primer 3 (PP3) blue, red, green, find, for it, said, we, that, what am, to, who, are, do	jat					Finds parts in compound words, e.g. cannot				
PRIMER all, am, are, at, ate, be, black, brown, but, came, did, do, eat, four, get, good, have he, into, like, must, new, no, now, on, our, out, please, ran, ride, saw, say, she so, soon, that, there, they, this, too, under, want, was, well, went, what, white, will, with, yes	sat, mat, gat lat, hat, nat, rat, fat, bat, tat, pat	*that *chat	Short a cat Short i bit		-it	Pronounces contracted forms: isn't I'm I'll	-ing			
	Final cat, cad, cam, can, cab	spat drat	Short o not Short e net		-ot -et		Inflects possessives: -'s Jane's			
FIRST READER after, again, an, any, as, ask, by, could, every, fly, from, going, had has, her, him, his, how, just, know, let, live, may, of, old, once, open over, put, round, some, stop, take, thank, them, then, think, walk, were, when	cap	blat brat	Short u nut Silent e at ate		-ut -ate					

*Digraph

in such matters, but pupils can play increasingly larger roles as they learn the process and progress in skill. Figure 14-3 illustrates such a contract. As you can see, the contract draws specific skills tasks from the needs signaled on Billy's Reading Checksheet. In setting up the contract, the teacher explains the procedure very carefully to Billy:

First / This contract represents the skills he needs to master to move forward in reading, and he is to perform the tasks. When he masters certain skills, he will not be required to practice them again unless he loses them.

Second / The first column represents the skills needs he is to work on (explains the meaning of each skill).

Third / The second column gives the material, page numbers, and so on that he will obtain himself and complete (explains material filing system). The teacher then goes through each task with him and blocks out the procedure so that he can do it on his own.

Fourth / The remaining columns represent the days of the contract period (normally a week). The teacher then explains how she wants the student to evaluate his daily work. This includes how he will use a self-correction key, how he will report the number of correct and incorrect responses, and whether he will indicate through some system his feelings about his success with each task—for example, NS, not successful; Su, suc-

Figure 14-2 (A) / Billy Jones' Checksheet (*Continued on page 232*).

Sight Words	Phonic Analysis Skills					Structural Analysis Skills				Dictionary
	Consonants		Vowels			Roots, Compounds, Contractions	Endings	Prefixes, Suffixes	Syllables	
	Single	Blends, Digraphs	Single	Digraphs, Diphthongs	Phonograms					
black + blue + enough+ (there – (where– please – know – pretty they yellow (then (when duck your	c- g- -h -b -m -t -d	ch – th – bl – st – sl – pr – tr – fr – dr – br – gr –	-d- -e- -i-		-an -ab -am -at -ad	something hen/house				

		Rd.												
Billy Jones pupil name		Expectancy Wd. Recog.	PP1	PP2	PP3	P	1²	②¹	2²	3¹	3²	4	5	6
WORD RECOGNITION		Lev.	PP1	PP2	PP3	ⓅP	1²	2¹	2²	3¹	3²	4	5	6
		Comprehension	PP1	PP2	PP3	ⓅP	1²	2¹	2²	3¹	3²	4	5	6

cessful; VS very successful. If students feel unsuccessful, they are to notify the teacher immediately.

Sample pupil papers can be left in the folder at the option of the teacher or student. They might be summaries of materials reviewed, summary pages of specific materials such as SRA stories tasks, sample pages from specific exercise materials, or materials that are being used for skills work (pages from workbooks).

The autotutorial

The autotutorial is that portion of school time in which the pupil actually tutors or teaches himself via the tasks prescribed in the reading contract. As a result of prior planning by both teacher and pupil, it is anticipated that the pupil will be able to direct his learning experiences completely on his own except for periodic teacher-pupil conferences (which will be discussed later).

Although the details will not be stressed here, the autotutorial is built around learning experiences and materials that will provide (1) needed and relevant skills practice and (2) the means for instant feedback and reinforcement. Autotutorials differ

Figure 14-2 (B) / (Continued).

COMPREHENSION _Billy Jones_ pupil name				
Predicting/ Extending	Locating Information	Remembering	Organizing	Evaluating Critically
Predict different story endings Restore omitted words State main idea of story	Use Table of Contents Locate specific sentences Locate animal words in picture dictionary		Outline orally the sequence of the story	Judge whether story is real or imaginary

greatly from the traditional individual pupil seatwork often used in conjunction with basal reading programs; tasks are individualized, and the evaluation procedure is primarily pupil-directed.

Following through with Billy Jones, we would expect to see him come to the reading period and do the following:

1. Without direction, obtain his reading packet.
2. Secure the materials called for in his current pupil contract.
3. Carry his materials to his assigned work place and begin work on his contract.
4. Utilize the self-checking features of his tasks periodically to ensure that he is responding correctly.
5. Near the end of the period, take the checklist, insert the number of the date, and evaluate in some prearranged fashion his feelings about his successes and needs in each of the areas completed.
6. Return the materials and packet to their respective places.

Figure 14-3 (A) / Pupil contract — word recognition (*Continued on page 234*).

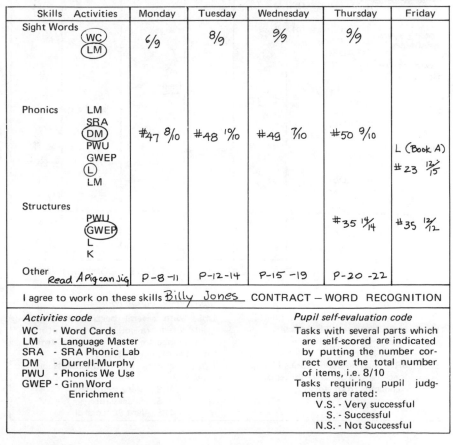

Skills	Activities	Monday	Tuesday	Wednesday	Thursday	Friday
Sight Words	(WC) (LM)	6/9	8/9	9/9	9/9	
Phonics	LM SRA (DM) PWU GWEP (L) LM	#47 8/10	#48 1%0	#49 7/10	#50 9/10	L (Book A) #23 13/15
Structures	PWU (GWEP) L K				#35 14/14	#35 13/12
Other	Read A Pig can Jig	P-8 -11	P-12-14	P-15 -19	P-20 -22	

I agree to work on these skills _Billy Jones_ CONTRACT — WORD RECOGNITION

Activities code

WC - Word Cards
LM - Language Master
SRA - SRA Phonic Lab
DM - Durrell-Murphy
PWU - Phonics We Use
GWEP - Ginn Word
     Enrichment

Pupil self-evaluation code

Tasks with several parts which are self-scored are indicated by putting the number correct over the total number of items, i.e. 8/10

Tasks requiring pupil judgments are rated:
    V.S. - Very successful
    S. - Successful
    N.S. - Not Successful

The evaluative conference

There is no magic formula for specifying how often a teacher should confer with each individual. Individual pupil circumstances, such as need for adult support, the type of task, and other variables must be closely observed by the teacher, who then sets a schedule for conferences with the particular student. The conference has the following goals:

First goal / The positive reinforcement of the pupil's confidence in his ability to produce good results on his own.

Second goal / The assessment of the pupil's (1) understandings of the tasks and (2) effectiveness in task mastery. Misunderstanding of tasks is often the prime reason for lack of success. Or, the tasks themselves may be inappropriate.

Figure 14-3 (B) / Pupil contract — comprehension.

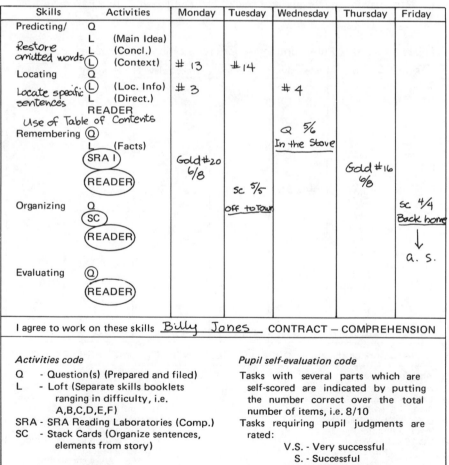

Skills	Activities	Monday	Tuesday	Wednesday	Thursday	Friday
Predicting/ Q						
Restore L	(Main Idea)					
omitted words L	(Concl.)					
Ⓛ	(Context)	# 13	#14			
Locating Q						
Locate specific Ⓛ	(Loc. Info)	# 3		# 4		
sentences L	(Direct.)					
READER						
Use of Table of Contents						
Remembering Ⓠ				Q ⁵⁄₆ _In the Stove_		
L	(Facts)					
(SRA I)		Gold #20 ⁶⁄₈			Gold #16 ⁹⁄₈	
(READER)			sc ⁵⁄₅			
Organizing Q			_off to Town_			sc ⁴⁄₄ _Back home_ ↓ a. s.
(SC)						
(READER)						
Evaluating Ⓠ						
(READER)						

I agree to work on these skills _Billy Jones_   CONTRACT – COMPREHENSION

Activities code

Q   - Question(s) (Prepared and filed)
L   - Loft (Separate skills booklets ranging in difficulty, i.e. A,B,C,D,E,F)
SRA - SRA Reading Laboratories (Comp.)
SC   - Stack Cards (Organize sentences, elements from story)

Pupil self-evaluation code

Tasks with several parts which are self-scored are indicated by putting the number correct over the total number of items, i.e. 8/10
Tasks requiring pupil judgments are rated:

V.S. - Very successful
S. - Successful
N.S. - Not Successful

Third goal / The creation of an attitude of accuracy on the part of the student so that he is not racing through tasks toward the goal of task completion. Many children think that getting through "quickest" is the measure of success, rather than what happens during the process. Teachers need to reward verbally and emphasize task accuracy.

Fourth goal / The informal evaluation of skills attainments. In a few seconds, the diagnostic teacher can check a pupil's ability to apply the skills that have been the focus of contract work. Pupils should anticipate such checking as another incentive to master the skill rather than complete the page.

Fifth goal / The evaluation of task accomplishments and the projection of subsequent contract tasks. In the early stages, these will be heavily teacher-directed. As pupils gain in skill and understanding of goals, they can carry much of the contract projection task.

Sixth goal / The actual writing of the new contract, which should be done as much as possible by the student. He can program in the agreed-upon skills goals as well as the materials to be used.

Evaluative conferences are the glue that keeps the autotutorial going. If students and teachers fail to communicate at this time, trouble is certain. In addition, if pupils fail to receive sufficient ego reinforcement, they cannot be expected to persevere. Extending the case of Billy Jones into the evaluative conference, we might observe the following meeting:

Teacher: From watching you work, it looks like you're learning many skills (positive reinforcement). Show me how it has gone.

Billy: Well, I think I know these words now (reads off sight words studied): *where, there, when, then*.

Teacher: Excellent. Do you have much trouble when you meet them in stories?

Billy: Not much. We'll see in a second (referring to the fact that he will read a segment of connected material for the teacher as a routine skills check). I think I can read anything you can give me by changing the first letter (consonant) of *cat*.

Teacher: Great. Read these for me, please. Teacher jots down the following:

cat	gat
bat	chat
fat	that
rat	stat
mat	what
nat	

Billy: (Correctly reads the words.)

Teacher: I thought I might catch you again on *what*, but I didn't (referring to the fact that Billy noted the changed vowel sound when *-at* was preceded by *wh-*).

Teacher: Would you like to read this page to me (pointing to a pattern page story that contains the elements he has been working on)?
Billy: (Reading aloud)

> That bat is fat.
> What bat is fat?
> That bat.
> Is the cat on the mat fat?
> No, but the nat on the rat is fat.

Teacher: You read that very well. How far do you feel that you can go before we meet again?
Billy: I think I can read all of the next story and maybe a little of the one after that.
Teacher: That would be very good. Please note that on your contract. Now, let's read a little from the last story you read in *Our Family*. Before we read, please give me a short rundown on what happened. (A short comprehension check is made, even though not much emphasis is given to this strength area at this point in Billy's contract.)
Billy: (Summarizes story.)
Teacher: (Referring to points mentioned by Billy) Where did Tom say that? Would you find that and read it for me please?
Billy: (Billy reads a few such elements and thus demonstrates location and word recognition skill.)
Teacher: You read with good expression. Would you read this sentence for me once more, please (locating a sentence with a missed word)?
Billy: (Reads line, repeating error.)
Teacher: (Writes word out and asks him if he sees any clues. He does, but they don't help, so the teacher tells him the word and puts it on his contract. Repeats process with two other words.) We've had a good conference. You're really moving. Now, what should we include in the next contract?
Billy: (Enumerates the sight words, sounds, stories, and so on and is prepared to write up the contract.)

The conference with Billy has taken about ten minutes. Some conferences will take longer; others can be even shorter. As we will see later, conferences may be held with individuals other than the teacher. The teacher's encouragement, coupled with the task accomplishments, should recharge Billy for the time between this and the next conference. Only occasional quick comments may be necessary to sustain his work habits.

Learning activities and materials for pupil-directed learning
Much of the effectiveness of pupil-managed learning experiences depends on the nature of the learning tasks. No amount of teacher support and structure can overcome a basic deficit in the quality

of auto-instructional learning activities and materials. Before describing what appear to be good experiences, we will examine the criteria for their selection:

Criterion 1 / The material must have an accompanying key so that the student can reinforce correct responses and redirect incorrect responses.

Criterion 2 / It must be possible to develop specific reading skills from the material. Some skills material has little validity.

Criterion 3 / The material must be so arranged that it is keyed to the specific skills elements of the checklists. For instance, pages on final consonant elements should be taken out of the workbook and keyed to the checklist, or some code arrangement should be used so that the pages can be located rapidly by the pupils.

Criterion 4 / Where possible, a variety of tasks should be available for each skill.

Criterion 5 / Response modes should be both simple and consistent so that pupils do not need long explanations about what they are to do.

Criterion 6 / Any related equipment must be simple enough to operate that any student can manage it with brief practice and explanation.

All the learning experiences and materials that follow should measure up to these criteria.

Word recognition experiences and materials

Contextual analysis / Pupil-managed learning experiences should include closure tasks varying from simple, carefully arranged closures to random, every-fifth-word closures. In the earliest cloze experiences, the emphasis is on the pupil's ability to construct a meaningful statement by choosing a word that fits the pattern. All the words should be in the pupil's sight vocabulary. Because of limited spelling and writing skills, such exercises as the following can be developed or found in the support materials of several basal readers.

Directions / Circle the word that belongs in the block.

1. Tom_____ run fast.

     is   can   Mary

2. Mother_____ , "Go away."

     said   Father   will

Directions / Cut out the words at the bottom and paste them where they belong in the sentences.

1. Tom _____ run fast.

2. Bob is _____ the car.

in	can

The sentences can be written with the answer words on the back of the exercise as a checking key for the pupil. Attention should be given to the omission of verb parts, noun markers, and other elements within statements. Quotations should also be included.

As pupils increase in skill (writing and spelling), the open closure task should be used. Spelling should not receive prime emphasis; the point is the legitimacy of the response in terms of closure. Because we assume that the students can understand most of the syntactic structures, the emphasis at this point is on words which may or may not be recognizable by the pupil. This, of course, is the assumption underlying the use of context for determining what words are by the logical meaning unit. The following exercises illustrate increasingly difficult tasks.

Sentence Task

Directions / Write in as best you can the words that should be in the spaces. Only one word is to be placed in each space.

1. Tom said, "I _____ and hurt my right leg."

2. Mary _____ Jack went to the store.

3. At the store they _____ some milk and bread.
(Key on back)

Paragraph Task

Directions / Write in as best you can the words that should be in the spaces. Only one word is to be placed in each space.

Dick and _____ were on their way to _____ . They _____ to town every Saturday. Jane wanted to _____ a new pair of _____ for school. Her _____ shoes were worn _____ . _____ wanted to buy himself a coat.

(Key on back)

Story Segment

The story segment is an extension of the paragraph task, except that usually every fifth or tenth word is omitted. For an example as well as information for evaluating task performance, refer back to Chapter 9.

Sight words / Independent learning devices for sight words are basically limited to word cards with picture referents and systems for auditory reinforcement. Naming words can be placed on cards in the following fashion so that the student can:

1. Attempt to read the word (if previously studied).

2. Check the word with its picture referent on the back.

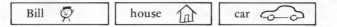

Pupils can be handed several such cards for independent learning practice.

Unfortunately, many basic words do not have picture referents. In order for pupils to guide their own practice with such words, it is imperative that they have some type of auditory cue or reinforcement against which to check their responses. These can set up with recorders (record and tape) and Language Masters (Bell and Howell).

Recorders allow children to follow along as the words or stories are played. There are already a number of programs employing this technique, which may be used simply for pleasure or for learning specific vocabulary. Teachers can, of course, prepare such materials themselves or with the help of parents and other students. Because time and equipment are restrictions, I would suggest the following:

On your own or through the school administration attempt to purchase the small, transistorized recorders that can and will be used by you and the pupils (preferably cassette types because of the simplicity of operation).

Prepare a simple file system so that the prerecorded cassettes can be managed and used.

Plan to make two or three "follow along" types of tapes each week so that you build up a good supply of these.

Perhaps one of the most potentially valuable aids to a pupil's management of his own learning in the early stages of reading is the Language Master. This machine, on which one can both record and play short pieces of tape, allows a degree of flexibility that cannot be provided by the reel or cassette recording devices. Card strips of varying lengths, usually ranging from 8 to 15 inches, have recording tape pasted to them. By inserting the card into the machine and depressing a specific button, you can record whatever you wish on the card within the boundaries of time (approximately 4 seconds' worth of recording on the 9-inch card and 7 seconds on the 15-inch card). The contents of the recorded message can then be written on the upper part of the card and read at the same time as the words are heard. Figure 14-4 shows a sample card.

Among the possibilities for self-reinforcing reading instruction are the following:

Language-experience stories / The teacher can record each pupil's sentence or story on several cards with a washable marker. The pupil can then record the sentences on the tape in his own voice for subsequent practice. The reverse of this would be for the student to dictate his story on the cards so that the teacher could listen and write it on the top of each card.

Basal series stories / The teacher can purchase extra copies of pre-primers and cut them up so as to make a talking book. The talking book would contain the pictures and sentence cards (Language Master cards with the sentences from the story recorded and pasted on), as shown in Figure 14-5. The student could proceed through the stories at his own pace, listening as often or as little as he needs to in order to remember the words. Check tests can be provided every few pages by inserting special sentence cards without the accompanying sounds so that the student can demonstrate his knowledge by recording the sentence on the card for later checking by the teacher or an assistant.

Learning new sight vocabulary / While the preceding tasks involve the learning of new sight vocabulary, the machine might also be used for learning new words, checking up on words via a special glossary of cards, and so on. When pupils experience continuing difficulties with words, a teacher could quickly transcribe the troublesome words on cards for practice. The pupils can then independently check themselves as they study the word cards or read new stories containing the troublesome words.

Figure 14-4 / A Language Master card strip.

My name is John. — Cards can be prepared so that message can be erased

Recording tape (2 recording-playback tracks)

Figure 14-5 / A talking book.

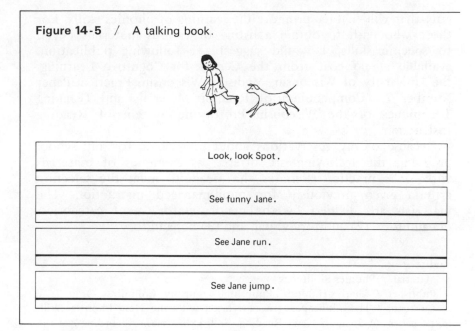

Look, look Spot.

See funny Jane.

See Jane run.

See Jane jump.

The ease with which the Language Master can be handled by teachers and children makes it an extremely valuable aid in the early stages of reading instruction. Of course, availability and use must be carefully scheduled so that it is not overused or misused. It also requires a work and time investment on the part of the teacher; the manufacturer up to now has offered few materials useful for the reading teacher. Other machines that combine both sound and visual components matched for learning to read, to perform phonic tasks, and so on are being developed, and teachers should study such materials to determine their potential for self-directing instruction. Manufacturers in this area include Hoffman, Mattel, and Educational Development Laboratories.

Phonic analysis / Phonic workbooks, games, tapes, records, and programs have literally flooded the market within the last few years. As a result of the increased emphasis on this dimension of reading, many programs have been purchased prematurely. Although evidence cannot be provided to justify my own feeling, I am concerned that some of these devices seem to be useless and even harmful. The point is that it is the teacher who must teach phonics, not a machine. If programs are not carefully chosen and tailored, conflicting systems can be presented simultaneously or there can be no reinforcement with connected reading. It is imperative that we secure materials that will in fact promote the learning of phonics skills. For those who wish to obtain a listing of various materials keyed to specific skills, I would suggest the following publication, available at no cost from the Center for Cognitive Learning, the University of Wisconsin, Madison, Wisconsin: Practical Paper Number 7, "Compendium of Reading Materials and Teaching Techniques of the Wisconsin Prototypic System of Reading Instruction."

Because of my reservations about prescribing for any school program, the following are offered as examples of materials with skills practice exercises that seem to meet the selection criteria given previously for pupil-managed instruction. The materials are divided by the major reinforcement categories: (1) auditory, (2) auditory-visual, and (3) nonauditory.

Auditory

Material / Phonics Skilltapes

Publisher / Charles H. Merrill Publishing Company, Columbus, Ohio

Contents / The Skilltapes are correlated with the New Phonics Skilltexts series (1-6) and New Reading Skilltexts series. According to the publishers, the material sequentially develops and spirally reviews three basic skills: sounds of words, structure of words, and understanding of words. The tapes are conventional reel tapes, recorded at 1 7/8 or 3 3/4 ips.

Material / The Phonics Program

Publisher / Bell and Howell Company, Chicago, Illinois

Contents / The Phonics Program is synthetically oriented with the initial synthesis focused on short vowel words such as *at*, *an*, *if*. Set I is labeled "Sound Blending and Phonetic Skill"; Set II is called "Consonant Blends and Irregular Patterns"; Set III is entitled "Word Building and Word Analysis Techniques."

Auditory-visual

Material / Talking Typewriter

Publisher / Responsive Environments Corporation, Englewood Cliffs, New Jersey

Contents / The "talking typewriter" is a computerized system that operates from a standard typewriter keyboard with keys divided into nine color groups. By responding to the keys the student pushes, the computerized "talking typewriter" teaches the child to recognize letters and words.

Material / Sesame Street Reading Program

Publisher / Children's Television Workshop

Contents / An offshoot of the successful *Sesame Street* program, this is a reading program for second-graders with reading difficulties (with failing third- and fourth-graders as outer targets). The programming utilizes the many possibilities of the television medium.

Material / Learning with Laughter
Publisher / Scott Education Division, Holyoke, Massachusetts
Contents / This series matches contemporary graphics with music and voices in thirty kits that teach the alphabet, initial consonants, initial consonant digraphs, and so on. Filmstrips are correlated with records or cassettes to develop the various word recognition skills.

Material / Hoffman Learning Systems
Publisher / Hoffman Company, Arcadia, California
Contents / The Hoffman reader program utilizes audiovisual equipment that correlates a filmstrip with a record for the development of phonic skills. Several children can plug earphones into the listening station and participate in the lesson simultaneously.

Nonauditory

Material / Ginn Word Enrichment Program
Publisher / Ginn and Company, Waltham, Massachusetts
Contents / Seven workbooks are designed to produce a sequence of phonic and structural analysis skills that closely parallels the Ginn Reading Program. Diagnostic tests determine specific skills needs. Mastery tests indicate subsequent skills mastery in terms of the consonant elements, vowel elements, syllables, and so on.

Material / Barnell Loft Specific Skills Series
Publisher / Barnell Loft, Ltd., Rockville Center, N.Y.
Contents / Working with sounds, the phonics portion of this series contains phonics skills through the various grade levels (Books A, B, C, D, E, F). Compiled in paperback books, the materials can be used for individualizing instruction for specific word attack skills. Pupil progress profiles are provided for individual charting.

Material / Durrell-Murphy Phonics Practice Program (1968)
Publisher / Harcourt Brace Jovanovich, New York
Contents / This material gives self-directing phonics practice on separate cards that contain initial consonants, initial digraphs and blends, final consonants, short vowel phonograms, long vowel phonograms, and other phonograms. The materials have a unique reinforcement feature: The pupil writes the response and checks it on the back with a picture clue.

Material / Individualized Phonics (reprinted masters for duplicator)
Publisher / Teachers Publishing Corporation, Darien, Connecticut
Contents / The material is arranged into four levels, each of which contains from 76 to 103 separate pages. The basic sequence focuses initially on consonant elements.

Material / SRA Reading Laboratory I Word Games
Publisher / Science Research Associates, Chicago
Contents / Utilizing a word game format and graduated from single initial consonants to vowel digraphs, this material provides a basic program for matching sound elements with guide words containing key sounds. Pupils can practice blending elements into words and check their accuracy by noting a picture referent on the back of each card.

Structural analysis / Of the programs listed in the phonics section, three have specific skills practice tasks on structural analysis elements: the Ginn Word Enrichment Program, Barnell Loft Specific Skills Series, and the SRA Reading Laboratory I Word Games.

Although the materials do not have self-checking features, the Kenworthy Word Cards provide extensive practice with root words, prefixes, suffixes, and compound words. Such materials could be used in pupil-to-pupil tutorial sessions.

Material / Kenworthy Word Cards
Publisher / Kenworthy Educational Services, Inc., Buffalo, N.Y.
Contents / Fold-over cards that provide practice with prefixes, suffixes, root words, and compound words.

Dictionary analysis / Direct practice in the use of the dictionary glossary and phonetic respellings are most often found in basal reader workbooks—for example, the Scott, Foresman series in which these lessons are keyed to the companion *Thorndike-Barnhart Beginning Dictionary* (1968). Because dictionaries may vary in such elements, teachers should construct their own tasks for pupil practice in locating and writing out phonetic respellings of words they cannot readily attack.

Reading comprehension experiences and materials

There are many separate skills materials for reading comprehension; most emphasize the literal comprehension elements with some emphasis on inferential tasks. The greatest emphasis in the last decade has been on the use of the Science Research Associates Reading Laboratory kinds of materials (Parker, 1961) in which the pupils:

Take an initial placement test to find at what level (keyed by color) they need to begin.

Start choosing short reading selections from their color level, reading the selections, and then answering comprehension questions, vocabulary questions, and so on.

Repeat this process, largely on their own, and progress to more difficult levels (as indicated by different colors).

Such materials have provided perhaps the greatest opportunity within standard school reading programs for pupils to read either below or above their assigned grade level. They have also been met with a great deal of interest, at least initially. There are some drawbacks, however: They (1) may sometimes restrict independent reading interest because of the highly detailed, built-in response system, and (2) they may condition children not to want to read book-type materials because of their length. Teachers should be aware that overpractice in tight programmed formats may limit many other valuable forms of comprehension practice. In offering a listing of programs for skills practice of the rather tight format sort, I would urge that they be fitted into a broader program in which provision is made for reading without direct comprehension checks every few pages.

Material / Barnell Loft Specific Skills Series
Publisher / Barnell Loft, Ltd., Rockville Center, N.Y.
Contents / Like the word analysis materials by the same publisher, these materials are graduated in difficulty from Book A to Book F. There is a book of skills tasks for each of the following skills areas: getting the facts, following directions, locating the answer, using the context, getting the main idea, drawing conclusions.

Material / EDL Study Skills Laboratory
Publisher / Educational Development Laboratories, A Division of McGraw-Hill Book Co., Huntington, N.Y.
Contents / These are boxed-type materials in which pupils can work on different types of locational skills. The skills included are: copyright notice, table of contents, card catalog, Dewey decimal system, dictionary (using it as an encyclopedia), almanac, bar graph.

Material / Macmillan Reading Spectrum
Publisher / The Macmillan Company, New York
Contents / This material is housed in booklet form and consists of six levels of increasing difficulty in the areas of vocabulary development and comprehension. Separate pupil record books are provided in order that pupils may maintain a record of their successes on each task. The materials were developed for the intermediate grade levels and do not provide for low-level primary reading. Placement tests, final reviews, and supplementary tests are provided.

Material / New Merrill Skilltexts
Publisher / Charles E. Merrill Company, Columbus, Ohio
Contents / The materials are basically workbooks ranging from first- to sixth-grade reading difficulty which are almost self-contained reading programs. There are short stories followed by various types of word recognition and comprehension exercises. Portions of the programs can be used for separate skills practice.

Material / Random House Pacesetters
Publisher / Random House, New York
Contents / This is basically a book reading program; children read pre-chosen selections, which come in multiples of ten. Ten books are contained in boxes labeled Interesting People, Marvelous but True, Fun and Fantasy, High Action, This Could Be You. Most of the books are geared to fifth or

sixth grade; there are only a few books as low as third grade. In conjunction with reading the books, the pupils have to answer questions (if the teacher wishes).

Material / Reader's Digest Reading Skill Builders
Publisher / Reader's Digest, Pleasantville, New York
Contents / Constructed in the *Reader's Digest* format, these materials contain short selections, frequently adapted from the magazine. The books are organized according to reading difficulty and have a basic format at the end of each story for checking comprehension, word meaning, rate, and so on.

Material / Reader's Digest Science Reader
Publisher / Reader's Digest, Pleasantville, New York
Contents / These materials are much like the other *Reader's Digest* materials except that they provide only science reading materials and have questions only at the end of the selection. The questions concern just major concepts. The illustrations are quite detailed and seem to be valuable for motivation, particularly for boys. Selections vary in reading level from about third to sixth grade, although the interest level seems much broader.

Material / Reading-Thinking Skills
Publisher / Continental Press, Oklahoma City, Okla.
Contents / This duplicator series provides reading-thinking skills tasks from kindergarten through the sixth-grade level. Some useful inferential tasks are readily obtainable in the series.

Material / SRA Reading Laboratories (several editions)
Publisher / Science Research Associates, Chicago
Contents / This widely used series presents all the materials in a box or laboratory. After the pupils are placed in an achievement level (keyed by color), they draw a short power builder story and accompanying questions from their color level. They complete the reading, the tasks, and check their work with the answer key provided. Pupil progress in comprehension and rate is often profiled in special books.

Fluency experiences and materials

Some of the materials in the comprehension section contain mechanisms for the pupil to check his fluency in terms of rate of silent reading. Usually, such aids provide either a timed test so that the pupil sees how far he has progressed in a given number of minutes or a word-count total so he can divide the elapsed reading time into the word count. Perhaps the easiest way for a pupil to determine fluency is to set a timer for 1 minute and mark the number of words read when the timer goes off. After completing the selection, he can determine how many words were read in the timed segment.

Summary

The value and necessity of pupils managing most of their own learning experiences in reading is the focus of this chapter, in which we have spelled out (1) the structure for organizing pupil-managed learning experiences and (2) useful learning activities and materials.

The structure was developed with the reading packet, the autotutorial, and the evaluative conference. The reading packet includes a reading checklist, checksheet, contract forms, and samples for each pupil. The autotutorial is the pupil-managed learning experience structured jointly by teacher and pupil in the evaluative conference.

In order to be effective, learning materials need to reinforce correct responses, redirect incorrect responses, develop specific skills keyed to checklist skills, vary in format, involve simple directions, and be easily managed by students on their own. Examples of specific skills materials in word recognition and comprehension were listed.

five
What the diagnostic reading teacher organizes and operates

Up to this point, we have been most concerned with the diagnostic teacher as one who diagnoses and prescribes for individual skills needs. But because most teachers will have to work with groups of 25 to 35 students, it is imperative that we consider how such a detailed program can be translated into normal classroom situations. Material, pupil, teacher, and program variables change sharply from one classroom situation to another, and we cannot anticipate every circumstance. We can, however, illustrate a logical progression that seems adaptable to most situations.

The first step in the transition process revolves around the use of the previously discussed concepts in a traditional, one-basal-reader, three-reading-group classroom (Chapter 15, "Diagnostic Reading Instruction in the Current Reading Program").

The second step of the progression is the emergence of a multigroup structure that shows increased recognition of individual differences and erases many of the practices associated with traditional reading (Chapter 16, "Diagnostic Reading Instruction in the Multilevel Program").

The final step is a highly individualized reading program that exists as one aspect of a larger "communications skills program" (Chapter 17, "Diagnostic Reading Instruction in the Individualized Program").

15 Diagnostic reading instruction in the current reading program

Bahavioral objective
1. Suggest basic modifications that can be employed in traditional reading classrooms.

This chapter is designed to indicate the basic points of departure for changing instruction from traditional to diagnostic. Some readers may be disturbed by the suggestion that you can have diagnostic instruction in the context of a so-called traditional program; they might well insist that the traditional program is then no longer traditional. Our point here is not correct labeling, however, but the spelling out of take-off points for those who are interested in modifying traditional practices, but are unaware of how best to begin. We will discuss these basic modifications according to the organizing scheme for this book: the diagnostic reading teacher knows, determines, and prescribes.

Basic modification, first grade

Depending upon the setting of the school, the first-grade teacher can anticipate greeting first graders who range widely in language and dialect, intelligence, physical well-being, social and emotional well-being, attitudes about learning, knowledge of letters and words, and willingness to listen. Because such differences will be apparent to some degree (even in the most "normal" situations), all first-grade teachers need to know, determine, and prescribe in the following ways:

What the first-grade teacher knows
1. The physical, understanding, and social-emotional components associated with reading readiness (Chapter 8) / Memorizing the contents of this text will not help the first-grade teacher, but if he uses the organizers as a means for expanding subsequent knowledge through observation and reading, there is a strong possibility that useful skills can be developed.
2. The meaning of independent, instructional, and frustrational reading levels as well as the most expedient means for making such judgments (Chapter 9) / These terms really cannot mean anything until the teacher has had numerous opportunities to observe children of varying levels as they read both orally and silently, and answer questions. Until a teacher can rec-

ognize the look of panic in the eyes of a frustrated reader or pick up other indexes of difficulty, he cannot conceive the importance of these concepts for reading instruction.

3. The specific sequence of reading skills developed by the school's basal reading program / Evidence suggests that most schools adopt a single basal series (Strickland, 1969), despite the opportunity to use two or more. The quality of the instruction in the single basal could be greatly strengthened if the first-grade teacher (as well as the other teachers) knew the skills program thoroughly enough to realize:

Which sight words were first introduced
Which elements in the sight words were used to teach children to attack similar words
Which comprehension skills could best be developed with which stories
The sequence of phonics elements taught

Because few of us can keep such things in mind unless we have taught the series for a number of years, it seems sensible to develop our own skills checklist (Chapter 11) so that we can periodically check to see where we are in terms of skills development as well as where we need to go. An example of such a checklist is shown in Figure 15-1. They may appear time-consuming, but such checklists can be of great value in establishing specific coverage goals. True, there is little value in coverage without adequate achievement (for example, finishing the first reader but being unable to read it at an instructional level), but there are times when we get bogged down with

Figure 15-1

SIGHT WORDS (Page number introduced)		PHONICS: Beginning Consonants	PHONICS: Ending Consonants	PHONICS: Phonograms	STRUCTURES: Compounds and Contractions	STRUCTURES: Endings	
1. go 2. Don 3. help 4. look 5. Janet 6. Susie 7. Tabby 8. here 9. Bozo 10. run 11. come 12. oh 13. at 14. me 15. get 16. down 17. jump	PP-1						
1. said 2. and 3. father 4. I 5. no 6. mother 7. you 8. can 9. that 10. not 11. is 12. want 13. to 14. with 15. play	PP-2	f-(father) d-(down) h-(here, help) m-(mother, me) s-(Susie, said)					
8. this 9. ride 13. in 17. will 19. for 20. one 22. house 24. do 25. who 26. car 28. a 29. book 30. like 31. what 34. up 35. something 37. it 38. but 40. now 41. work 43. my 44. little 45. dog 46. us 47. have 49. guess 51. red 54. two 55. three 57. fun 58. big 69. funny 70. cat	PP-3	c(hard c) come, can, cat. b-(book, Bozo, but, big)		-an -at -et	-something	5 gets wants cars comes dogs likes	
7. hat 10. yes 12. hello 15. out 18. maybe 20. blue 24. there 26. too 29. pretty 31. on 34. Sally 36. don't 39. fast 42. horse 46. wagon 49. home 55. know 57. let's 60. all 62. he 66. they 67. went 70. then 73. birthday 74. happy 76. dear 79. pony 81. black 88. try 91. let 93. her 95. back 97. came 100. toy 102. games 105. had 106. where 108. Billy 110. thank 112. can't	1¹	n-(not, now, no) t-(Tabby, two, toy) r-(run, ride, red) w-(want, with will, work)		-ake (wake, take) -ow (how-now) -ot (got-not)	-can't -don't		
5. school 8. shoes 9. rain 11. way 12. Patty 13. show 15. Miss 17. about 19. has 21. which 22. laugh began 23. name 24. hand right march 26. left 27. foot 28. be 29. first tell 33. his 35. sleep 36. story 38. last legs 39. chair 41. off 42. TV cut 44. hair 45. man 47. street 49. kitten 50. lost 51. live call 52. Bill 54. found 55. spring green 56. tree 57. bird 60. picture 61. color 62. of when 64. wash 65. our 68. just 69. year 70. more than things 71. old 75. stones some 76. sticks turtle 78. could 79. from 80. room 81. why bunny 83. feed 84. pen 85. yard over steps 86. basket 89. puppy 90. food	1²			-im (him, Jim) -oy (toy, boy)			

manual directions and neglect to move the children as far as they are capable of moving. We have seen many teachers, young and old, suddenly realize that the end of the year is in sight and the completion goal is not and lose their perspective in a mad rush to the finish line that produces nothing for the children.

What the first-grade teacher determines

1. The unique physical, understanding, and social-emotional needs of those pupils experiencing difficulty in reading / This is the action step. First-grade teachers who equip themselves with the observational skills suggested in Chapter 8 are in a unique position to note possible needs. Such determinations are usually made only when we, as teachers, are consciously looking for specific behaviors that identify specific needs.

2. The relative difficulty (independent, instructional, frustrational) with which the various students read orally and answer story questions / Despite the attacks on "round robin" oral reading, a considerable amount of such reading exists in most first-grade programs. It persists because teachers believe that children need the practice and because it gives the teacher a means for checking student skill. We do not recommend the "round-robin" practice, but we do endorse the value of oral reading in initial instruction. The second consideration—checking pupil skill—seems valid too, *if the skill is actually checked* by the teacher. Observations such as the following raise the question of whether or not we are really checking anything.

	Reading group 3	
Pupil	No. words in selection	Words missed
Billy	31	up
Bobby	22	—
Drew	24	down, get, didn't
Nancy	18	down, get, come, it
Sarah	32	—
Sue	20	not
Tom	18	to, and, here, come, not
Will	27	here

Although the reading samples were small, we might wonder about the difficulty level of this material for Drew, Nancy, and Tom.

3. The listening comprehension level of each child and the relationship of this level to the child's reading level / If we apply this to the pupils in the table above, we might wonder about the understanding levels of Drew, Nancy, and Tom. Subsequent checking could reveal no basic understanding problems, and we could discount the possibility of limited understanding ability and seek to alter their rate of instruction, and so on. On the other hand, we might find that some of the students with few problems are capable of working successfully in more advanced reading materials.

4. The specific skills needs of individual pupils through nonsystematic diagnosis / By simply noting the words that were missed by the individual pupils in Group 3, we employed nonsystematic diagnosis. Such daily checks might provide us with better insights into the specific problems; for ex-

ample, in addition to problems with sight words, we might find that Nancy neglects inflectional endings and has trouble with words beginning with consonant blends. Other examples of errors noted by the teacher are these:

Billy   up

Drew   do~~w~~n, get, didn't, can't, jump(ed,) look(ed)

Nancy   down, g~~e~~t, come, ~~it~~, (th)at, (th)is, what, (th)ere, look(ed)

Sue   no~~t~~, (wh)en/(th)en

Tom   and, h~~e~~re, come, n~~o~~t, to

Will   h~~e~~re

By noting errors from day to day and subsequently stressing the needed elements with the individuals involved, the teacher may be able to mark off words and elements that are learned (as illustrated above).

What the first-grade teacher prescribes

1, Special tasks for children who have certain readiness deficiencies / Actions such as those suggested in Chapter 8 may be taken for meeting specific skills needs. These tasks can be prescribed in addition to or in lieu of the regular group seatwork assignments. Certain slow-starting children can profit greatly from tasks such as these contained in the Fitzhugh Plus Program (Fitzhugh, 1968), which they can work on independently in lieu of other tasks beyond their visual skill. Other individual as well as group skills tasks could be managed with record players, tape recorders, and so on.

2. Special reading tasks for those children who have specific skills needs / Sources of such tasks can be found in Chapter 14. The tasks may be as simple or involved as the teacher wishes. Simple but potentially useful tasks might involve the following:

Asking Nancy to take home some sentence cards with troublesome sight words and to read these to her mother.

Requesting Bobby to listen to and help Tom read his story aloud.

Giving Sara word cards and asking her to group them by beginning sounds (consonants).

Basic modifications, second and third grades

Second- and third-grade reading teachers need to be able to direct pupils whose reading levels range from beginning to intermediate. The normal range of reading differences found within these two grades, as shown in Figure 15-2, is quite diverse.

What the second/third-grade teacher knows

1. The specific sequence of reading skills developed by the school basal reading program / A simple, teacher-constructed checklist as illustrated for the first-grade teacher would provide such direction. The checklist should range from preprimer 1 to at least the fourth or fifth grade.

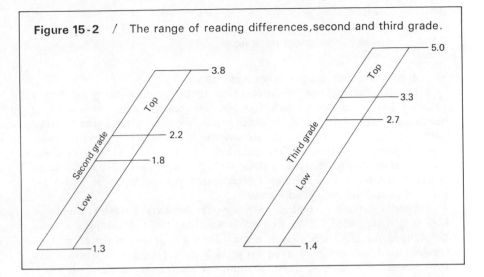

Figure 15-2 / The range of reading differences, second and third grade.

2. The types of reading materials and approaches the various pupils have been exposed to in their previous instruction / For teachers and pupils who have been in the same school for the same number of years, it is often possible to know a great deal about the child's program and his adaptation to it. If, however, the teacher or the child is relatively new to the program, such assessments are difficult. When we realize that children have had certain reading materials but have not been successful with them, it is very difficult to ask them to repeat those materials. Similarly, if we know that certain children have not prospered with a given approach (such as a sight word approach), we have information for making program adjustments.

The second/third-grade teacher determines

1. The relative difficulty (independent, instructional, frustrational) with which the various students read orally and silently and answer questions about the story / As readers develop independent word recognition means, silent reading becomes the prominent mode. Because the variations between readers are increasing, the teacher needs to be aware of those children who are moving with little or no difficulty as well as those who appear not to be moving at all.

2. The listening comprehension level of each child and the relationship of this level to the child's reading level / The importance of this measure of reading potential has been discussed in brief in the first-grade section as well as in Chapter 10. By noting wide discrepancies between achievement and potential in these early years, teachers can single out pupils with reading problems for special attention before it is too late.

3. The specific skills needs of individual pupils / No longer will the teacher's nonsystematic diagnosis be limited primarily to sight word and beginning consonant elements; it will reflect basic difficulties in attacking vowel situations, structural situations (other than a few endings), and so on. We might expect a second-grade teacher to make the following kind of notation about the children reading on grade level:

Billy	Sarah
Bobby	Sue
Drew	Tom (not in group any longer)
Nancy	Will

What the second/third-grade teacher prescribes

1. Special learning tasks for individuals in the reading group meeting / Utilizing her notes on individual needs, the teacher keys corresponding questions to the children. Rather than randomly seeking tell-backs of story parts, the teacher may provide Johnny (who needs more practice) with more opportunities to work on this skill. The teacher has Mary read the sections amenable to context analysis skills practice. Certainly, the concept is not novel, but a well-developed prescription system might be useful for those of us without such good memories.

2. Special tasks for children in nongroup contexts / This is the same idea as that suggested for the first grade. Learning tasks of various sorts can be planned for pupil self-direction, peer direction, or parent direction. One teacher we know designed a parent-participation program in which every slow reader has a planned session at home for about thirty minutes each day. The teacher feels that when the parents follow the directed program, the children inevitably make significant progress in reading.

Basic modifications, fourth grade and above

We often do not realize that the intermediate-grade teacher must possess the most detailed knowledge of the reading program because of the wide range in reading achievement levels among the children in her class. Figure 15-3 shows the ranges in graphic form.

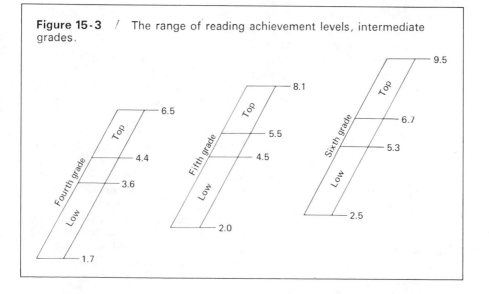

Figure 15-3 / The range of reading achievement levels, intermediate grades.

What the intermediate teacher knows

The teacher of an intermediate grade must have the widest possible knowledge of reading skills sequences, programs, materials, and techniques. Descriptive skills sequences, program summaries, and other outline materials must be procured or developed if these teachers are to function effectively in determining and prescribing.

What the intermediate teacher determines

1. The relative difficulty with which the various students read silently and answer comprehension questions in the graded content materials / The old adage that "children learn to read in the primary grades and read to learn in the other grades" takes on added meaning when one contrasts the emphases that often characterize the two levels. In the intermediate grades, there is less emphasis on "learning to read" as the students encounter increasingly complex reading assignments in social studies, science, math, and English texts. If they have not learned to read, they are frequently lost in the content assignments, which are developed on the erroneous assumption that all pupils in a grade have the same reading skill. Because many children vary in ability from the grade level, the teacher must make assessments and determinations to put pupils at work on tasks they can manage. The cloze test as described in Chapter 9 is valuable for the intermediate grades, because teachers can determine which pupils can and cannot profit from the assigned reading.

2. The listening comprehension level of each child and the relationship of this level to the child's reading level in the various content areas / When we find a number of fifth-graders who cannot read the fifth-grade text, our next course of action is to determine whether or not they can understand such material if it is read to them. If they can and we feel it is important that they learn the concepts, we can tape the material or make arrangements for someone to read part or all of it to them. If they do not grasp the concepts from listening, then other means must be devised. The important thing, however, is that we determine a "potential" to understand in some children which will give us direction toward word recognition instruction in reading. For those who do not have the potential, we will seek to find their understanding skills and build on them.

3. The specific skills needs of individual pupils.

What the intermediate teacher prescribes

Because reading groups are less used in the intermediate grades (usually only one or two), achievement opportunities for many children become exceedingly limited. As long as reading groups contain children who cannot read the assigned material, little can be done for them; nor can we do much for students who are asked to read science and geography assignments that are beyond their reading levels. For such children, the intermediate grades are intellectual wastelands where much of their basic curiosity is drained away. In order to change this situation, efforts must be made to obtain various levels of reading materials and media to increase the accessibility of the knowledge.

Summary

Diagnostic reading instruction can be initiated in the current program when the teacher uses the preceding chapter information to:

Know specific reading skills
Determine specific pupil needs (of skills)
Prescribe specific tasks for the pupil needs.

16 Diagnostic reading instruction in the multilevel program

Behavioral objectives
1. Describe the physical organization and operation of the traditional reading program (as carried out by Mrs. Jones).
2. Describe the process guiding the development of a new grouping arrangement.
3. Indicate what is meant by "cluster grouping" as well as the rationale behind it.
4. Contrast teacher time scheduling and direct actions in traditional and multilevel instruction.

With increasing awareness of individual reading differences, traditional three-group reading programs can crack and splinter into multilevel programs with more groups. The following story of Mrs. Jones and her second-grade class will illustrate the process.

October and traditional reading

School had been in session over a month, and Mrs. Jones had become well acquainted with her thirty cherubs. Through observation and the results of the achievement test they had taken earlier, she had some notion of their relative reading skills. Let us look at the physical makeup of the room, including the reading groups and seating arrangements.

Scene 1

Each circle in the scene represents a pupil seat. The numbers in the circles indicate the reading achievement levels of the various pupils as obtained by the Metropolitan Achievement Test-Reading Test (Durost et al., 1962). The empty circles indicate the reading circle seats, which in this case are alternately filled by the top, middle, and low groups. During the 90-minute reading period, Mrs. Jones works for approximately 30 minutes with each group:

9:00	Assigns seatwork to middle and high groups
9:05	Works with low group in circle
9:30	Works with middle group in circle
10:00	Works with high group in circle

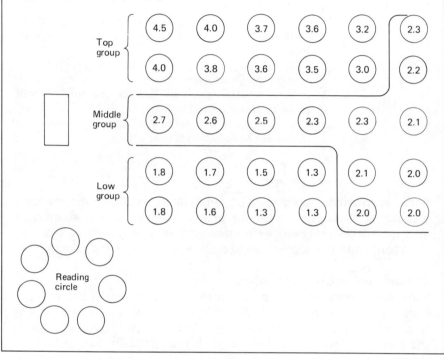

Figure 16-1 / Space arrangement in the traditional program.

Situation: Mrs. Jones' second-grade reading class

Time: Mid-October, the ninety-minute reading period

Reading program: Traditional basal, composed of three reading groups

An overhead view of Mrs. Jones, the children, and their spatial arrangements is suggested by the following drawing:

In order to give her full attention to the group with which she is working, Mrs. Jones set up work tasks for the other children in such a way that they will be able to work without interrupting her. When this is done, she turns her attention to the low group, which consists of the following members:

Low reading group	
Pupil name	Reading achievement score
Terry	1.8
Jerry	1.8
Mary	1.7
José	1.6
Al	1.5
Carol	1.3
Eddie	1.3
Bobby	1.3

Because all these children appear to be too slow and inaccurate readers for the 2^1 reader prescribed for her grade, Mrs. Jones uses the 1^2 (first reader) as the instructional material for the group. Even this material seems too hard for some of the pupils, for they make many mistakes in oral reading and have problems doing the accompanying assignments in the basal workbook.

After the low group is sent to their seats with enough work to hold them for the remainder of the hour, Mrs. Jones meets her largest group, the middle group. The twelve students in this group are reading from the 2^1 basal, but at not quite the same pace as the high reading group. Within the group of twelve, Mrs. Jones notes many differences in oral reading skill, answering skill, and workbook skill. A few students appear to have almost all the answers, while some children never seem to finish reading the assignment. When the teacher waits for the slowest pupils to finish, the quick readers tend to talk among themselves, read ahead, or fiddle with something.

By the time Mrs. Jones reaches the last and best group of readers, she usually finds herself regenerated by the way most of the students breeze through the story, answer questions, and discuss skills and story happenings. She often thinks to herself how great it would be if all the groups were this good.

Mrs. Jones becomes dissatisfied
Although her organization works smoothly and she has no major discipline problems, Mrs. Jones clearly sees that:

The low group is a disaster area, several children cannot read the materials and appear to be gaining little or nothing.

Seatwork does not seem to challenge some of the students, while others seem to struggle with it and never finish.

Much of the seatwork is wrong, and there is seldom time enough to correct the responses and go over them with the children concerned.

A few pupils dominate the reading circle and do all the answering, while others appear to be thinking of other things.

Certain children like Karen in the top group and Eugene in the middle group never experience any difficulty with seatwork tasks and seem to be concerned only with quickly jotting down answers so they can read library books.

Dissatisfied with the results of her program because of the evident pupil variance, Mrs. Jones decides to check the validity of her placements by informally testing the various children in the basal series to determine each child's instructional level as precisely as possible. She makes the discoveries revealed in Table 16-1. Subsequent checks reinforced Mrs. Jones' determinations of the instructional levels. Simple moves, such as putting Terry into the middle group or Kris, Susan, and Arnold into the low group, did not really seem to be the answer, because the distance between the top and the bottom of the low group was already too great. Giving thought to instructing each child on his or her own instructional level, Mrs. Jones found that she would have the following nine reading groups:

Level	Group
5th	Karen
3^2	Arthur, Robert, Willis, Jean
3^1	Martha, Ann, Alice, Eugene
2^2	Tanya, Geof, Thomas, Liz, Fran
2^1	Richard, Ronda, Allen, Sally, Charles, Terry
1^2	Susan, Kris, Arnold
1^1	Jerry, Mary, José
PP 2	Carol, Bobby
PP 1	Al, Eddie

"I'm a good teacher," thought Mrs. Jones, "but not that good." Frankly doubting the possibility of anybody working effectively

Table 16-1 / Achievement Score (AS) and Informal Inventory Score (IIS) for each of Mrs. Jones' pupils

Top reading group			Middle reading group			Low reading group		
Pupil	AS	IIS	Pupil	AS	IIS	Pupil	AS	IIS
Karen	4.5	5	Thomas	2.7	2^2	Terry	1.8	2^1
Martha	4.0	3^1	Eugene	2.6	3^1	Jerry	1.8	P
Arthur	4.0	3^2	Richard	2.5	2^1	Mary	1.7	P
Robert	3.8	3^2	Ronda	2.3	2^1	José	1.6	P
Tanya	3.7	2^2	Liz	2.3	2^2	Al	1.5	PP 1
Willis	3.6	3^2	Susan	2.3	1^2	Carol	1.3	PP 2
Ann	3.6	3^1	Allen	2.2	2^1	Eddie	1.3	PP 1
Geof	3.5	2^2	Kris	2.1	1^2	Bobby	1.3	PP 2
Alice	3.2	3^1	Sally	2.1	2^1			
Jean	3.0	3^2	Arnold	2.0	1^2			
			Fran	2.0	2^2			
			Charles	2.0	2^1			

with nine reading groups, she sought to find some kind of organization that would enable her to be better able to meet the various needs, but still be manageable.

November and multilevel reading

Rather than nine groups, Mrs. Jones developed four which were called "clusters" or "cluster groupings." Although there was only one more group than previously, she felt she had made some significant changes.

Scene 2

Mrs. Jones' reasoning for the development of these groupings represented not only an element of compromise, but also a different concept about the nature of group work.

Pupil Content of cluster		Rationale for placement
Cluster 1		
5	1	The difference between 3^1 and 3^2 connected
3^2	4	reading is not great. Karen (5) can read at a
3^1	4	higher level most of the time.
Cluster 2		
2^2	5	Group instruction will be keyed to the most
2^1	6	needed word attack skills. Seatwork will be
		planned to permit the better readers to read
		more difficult materials according to their interests.
Cluster 3		
1^2	3	Group instruction will be focused on common
P	3	needs, while independent reading will be at instructional levels.
Cluster 4		
PP 2	2	The rationale is essentially the same as above.
PP 1	2	

In addition to establishing groups where the lowest achievers might succeed better, the teacher had established very different ways of working. The children might encounter some wheel spinning in the group situation with the teacher, but they would not be doing the same reading tasks when they returned to their seats. Rather, they would be reading in accordance with their individualized needs and levels. Concurrent with the plan was the beginning of a contract program like that described in Chapter 14 for work on individual skills needs.

Any number of seating arrangements could have been employed, but Mrs. Jones sought to provide seating that would facilitate varying needs such as special projects, peer assistance, and materials usage. Consequently, pupils were not segregated by reading ability or inability. As before, there was the reading corner where Mrs. Jones held forth with the various reading clusters as well as with individuals. But now time deployment and instructional strategy were very different. To Mrs. Jones, meeting every group every day no longer seemed to be critically important; her concern was focused on the kinds of learning experiences that could be most useful in bringing about desired skills. She decided that direct teaching actions were most important for the slower readers, while self-directed experiences would be most valuable for the stronger readers. The result was a schedule revision that established the following time priorities:

	Direct teacher actions with groups				
Period	Monday	Tuesday	Wednesday	Thursday	Friday
9:00-9:15	All pupils begin independent assignments as the teacher moves about and troubleshoots, structures, and so on.				
9:15-9:40	PP	PP	PP	PP	PP
9:40-10:05	P 1^2	P 1^2	P 1^2	P 1^2	P 1^2
10:05-10:30	2	3	2	3	2

The justification for spending most of her teaching time on a third of the class (10 students in this instance) may be that Mrs. Jones can see different results in behavior worth the extra attention to the ten slow students. A description of a single reading period will provide some insight into Mrs. Jones' multilevel program.

Observation

9:00-9:15 / At the appointed time, pupils went to work on their respective tasks. There was little incidence of somebody waiting to be told what to do. Part of the reason for the apparent industry may have been the individual pupil contracts. A close inspection of the contracts revealed strong similarities between certain contracts. Mrs. Jones moved rather swiftly around the room, pausing momentarily to ask a question, offer a comment, and so on. The observer sensed that the teacher's goal was to evaluate and reinforce by positive comment.

9:15-9:40 / During the first five or six minutes, Mrs. Jones worked with the combined group (four children) on auditory and visual discrimination of four common consonants:

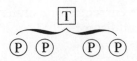

At the completion of the task, the teacher asked the PP 2 pair to take turns reading some sentences (containing their sight vocabulary) to one another while she worked with the other pair on oral reading:

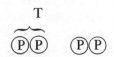

In working with the oral reading group, Mrs. Jones had the pupils read sentences containing unknown words that could be attacked by contextual meaning. She wanted to cue the children to read through the material repeatedly so that they could anticipate the unknown word. After the assignment, the pupils were asked to read the story to one another in a shared fashion. Mrs. Jones then turned her attention back to the other pair:

Her work with this pair was a review of the sentence reading they had practiced and then oral reading of a story (at which time Mrs. Jones noted specific difficulties and attack efforts). At the end of the session, she outlined the continuing tasks that the two pairs would do for the balance of the period and the first part of the next day.

9:40-10:05 / Most of the period was spent on phonic word attack. The teacher worked with the group as a whole on blending single initial consonants to three short vowel phonograms (*-an,* *-in, -en*). Each pupil had a set of consonant cards arranged on his desk; on teacher command, he would form the word spoken:

$$\boxed{c}\ a\ n$$
$$\boxed{p}\ i\ n$$
$$\boxed{t}\ e\ n$$

The remaining few minutes were spent with the pupils divided into pairs to read their current story orally to one another as the teacher moved about and listened:

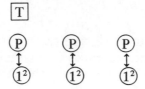

Continuation tasks had apparently been set previously, for the teacher did not spend any time discussing what these children would be doing while she worked with the other groups.

10:05-10:30 / Perhaps because of the size of Cluster 2, Mrs. Jones worked differently with this group than with the others. Most of the time was spent on a common skills lesson and a brief discussion of specific points about a story read by all the students prior to the group meeting. The emphasis of the discussion appeared to be on eliciting various viewpoints about specific characters. Evidently, the teacher had in mind a specific set of comprehension objectives that were to be triggered by a certain questioning set. It was interesting to note that the teacher contributed little to the discussion other than a few questions.

Mrs. Jones evaluates

Although pleased with more accurate reading placements and the new procedures, Mrs. Jones was not completely content. Like any person dissatisfied with something to the extent of taking action to change it, she was destined never to be satisfied with her program. It could always be improved. In weighing the satisfying feelings, she noted such things as:

Increased interest on the part of all students, especially the slower ones.

Increased amounts of reading. Individuals were quadrupling the amounts previously read during class time (especially the more able readers). There was already a problem in terms of the availability of enough reading materials.

A sense of accomplishment on the part of the slowest learners.

On the dissatisfying side, Mrs. Jones was concerned about:

The failure of certain individuals to use their time well when they were on their own.

The reluctance of some pupils to master their learning tasks rather than "go through the motions."

The haste with which some of the better readers met contract obligation (because it resulted in low-quality work).
The usefulness of the outdated reader used as the base reader for Cluster 1.

In thinking back to her traditional program and comparing, Mrs. Jones felt that although she still had many of the same deficits, there were not a great many more positive elements. Her subjective conclusion was that her reading program was better, but still needed more work.

Summary
Mrs. Jones' traditional three-group pattern fell, a victim of increasing concern for individual differences coupled with a growing knowledge of how to cope with them. In its stead arose such things as "instructional level clusters," groups designed to better accommodate the range of differences. We have described the metamorphosis of a traditional second-grade reading program into a multilevel reading program utilizing individual contracts, varied time allotments, varied teaching strategies, and so on.

Diagnostic reading instruction in the individualized program

Behavioral objectives
1. Describe the sequence of and rationale behind the phasing out of instructional groups.
2. Contrast the following characteristics of the traditional and diagnostic reading programs illustrated: materials, time, grouping arrangements, space arrangements, teaching strategies, integration with other language skills, evaluation standards and mechanisms, and instructional responsibilities of parents and peers.
3. Implement the techniques of diagnostic instruction in the classrooms so that pupils will read more widely and critically in such a way that they solve their problems in highly reasoned ways, entertain themselves and others, and gain greater appreciation of the joys and hardships of living.

Although Mrs. Jones obtained a certain amount of individualization in her cluster grouping plan, she recognized the possibilities for further changes in this direction. In this chapter we will describe the implementation of a fully individualized reading program. With increasing knowledge of individual needs and management means, Mrs. Jones began phasing out her four reading clusters in the following sequence:

First / Top groups were phased out first because of the pupils' greater reading skill and concomitant ability to assist themselves in independent reading. Rather than saying "You're individualized today," Mrs. Jones progressed toward individualization by increasing student responsibility for developing and managing their own contracts and study projects.

Second / The lowest groups were phased out next because of the diverse needs of the individuals concerned. Even though she recognized these children's needs for teacher direction in structured situations, Mrs. Jones was painfully aware that their unique skills needs were seldom satisfied with group tasks. Such skills work would have to be accomplished with the assistance of special reinforcement agents such as the Language Master and other self-reinforcing materials. Despite their phased-out status, the teacher still managed her time in order to give these readers the greatest amount of direction.

Third / Middle groups were held intact the longest because of their homogeneity. Group instruction seemed most appropriate for these children in terms of the total picture, but they too needed to pursue individual needs and projects. As these pupils became involved in other work projects, they were released from the group.

Characteristics of the individualized program

Changes occurring in the transition from traditional to diagnostic reading instruction are described in terms of materials, time, grouping, space arrangements, teaching strategies, integration with other language skills, evaluation standards and mechanisms, and the instructional responsibilities of parents and peers.

Materials

In the traditional reading program, with its plodding pace, Mrs. Jones seemed to have enough reading materials. With the identification of the wide range of instructional levels ranging from preprimer 1 to fifth grade, the need for (1) new basal-type materials for the slowest readers and (2) new basal-type materials for those moving ahead into the previously sacred provinces of the third-, fourth-, and fifth-grade teachers, Mrs. Jones had to act. She first traded the inappropriate basals in her possession to other schools in the system using different reading series.

As one might anticipate, the other teachers were affected by Mrs. Jones' program. Although their actions might have been different, they chose to move in the same direction. Rather than sharing pupils (by establishing four supposedly homogeneous groups that would each use a single reader), these teachers pooled their reading resources—basals, basal workbooks, room libraries, reference sets, and skills materials—and placed them in the new learning materials center (the hall adjacent to the four classrooms). Figure 17-1 indicates the vast array of reading resources available to Mrs. Jones' students as well as to the students in the cooperating three rooms. In September Mrs. Jones and the other teachers had only the basal texts assigned to their grade level (and possibly a few from the preceding level for slow readers). After the trading, each of the teachers had a pool of varied materials:

Before trade		After trade		
		Basal A	Basal B	Basal C
Mrs. Jones (2nd grade)				
60 (30 copies each of 2^1 and 2^2 Basal A)	PP	5	5	5
	P	10	10	10

Before trade	After trade		
Mrs. Smith (2nd grade)	1^2 10	10	10
60 (30 copies each of 2^1 and 2^2 Basal A)	2^1 10	10	10
	2^2 10	10	10
Mrs. Black (3rd grade)	3^1 10	10	10
60 (30 copies each of 3^1 and 3^2 Basal A)	3^2 10	10	10
	4 10	10	10
Mrs. Adam (3rd grade)	5 5	5	5
60 (30 copies each of 3^1 and 3^2 Basal A)	*6 5	5	5

*15 out-of-adoption readers given free.

Similarly, the group of teachers diversified the meager supplemental readers through pooling and swapping to spread out the number of titles while reducing the big stockpiles of a few titles. Being aware that the supplemental skills materials had to be fitted to the readers in accordance with needs, the four teachers also pooled workbooks, with some being traded off to other schools for supplemental workbooks accompanying the newly acquired basals. The fifty library books in each room collection proved to be almost meaningless after the first month or two of school and were soon gathering dust. Through the pooling of these materials in the new learning center, accessibility to library books was increased fourfold. The same was done with reference and other reading materials (reading labs, phonic games, tapes, records). For Mrs. Jones and her co-workers, diagnostic reading instruction necessitated books in numbers they had never anticipated.

Working in another vein, they sought means for providing simply operated audiovisual materials that would permit poorer readers to enjoy books taped by excellent readers. They searched for inexpensive audiovisual aids to increase opportunities for children to experience the pleasures of literature beyond their word recognition skills but not beyond their understanding and appreciation. Small tape recorders were now used by the pupils for listening to stories and for developing oral stories and communications of various kinds (newscasts, plays).

Time

Instead of sequentially meeting her three reading groups during the course of each 90-minute reading period, Mrs. Jones served as the consultant and resident troubleshooter for any of the various communication concerns of her charges in the expanded 2-hour block of communication time. As we will discuss in detail in a subsequent section, the great amount of time devoted to the

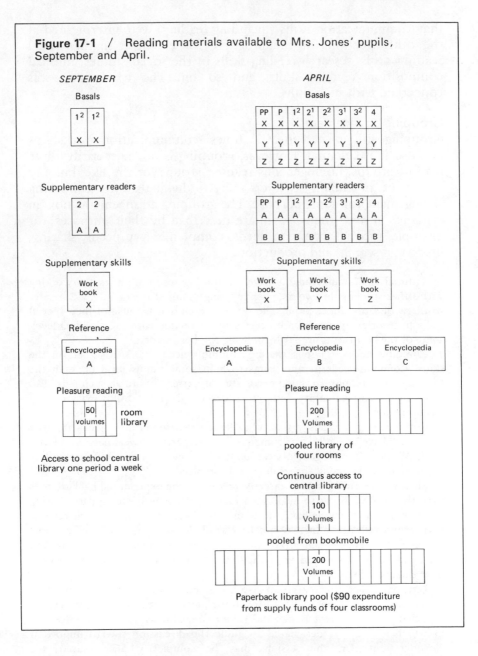

Figure 17-1 / Reading materials available to Mrs. Jones' pupils, September and April.

interrelated skills permitted a logical support of all aspects of communication often hampered by discrete reading, spelling, writing, and English periods. Although the two hours was designated as the communication workshop, Mrs. Jones realized that communication skills (including reading) were intermeshed in the other portions of the program—for example, mathematical reading skills, research reading skills in the social studies, musical composition reading skills, and so on. The whole day was concerned with such skills.

Grouping arrangements

Grouping still existed in Mrs. Jones' communication workshops because it is essential. However, grouping is not necessarily three reading groups, homogeneous reading groups, or the like, but any means of organizing two or more individuals into a working arrangement for some purpose. The grouping arrangements now in evidence in Mrs. Jones' room are described by their purposes; for example, tutorial, common needs, complementary needs, sharing, literary, research, and production.

Tutorial / Certain students have continuing responsibilities for working with other students in two-member tutoring teams—for example, a 2^1 reader works with a preprimer pupil. The tutors are chosen because of their special skills in tutoring, which are not necessarily correlated with their reading level; some of the best tutors are far from being the best readers.

Common needs / Pupils sharing common needs work together on the skills. Common-needs pairing seems to help some pupils push on with the learning task. Because common needs are not extremely broad, such pairs also work in a complementary fashion as described in the following grouping arrangements.

Complementary needs / Careful skills analysis sometimes reveals that the pupils will have strengths that compensate for a partner's weaknesses, and vice versa. When such arrangements can be made, they seem valuable for building group skills well beyond the reading skills involved.

Sharing / Reading skill is directly related to the experiential backgrounds that the readers bring to such situations. Consequently, legitimate sharing sessions in which pupils have the chance to share the fruits of their reading with others (who may or may not have read the same materials) offer a real learning experience. Such arrangements may be informal and center around each individual's own reading or they may be more formal and fall into the next category (literary).

Literary / The literary group also brings pupils together for the purpose of relating to some material read by all the participants. Such sessions can be modeled after the Great Books and Junior Great Books discussions (Worley), in which a leader is designated to guide the discussion toward important considerations. Or, the sessions may be completely unstructured; the participants may develop their own structure. Certain texts permit pupils of different levels to read the same stories in look-alike texts of variant difficulty levels (Bond and Cuddy, 1962). One publisher provides a group of texts that contain stories of increasing difficulty (Pacesetters in Personal Reading, Lyons and Carnahan, 1969). Pupils at different levels thus may be reading from the same text, although in different places.

Research / Pupils can bring common goals and interests and complementary skills to research tasks. Although the term *research* has a formal connotation, the research envisioned here is as simple or complex as the group wishes to make it. Initially, research groups in the primary grades seek to answer important questions by delving into sources such as children's reference books. Such research practice can become rather sophisticated in a program that provides the necessary time, materials, and incentives to young researchers.

Production / A production group should prepare a product of some sort. Consequently, research groups as well as other groups could also be called production groups. Group goals may involve the preparation of a newspaper, magazine, research project, television report, radio broadcast, and so on. Production groups involve students in the construction of a product that presumably has value both to them and to other students who will be the recipients of the products.

Space Arrangements

Seating arrangements in the new plan no longer seek to separate individuals spatially so that they will not copy one another's work, but are designed to meet continuing needs such as work space for major projects and all types of short-term needs. Figure 17-2 graphically illustrates the spatial arrangement at one given moment, because furniture placement must be temporary in a dynamic program. At the moment shown, the children are dispersed in the following arrangements:

The four children who occupy the den area are discussing the various books they have brought. As their discussion progresses, it becomes evident that they are united by the purpose of making specific recommendations to the larger class about the relative values of the newest books. Although the discussion is dominated by two of the children, the other children seem attentive and insert brief comments at various times.

Several pairs of children are involved in common needs or complementary needs groupings; they are using the same texts and performing a number of the same types of tasks. Two boys working near the den appear to be developing contract modifications as a result of meeting the assigned tasks well in advance of their earlier expectations. Three children at the center of the room appear to be employing the "prediction and verification" approach to a story they have not previously read or heard. Each speculates about the contents of the story from the title and then reads certain amounts silently (they set the boundaries for testing their predictions). One child seems obviously pleased that his predictions are proving to be the most accurate. Two children have formed a common needs group almost beside the group just described. At the moment of observation, they appear to be taking

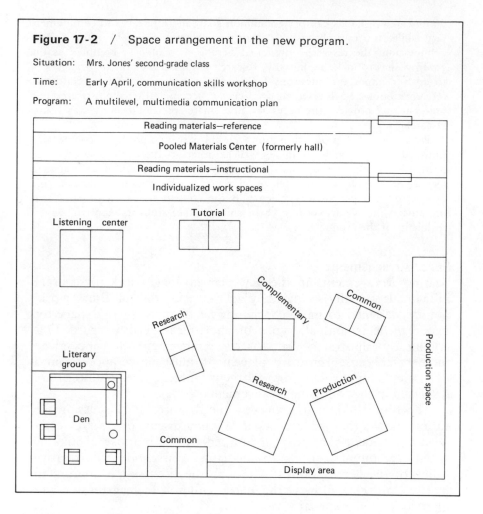

Figure 17-2 / Space arrangement in the new program.

Situation: Mrs. Jones' second-grade class

Time: Early April, communication skills workshop

Program: A multilevel, multimedia communication plan

turns in reading orally to one another from a very easy set of reading materials.

Two small groups (four pupils in one, three in the other) appear to be developing products. The group at the table near the display area is working on the layout of a class newspaper. Although each child appears to be working individually, there is frequent consultation about ideas, spellings, division of work. Nearby in the production space area, the other group seems to be occupied with the development of some sort of pictorial "time line" that demands artistic as well as written composition skills. Little is said within this group; concentration appears intense.

Individualized tasks are in evidence in the space against the hall wall. A quick look over the various shoulders reveals many reading levels and a wide variety of learning tasks. Each pupil seems more concerned about his own tasks than those of his neighbors, although common questions such as "What's this word?" do occur. Contract sheets usually occupy a prominent portion of the pupil's working space. The three children at work in the listening center appear to be doing very different tasks. One of the children is evidently using the Language Master and a talking book. His infrequent use of the Language Master suggests that he feels only a limited need for checking the words in the particular story. (Earphones are used by all three children so there is no disturbing noise.) The other two children appear to be listening to specially taped stories, but it is not clear whether or not they are listening for specific purposes such as "to follow spoken directions" or for the pleasure of hearing a special story.

Two boys just behind the listening center have a small transistorized tape recorder and are preparing a narrative of some sort. The teacher later explains that they are preparing an oral description of their trip to the governor's mansion, where one of the boy's brothers received a scouting award. An important news event in the school, the award ceremony and an interview with the award-winning brother will occupy five minutes of the school newscast that afternoon. The concern of the boys seems to be registered by their intensity in writing down the most important points to be sure their report is accurate.

Teaching strategies

Mrs. Jones' vital role in this operation is unmistakable, because it is her supportive behavior that is a good part of the stimulus. Rather than mechanically making rounds and complimenting, she seems to sense when and where she is needed. She may spend 10 minutes with one individual and 30 or 40 seconds with another, with apparent success in both instances. Mrs. Jones is the diagnostic teacher in a highly developed sense; her diagnosis obviously extends beyond the simple mechanics of reading to the intricate interpersonal relationships and needs of children.

By contrast with the beginning of the year, Mrs. Jones had moved an enormous distance from the building backgrounds, introducing vocabulary, guided reading, rereading, and extending skills cycles with the three groups. No longer was all learning dependent upon her arrival in the group or her explicit assignment of tasks. Students were given responsibilities and opportunities to assume greater ones in terms of reading and producing. Nevertheless, Mrs. Jones was the master diagnostician who possessed both the knowledge and the skill to steer errant learners in directions that would prove beneficial to language arts, thinking, and self-directing achievement. Within her there was still an element of

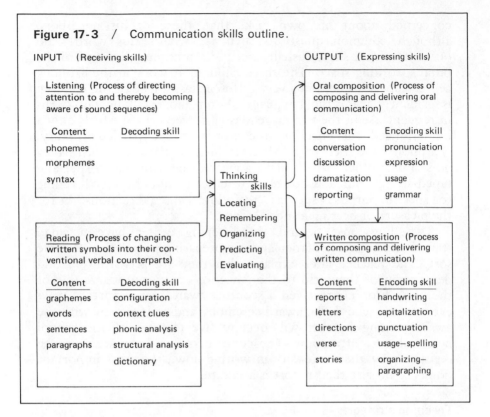

Figure 17-3 / Communication skills outline.

INPUT   (Receiving skills)   OUTPUT   (Expressing skills)

Listening (Process of directing attention to and thereby becoming aware of sound sequences)

Content	Decoding skill
phonemes	
morphemes	
syntax	

Thinking skills

Locating
Remembering
Organizing
Predicting
Evaluating

Oral composition (Process of composing and delivering oral communication)

Content	Encoding skill
conversation	pronunciation
discussion	expression
dramatization	usage
reporting	grammar

Reading (Process of changing written symbols into their conventional verbal counterparts)

Content	Decoding skill
graphemes	configuration
words	context clues
sentences	phonic analysis
paragraphs	structural analysis
	dictionary

Written composition (Process of composing and delivering written communication)

Content	Encoding skill
reports	handwriting
letters	capitalization
directions	punctuation
verse	usage–spelling
stories	organizing–paragraphing

the teacher as "the giver of information," but she was usually able to foresee the limitations of telling situations and resisted the urge.

Integration with other language skills

October's segmented program of reading (90 minutes), spelling (20 minutes), handwriting (20 minutes), and English (15 minutes here and there) became the communication workshop in which all these elements were simply segments of basic input (receiving) and output (expressing) skills. Figure 17-3 indicates the nature of these skills.

The reader has already observed that Mrs. Jones has broken down many of the artificial barriers to communication through providing access to more verbal exchange and high-value listening experiences. She has taken many specific steps that have allowed pupils to have both increased input and output opportunities:

Input	Output
Vital listening experiences in small groups	Oral composition in varied tasks
Taped stories	Oral compositions in the various types of small groups
Less restricted sharing of ideas	Dramatizations
Greatly increased reading	News reports
	All types of written communications

Mrs. Jones realized that students do not carry out these functions without increasing their stores of concepts, vocabulary, usage skills, composing skills, spelling skills, handwriting skills—in fact, all their communication skills. If the students create important products (oral or written), they implement their own self-correction process—for example, they start to look up spellings, reread their materials for accuracy, check punctuation, look up elements of usage, check the formation of certain letter shapes, and so on. She realized one of the things we often fail to see; namely, that communication skills are improved through the practice of purposeful communications and not through the completion of meaningless exercises.

Evaluation standards and mechanisms

In October, the word *evaluation* meant "grading" to Mrs. Jones. She evaluated each pupil's reading skill and gave him or her a grade that reflected both his standing in the group and his own level of effort. While feeling happy that she did not just have to compare the poor readers (who came poor) with the good readers (who came good), she always wondered about the effects of the grades as stimulators to the children and as indicators to the parents because: (1) The best readers knew they were best and were not threatened by the grades. (2) The poor readers similarly knew where they were and knew that even though they might get an E for effort, they would not get much higher on the comparative achievement totem pole. (3) The parents probably did not know too much more about their child's reading as a result of the report card than they did before.

With the advent of individualized skills goals, Mrs. Jones could report specific achievement needs to both pupils and parents. By looking at the checklist of skills gains, the increments of the slower pupils, all could place real value on the individual's gains as measured against his personalized goals. With products becoming increasingly important, individuals could often parlay drive and determination into products that gave them the recognition they were often denied in the previous situation.

Evaluation was becoming more and more a pupil process in the sense that each pupil was carefully assessing his skills growth as measured by the checklist, checksheet, and product improvement. Students become increasingly competent in the evaluation of their products as they have opportunities to create and compare them with those of others. We cannot overemphasize that the greater the skill the student can attain in self-evaluation, the greater his subsequent skill in determining strengths and weaknesses in all areas of skill and affect. Mrs. Jones' role in the development of self-evaluation skill is largely one of approval of effort. She provides support and an environment that nurtures the development of positive self-concepts.

Instructional responsibilities of parents and peers

Pervading this classroom is the idea of interdependence; the group assumes responsibility for all its members. Actual instructional responsibilities are therefore expected of both peers and parents. In the section on grouping arrangements, we described tutorial arrangements, common needs groups, and complementary needs groups. Mrs. Jones learned a great deal in her initial months with the peer tutorials. She learned that interpersonal relationships were important concerns and that she needed to observe such arrangements closely in order that both tutor and tutored would experience success and satisfaction in their work. Much effort was expended to prevent the situation from becoming one that would "put down" the child being tutored or unduly raise the ego of the one doing the teaching.

Certain pupil needs exceeded the help Mrs. Jones and her peer tutoring arrangements could provide. Realizing that if these children were ever going to approach their reading potential they must have more assistance than what could be provided during the school day, she called in the parents of the affected children and explained the needs as clearly as she could. She indicated that success might be achieved if they were willing to respond to some directive suggestions. The suggestions varied sharply and depended upon Mrs. Jones' assessment of the kinds of experiences that seemed most productive for various situations. For example:

Child A / The parents of this child read very little themselves, and he had not developed any sustained interest toward books of any sort. Rather than prescribing a pupil reading program, she obtained commitments from the parents that they would set aside thirty minutes to read to their several children from a book provided by Mrs. Jones. The means of operating the reading session were clearly defined and evaluated regularly through conferences.

Child B / The mother learned from Mrs. Jones how she could assist this child by listening to him read stories sent home by Mrs. Jones. The mother learned to bite her lip and resist the urge to scream and demean the child, and to substitute in their stead periodic reinforcement statements (suggested by Mrs. Jones). In time, this mother and child learned to appreciate their daily sharing session, though at first it was difficult for both.

Child C / As a result of their unique knowledge and understanding, the parents of this child operated what was, in essence, an individualized school for their child at specific times.

"Results, positive reading results, that's what it's all about," explained Mrs. Jones over and over to those who criticized her on the grounds that she was "ruining children's development in other areas," "subjecting families to unnecessary tensions," and so on. Although positive reading results did not occur in every instance, the impression was strong that positive things were happening.

A close-up of two children

In describing the new communications workshops, we have described materials usage, time involvement, grouping arrangements, and several other pertinent factors. We have not, however, focused on the individual pupils. In the paragraphs that follow we shall have the unique opportunity to note two very different pupils, Bobby and Karen, and some of the specific things they are doing with their new freedom.

Bobby

Bobby's preprimer 2 instructional level at the beginning of the year was nearly the lowest in the room. In the course of the year Mrs. Jones undertook an all-out attack on his reading problems and developed a highly organized program that involved not only her help, but also pupil and parent tutorial help. The program was so effective that Bobby and two of the other four lowest readers had progressed to the 2^1 level or better by April. Because Bobby remains one of the slowest readers in the room despite significant achievement, it seems useful to follow him through the course of a given communication skills period to determine what he does. His work involves the following basic segments:

1. The completion of certain fixed tasks on his contract.
2. Participation in a production task of his choice.
3. Free time to read, continue work on his production task, or assist someone else.

Upon entering the room, Bobby organizes his materials and proceeds to work on his contract (Figure 17-4). After completing the contract tasks and evaluating his performance, he seeks out Allen, his friend, to see if Allen will listen to him read the story just completed. Allen agrees, so Bobby reads the first few pages of the story to him. Since Bobby and Allen are working on a special feature story for a subsequent newsletter, they continue working together on a report on lighter-than-air aircraft, which was prompted by their visit to the Goodyear Blimp. Much of the reading and location of material in reference books is too difficult for Bobby but not for Allen, whose reading skill has increased to roughly that of fourth grade. Bobby's complementary drawing and planning skills enable him to be a valuable contributor to the enterprise.

Early in the year, Mrs. Jones and Bobby agreed that his reading skill would be strengthened by reading something in which he was interested at a specific time every day. Although he enjoyed very few reading tasks at the outset because of his limited skill, he did read the books Mrs. Jones helped him select. He read these for the

Figure 17-4 / Bobby's contract — word recognition.

Skills	Activities	Monday	Tuesday	Wednesday	Thursday	Friday
Sight Words *most known* (WC) *brought* LM *phone* *shout*		WC 5	WC 5			
Phonics LM *br-* (SRA) *tr-* (DM) *gr-* (PWU) GWEP				DM # 41	DM #42	PWU p13
r cont. vowels (L) BookD		#13	SRA #35			
Structures *-ed* (PWU) *dropping e+* *adding -ing,* (GWEP)5 *i.e. placing* L *doubling* K *final consonant*		PWU		PWU. p.77	GWEP p.	GWEP p.
Other			PWU p20			

I agree to work on these skills *Bobby* CONTRACT—WORD RECOGNITION

last 30 minutes of each period, despite the fact that it did interrupt his project work. While Mrs. Jones questioned herself about all the inherent negative factors, she concluded that it seemed like a "strong hope" for fixing a habit of reading. Therefore, at the preordained time he sought out some recreational reading material of his own choosing and read for the balance of the period. It was interesting to note that he put in a marker where he left off, presumably so he could continue when time permitted.

Karen

Karen started school as a reader. The youngest of the family's three girls, she had learned to read by association with her older sisters as they learned. Durkin (1970), in a study of children who entered first grade able to read, found such support to be common in the lives of early readers. For Karen, much of the first grade was meaningless because she was quite unique in her reading skill and really did not fit the fastest group. Consequently, as often happens, she was given the freedom to read pretty much what she

Figure 17-4 / Bobby's contract — comprehension.

Skills	Activities	Monday	Tuesday	Wednesday	Thursday	Friday
Predicting	Q					
	Ⓛ(Main Idea)	L-B #10				
	L (Concl.)					
	Ⓛ(Context)	L-B # 15				
Locating	Q					
	Ⓛ(Locat.)		L-B # 20	L-B #21		
	L (Direction)				L-B # 2	
	READER					
Remembering	Q		twice upon a time	"A Tiger"		The Sad Tree SC
	L (Facts)		Q 7/8	Q 4/5		
	ⓈⓡⒶ	orange#2		orange		
	ⓇEADER					
Organizing	Q					
	L					
	SC					
	ⓇEADER					
Evaluating	Q					
	READER				RTS #8	
	ⓇTS	The Lady Monster	NOBODY	The Deer		
	FREE READING					

I agree to work on these skills _Bobby_ CONTRACT—COMPREHENSION

wanted from the materials provided by the room, school, and public library. This she did. At the onset of her second year in school, Mrs. Jones found her capable of reading fifth-grade materials with some assistance.

For Karen, school meant that she attended regularly, but read essentially what interested her. Perhaps as a result of her exceptional skill, she appeared not to be readily accepted by the other children. Perceiving that Karen's choices of work as well as her social experience needed broadening, Mrs. Jones sought to have her assist the poorer readers. Unfortunately, Karen's help did not prove to be very effective either for her or for the children assisted. Mrs. Jones felt Karen's achievement needed to be channeled toward production rather than simply reading fiction most of the day. Thus, she sought, with success, to have Karen broaden her scope of reading through increased involvement in the staff work of a school newspaper. To the delight of the teacher, Karen began to produce and soon was moving toward being one of the most active contributors to the writing of and decision making on the paper. The contracts necessitated by her newspaper work not only caused Karen to read more broadly, but also brought her into social interaction situations with a broad range of pupils and adults.

Due to her highly developed skills, Karen's contract was not focused on the types of skills materials and activities of children such as Bobby. Rather, her contract was a chronicle of her contributions to the newspaper production task. In Figure 17-5, Karen gives her own account of her work in the communications workshop period.

Although it may be argued that Karen is too involved in her newspaper work, this contention seems dubious. It can be argued rather strongly that through the multitude of things revealed in her contract, she is having an unusually rich program for a child at the end of the second grade. Her unique skills and the unique curriculum permit her to develop:

Oral communication skills via interviewing, planning, and relating to many people.

Reading skills necessitated by the backgrounds for the various types of news and feature coverage she meets in different assignments.

Writing skills in the most meaningful way—namely, by writing things that will communicate to a larger audience.

It is certain that the Bobbys of the classroom will want to move into opportunities in which they can produce communications for the other members of the class, the school, and so on. As noted, Bobby was participating by developing an oral taped segment. When the production means become more developed, there will undoubtedly be a lessening of emphasis on the types of skills materials used by Bobby, because special skills practice will emerge more naturally as the result of doing "more meaningful" things.

Summing up

Karen, Bobby, and Allen are only three of thirty children, obviously not a large enough sample to portray the interworkings of the type of instruction we have suggested in this text. Yet, from such descriptions, along with the capsule explanations of the operations, the reader can expand the concepts to fill the mental screen with a three-dimensional image, complete with high-fidelity sound.

If we, as teachers, do not know what the important word recognition, comprehension, and fluency skills are, it is doubtful that we can diagnose and prescribe for their development. When

Figure 17-5 / Karen's Contract (Special)

Monday	Tuesday	Wednesday	Thursday	Friday
I interviewed Mrs. Walsh, the gym teacher, about the President's Physical Fitness Program	Working on story of Physical Fitness Program	Saw Mrs. Walsh again and got some more information. Called Mr. Jones at Able School	Finished story. It will be in tomorrow's paper.	Gave out the papers in Rooms 1, 2, 3. Met with editors to discuss comments
Worked with group to select stories for "the Most..." Feature Read + checked second page stories for content, spelling, and names.	Worked on story, selected for "The Most ..." Helped Joe Berry make some changes.	Wrote poem for poetry section of paper. It's not too good. Met with editors to plan next week's papers.	Wrote a better poem called The Rain. I think it may be next week. Wrote notes to people to be interview to set up appointments. Helped staple, count, and stack papers.	about paper, plan next page Assigned to do a story on what the students think about the President's Physical Fitness Program. Started to make out interim sheet.
Reading Clara Barton in spare time.				

we do know such skills, we can attempt teaching procedures (either directed by us or the children themselves) that will get results. Little of what we have described will "just happen." It did not just happen in the example of Mrs. Jones and her second-grade class; it happened because she could see children as individuals, which for the purposes of reading instruction meant that she could see different needs. She realized that despite its comfort, the three-group approach would not meet the needs. Rather than saying "Well, what can you do when you have only one basal," she determined what she, as an individual, could do about it. In other words, she acted intelligently by effecting small but significant changes.

We suspect that Mrs. Jones' program lost nothing that was valuable. We suspect that with her metamorphosis from ringmistress of a three-ring circus to a diagnostic teacher, she began the development of children who would:

Assume greater responsibility for their own actions of all sorts, especially self-instructional ones.

Read more material more effectively than if they had remained in the lock-step pattern of limited reading.

Read for purposes more varied than trying to remember "things that will be on the test."

Be far more capable of evaluating judgments that seem to be made on the slightest bit of testimony or evidence.

Actually entertain themselves by reading and producing useful products rather than constantly watching television.

Have increased potential to act as intelligent, well-informed citizens in the management of the complex problems that threaten our society today.

Everybody recognizes that something has to be done and done soon, yet almost no one gets beyond the talking stage. What are you going to do?

Bibliography

Aaron, I. E. What Teachers and Prospective Teachers Know about Phonics and Syllabication. *The Reading Teacher,* 14 (1961), 326-330.

Ammerman, H. L., and W. H. Melching. *The Derivation, Analysis, and Classification of Instructional Objectives.* Alexandria, Va.: George Washington University, 1966.

Aschner, M. J., J. J. Gallagher, J. M. Perry, S. S. Afsar, W. Jenne, and H. Farr. *A System for Classifying Thought Processes in the Context of Classroom Verbal Interaction.* Champaign, Ill.: Institute for Research on Exceptional Children, 1965.

Austin, M., and C. Morrison. *The First R: The Harvard Report on Reading in the Elementary School.* New York: Macmillan, 1963.

Bailey, M. H. "The Utility of Phonic Generalizations in Grades One Through Six," *The Reading Teacher,* 20:413-18, Feb. 1967.

Barrett, T. Performance on Selected Prereading Tasks and First-grade Achievement. A research paper presented at the International Reading Association Convention in Dallas, May 6, 1966.

_____. Taxonomy of Cognitive and Affective Dimensions of Reading Comprehension. Included in the chapter by T. Clymer in *The Sixty-seventh Yearbook of the National Society for the Study of Education,* Part 2. Chicago: University of Chicago Press, 1968.

Barton, A., and D. Wilder. Research and Practice in the Teaching of Reading: A Progress Report. In *Innovations in Education,* ed. M. Miles, pp. 361-398. New York: Teachers College, Columbia University, 1964.

Beldin, H. O. Informal Reading Testing: Historical Review and Review of Research. A symposium paper presented at the fourteenth annual convention of the International Reading Association, Kansas City, Mo., 1969.

Bell and Howell Corporation. Language Master. An electronic recording and playback machine, useful for reading instruction. Chicago: Bell and Howell.

_____. *The Phonics Program* (for the Language Master). Chicago: Bell and Howell.

Bellack, A., and J. R. Davitz, in collaboration with H. M. Kliebard and R. T. Hyman. The Language of the Classroom. New York: Institute of Psychological Research, Teachers College, Columbia University, 1963. (mimeographed)

Betts, E. A. *Foundations of Reading Instruction.* New York: American Book, 1946.

Black, M., and L. Whitehouse. Reinforcing Reading Skills Through Workbooks. *The Reading Teacher,* 15 (1961), 19-24.

Bloom, B. *Stability and Change in Human Characteristics.* New York: Wiley, 1964.

Bloom, B. S. *Taxonomy of Educational Objectives: Handbook 1, Cognitive Domain.* New York: McKay, 1956.

Bloomfield, L. Linguistics and Reading. *The Elementary English Review,* 19 (1941), 125-130.

————, and C. L. Barnhart. *Let's Read: A Linguistic Approach.* Detroit: Wayne State University Press, 1961.

Bond, G., and M. Cuddy. *Classmate Editions: The Developmental Reading Series.* Chicago: Lyons and Carnahan, 1962.

Bond, G., and R. Dykstra. *Final Report: Coordinating Center for First-grade Reading Instruction Programs.* Cooperative Research Project X-001. Minneapolis: University of Minnesota, 1967, p. 2.

Bond, G., et al. *Silent Reading Diagnostic Tests.* Chicago: Lyons and Carnahan, 1955.

————, and M. A. Tinker. *Reading Difficulties: Their Diagnosis and Correction,* third edition. New York: Appleton-Century-Crofts, 1968.

Boning, R. A. *Specific Skills Series.* (Contains both a word analysis series and a comprehension series.) Rockville Center, N.Y.: Barnell Loft, 1967.

Bormuth, J. R. Comparable Cloze and Multiple-choice Comprehension Test Scores. *Journal of Reading,* 10 (1967), 291-299.

Botel, M. A Comparative Study of the Validity of the Botel Reading Inventory and Selected Standardized Tests. A paper presented at the thirteenth annual convention of the International Reading Association, Boston, April 26, 1968.

Brekke, G. W. Actual and Recommended Allotments of Time for Reading. In *Elementary Reading Instruction: Selected Materials,* ed. A. Beery, T. Barrett, and W. Powell, pp. 129-132. Boston: Allyn and Bacon, 1969.

Burmeister, L. E. Vowel Pairs. *The Reading Teacher,* 21, 5 (February 1968), 445-452.

Burnett, R. W. Problem-solving Proficiencies among Elementary School Teachers. Institute of Educational Research, University of Indiana, 1963. (mimeographed)

Buros, O. K. *Reading Tests and Reviews.* Highland Park, N.J.: Gryphon Press, 1968. (Summarizes mental measurement yearbooks.)

Burrows, A., and Z. Lourie. "When Two Vowels Go Walking," *The Reading Teacher* 17:79-82 (Nov., 1963).

Carmichael, L., and W. Dearborn. *Reading and Visual Fatigue.* Boston: Houghton Mifflin, 1947.

Center for Cognitive Learning. Compendium of Reading Materials and Teaching Techniques for the Wisconsin Prototypic System of Reading Instruction. Practical Paper No. 7. The University of Wisconsin Center For Cognitive Learning, February 1969.

Chall, J. *Learning to Read: The Great Debate.* New York: McGraw-Hill, 1967.

Children's Television Workshop. *Sesame Street.* A daily one-hour television series transmitted over the National Educational Television Network, 1969.

Clark, C., and H. Wahlberg. The Influences of Massive Reward on Reading

Achievement in Potential Urban School Dropouts. *American Educational Research Journal,* 5 (1968), 305-310.

Clymer, T. What Is "Reading"? Some Current Concepts. In *Innovation and Change in Reading Instruction, The Sixty-seventh Yearbook of the National Society for the Study of Education,* ed. H. M. Robinson, pp. 18-23. Chicago: University of Chicago Press, 1968.

————, and T. Barrett. *Clymer-Barrett Prereading Battery.* Boston: Personnel Press, 1967.

————, and L. Burmeister. *Ginn Word Enrichment Program.* Boston: Ginn, 1967, 1968.

Cohen, D. H. The Effect of Literature on Vocabulary and Reading Achievement. *The Elementary English Review,* 45 (1968), 209-215, 217.

Cohen, S. Implications for High School Teachers. In *Reading for the Disadvantaged: Problems of Linguistically Different Learners,* ed. T. Horn. New York: Harcourt Brace Jovanovich, 1970.

Coleman, J. *Equality of Educational Opportunity.* Washington, D.C.: U.S. Department of Health, Education and Welfare, 1966.

Columbia Broadcasting System. *Captain Kangaroo.* A daily television series transmitted over the Columbia Broadcasting System, 1971.

Combs, A. *The Professional Education of Teachers.* Boston: Allyn and Bacon, 1965.

Decker, S. *An Empty Spoon.* Harper and Row, 1969.

Deighton, L., et al. *The Macmillan Reading Spectrum.* New York: Macmillan, 1964, 1966.

Della-Piana, G., et al. The Influence of Parental Attitudes and Child-parent Interaction upon Remedial Reading Progress, Final Report. Cooperative Research Project S-266, U.S. Office of Education, 1966.

Doctor, R. Reading workbooks: Boon or Busy Work? *The Elementary English Review,* 39 (1962), 224-228.

Dolch, E. Fact, Burden, and Reading Difficulty. *The Elementary English Review,* 16 (1939), 135-138.

————. *Teaching Primary Reading.* Champaign, Ill., Garrard Press, 1941.

Duell, O. K. An Analysis of Prompting Procedures for Teaching a Sight Vocabulary. *American Educational Research Journal,* 5 (1968), 675-686.

Durkin, D. *Teaching Them to Read.* Boston: Allyn and Bacon, 1970.

Durost, W. N., et al. *Metropolitan Achievement Tests.* New York: Harcourt Brace Jovanovich, 1955.

Durrell, D. D. *Durrell Analysis of Reading Difficulty.* New York: Harcourt Brace Jovanovich, 1962.

Durrell, D., and H. Murphy. *Durrell-Murphy Phonics Practice Program.* N.Y.: Harcourt Brace Jovanovich, 1968.

Dykstra, R. The Use of Readiness Tests for Prediction and Diagnosis: A Critique. In *The Evaluation of Children's Reading,* ed. T. Barrett, pp. 35-52. Newark: International Reading Association, 1967.

————. The Effectiveness of Code and Meaning Emphasis in Beginning Reading Programs. *The Reading Teacher,* 22 (1968), 17-23.

Eisner, E. W. Educational Objectives: Help or Hindrance? *School Review,* LXXV, 3 (1967).

Emans, R. Teacher Evaluations of Reading Skills and Individualized Reading. *The Elementary English Reviews,* 42 (1965), 258-260.

Fader, D., and E. McNeil. *Hooked on Books: Program and Proof.* New York: Berkley, 1968.

Farr, R. C., et al. The Problem with Reading: An Examination of Reading Programs in Indiana Schools. Indiana University, *Bulletin of the School of Education,* 45, 2 (March 1969).

Fitzhugh, K., and L. Fitzhugh. *The Fitzhugh Plus Program.* Galien, Mich.: Allied Education Council, 1968.

Flesch, R. *Why Johnny Can't Read.* New York: Harper and Row, 1955.

Fowler, H. *Curiosity and Explanatory Behavior.* New York: Macmillan, 1965.

Frase, L. Learning from Prose Material: Length of Passage, Knowledge of Results, and Position of Questions. *Journal of Educational Psychology,* 58 (1967), 266-272.

————. Some Unpredicted Effects of Different Questions upon Learning from Connected Discourse. *Journal of Educational Psychology,* 59 (1968), 197-201.

Fries, C., et al. *Merrill Linguistic Readers.* Columbus, O.: Charles E. Merrill, 1966.

Frost, J., and G. Pilgrim. Research Report on the Reading Program at the Camp Gary Job Corps. An unpublished report, the University of Texas at Austin, 1969.

————, and T. Rowland. *Compensatory Programming: The Acid Test of American Education.* Dubuque, Iowa: William C. Brown, 1971.

Gagné, R. The Analysis of Instructional Objectives for the Design of Instruction. In *Teaching Machines and Programmed Learning II,* ed. R. Glazer, Washington, D.C.: National Education Association, 1965.

Gates, A. The Necessary Mental Age for Beginning Reading. *Elementary School Journal* (1937), 497-508.

————, and C. Peardon. *Gates-Peardon Reading Exercises.* New York: Teachers College, Columbia University, 1932.

Gattengo, C. *Words in Color.* Chicago: Xerox Company, 1969.

Gilmore, J. *Gilmore Oral Reading Test.* New York: Harcourt Brace Jovanovich, 1951.

Ginn Publishing Company. *Ginn 360 Reading Program.* Boston: Ginn, 1969.

Ginott, H. *Between Parent and Child.* New York: Macmillan, 1965.

Goldberg, L., and D. Rasmussen. *S.R.A. Basic Reading Series.* Chicago: Science Research Associates, 1965.

Goldberg, M., et al. *The Effects of Ability Grouping.* New York: Teachers College, Columbia University, 1966.

Goodlad, J. The Schools vs. Education. *The Saturday Review,* April 19, 1969, 59-61, 80-82.

Goodman, K. A Linguistic Study of Cues and Miscues in Reading. *The Elementary English Review,* 42 (1965), 639-643.

Goudey, C. A Comparison of Children's Reading Performance Under Directed and Nondirected Conditions. Unpublished Ph.D. dissertation, University of Minnesota, 1969.

Guilford, J. Three Faces of Intellect. *American Psychologist,* 14 (1959), 469-479.

Guszak, F. Relations Between Teacher Practice and Knowledge of Reading Theory in Selected Grade School Classes. U.S. Office of Education Report S-437, Madison, Wis., 1967. (mimeographed)

————. Teacher Questioning and Reading. *The Reading Teacher*, 21 (1968), 227-234.

Hamacek, D. Characteristics of Good Teachers and Implications for Teacher Education. *Phi Delta Kappan*, L, 6 (1969), 341-344.

Harmer, W. The Selection and Use of Survey Reading Achievement Tests. In *The Evaluation of Children's Reading*, ed. T. Barrett. Newark: International Reading Association, 1967.

Harris, A. *How to Increase Reading Ability, fifth edition.* New York: McKay, 1970.

Harrison, L., and J. Stroud. *Harrison-Stroud Reading Readiness Profiles.* Boston: Houghton Mifflin, 1956.

Head Start Program, Office of Economic Opportunity, 1964.

Hildredth, G., et al. *The Metropolitan Reading Readiness Test*, New York: Harcourt Brace Jovanovich, 1964.

Houghton Mifflin Company. *Houghton Mifflin Reading Program*, 1970.

Hughes, M. *Development of the Means for the Assessment of the Quality of Teaching in the Elementary School.* Salt Lake City: University of Utah Press, 1959.

Hunt, L. The Key to the Conference Lies in the Questioning. In *The University of Toledo Educational Comment*, ed. H. Sandberg, pp. 25-34. Toledo, O.: The University of Toledo, 1966.

————. Evaluation Through Teacher-Pupil Conferences. In *The Evaluation of Children's Reading*, ed. T. Barrett, Newark: International Reading Association, 1967.

————. The Effect of Self-selection, Interest, and Motivation upon Independent, Instructional, and Frustrational Levels of Reading. A symposium paper presented at the fourth annual convention of the International Reading Association, Kansas City, 1969.

Inhelder, R., and J. Piaget. *The Growth of Critical Thinking.* New York: Basic Books, 1958.

Jensen, A. How Much Can We Boost IQ and Scholastic Achievement? *Harvard Educational Review*, 39 (1969), 1-12.

Kelley, T., et al. *Stanford Achievement Test: Reading Tests.* New York: Harcourt Brace Jovanovich, 1965.

Kerfoot, J. Problems and Research Considerations in Reading Comprehension. *The Reading Teacher*, 18 (1965), 250-256.

Kilgallon, P. A Study of Relationships among Certain Pupil Adjustments in Language Situations. Unpublished Ph.D. dissertation, Pennsylvania State College, 1942.

Klausmeier, H. *Learning and Human Abilities.* New York: Harper and Row, 1961.

Klineberg, O. Life Is Fun in a Smiling, Fair-skinned World. *The Saturday Review*, 1963. (Reprinted in *Issues and Innovations in the Teaching of Reading*, ed. J. Frost. Chicago: Scott Foresman, 1967.)

Kohl, H. *36 Children.* New York: Signet, 1967.

Krathwohl, D., et al. *Taxonomy of Educational Objectives—The Classification of Educational Goals, Handbook II: Affective Domain.* New York: McKay, 1964.

Kress, R., and M. Johnson. *Informal Reading Inventories.* Newark: International Reading Association, 1965.

Ladd, E. A Comparison of Two Types of Training with Reference to Developing Skill in Diagnostic Oral Reading Tests. Unpublished Ph.D. dissertation, Florida State University, 1961.

LaPray, M., and R. Ross. The Graded Word List: Quick Gauge of Reading Ability. *Journal of Reading,* 12 (1969), 305-307.

Lee, J., et al. Measuring Reading Readiness. *Elementary School Journal,* 34 (1934), 656-666.

Lerner, J. Dyslexia or Reading Disability: A Thorn by Any Name. A paper presented at the Association for Children with Learning Disabilities, Fort Worth, March 6-8, 1969.

Lindvall, C. *Defining Educational Objectives.* Pittsburgh: University of Pittsburgh Press, 1964.

Mager, R. *Preparing Instructional Objectives.* Palo Alto, Calif.: Fearon, 1962.

Maney, E. *Reading-Thinking Skills.* Oklahoma City: Continental Press, 1967.

McCracken, G., and C. Walcutt. *Basic Reading.* Philadelphia: Lippincott, 1963.

McCracken, R. *Standard Reading Inventory.* Klamath Falls, Ore.: Klamath Printing Company, 1966.

————. The Informal Reading Inventory as a Means of Improving Instruction. In *The Evaluation of Children's Reading,* ed. T. Barrett, Newark: International Reading Association, 1967.

————. Do We Want Real Readers? A guest editorial in *Journal of Reading,* 12 (1969), 446-448.

McCullogh, C. Recognition of Context Clues in Reading. *The Elementary English Review,* 22 (1955), 1-5.

McDonald, M., and E. Zaret. Report of a Study of Openness in Classroom Interactions. University of Wisconsin at Milwaukee, 1967. (mimeographed)

McKee, P., et al. *Reading for Meaning.* Boston: Houghton Mifflin, 1966.

Merrill Company. *New Modern Reading Skilltext Series.* Columbus, O.: Charles E. Merrill, 1966. (*Phonic Skilltapes* available from the same source.)

Metfessel, N. Instrumentation of Bloom's and Krathwohl's Taxonomies for the Writing of Educational Objectives. *Psychology in the Schools,* 6 (1969), 227-231.

Miller, W. The Joplin Plan: Is It Effective for Intermediate Grade Reading Instruction? *The Elementary English Review,* 46 (1969), 951-954.

Money, J. *The Disabled Reader: Education of the Dyslexic Child.* Baltimore: John Hopkins Press, 1966.

Moskowitz, M., and A. Orgel. *General Psychology.* Boston: Houghton Mifflin, 1969.

Murphy, H., and D. Durrell. *Murphy-Durrell Diagnostic Reading Readiness Tests,* revised edition, New York: Harcourt Brace Jovanovich, 1964.

Newsome, V. *Structural Grammar in the Classroom.* Oshkosh, Wis.: Wisconsin Council of Teachers of English, 1961.

Nurss, J. Oral Reading Errors and Reading Comprehension. *The Reading Teacher,* 22 (1969), 523-527.

Parker, D. *S.R.A. Reading Laboratory I.* Chicago: Science Research Associates, 1961.

Popham, W., and E. Baker. *Establishing Instructional Goals.* Englewood Cliffs, N.J.: Prentice Hall, 1969.

Powell, W. R. Reappraising the Criteria for Interpreting Informal Inventories. A paper presented at the thirteenth annual convention of the International Reading Association, Boston, 1968.

Project Follow Through, authorized under Title II of the Economic Opportunity Act, 1968.

Random House. *Random House Reading Pacesetters.* New York: Random House, 1968.

Rankin, E. F., and J. W. Culhane. Comparable Cloze and Multiple-choice Comprehension Test Scores. *Journal of Reading,* 13 (1969), 193-198.

Readers' Digest. *Readers' Digest Reading Skills Builders.* Pleasantville, N.Y.: Readers' Digest Services, 1958.

Right to Read Program. U.S. Office of Education, 1969.

Robinson, H. A. *EDL Study Skills Laboratory.* Huntington, N.Y.: Educational Development Laboratories, 1961.

Robinson, H. M. *The Open Highways Readers.* Chicago: Scott Foresman, 1966.

————, et al. *The New Basic Readers.* Chicago: Scott Foresman, 1962.

————, et al. *Widening Horizons.* Chicago: Scott Foresman, 1966.

Rosenthal, R., and L. Jacobsen. *Pygmalion in the Classroom.* Holt, Rinehart, and Winston, 1968.

Rothkopf, E. Learning from Written Instructive Materials: An Exploration of the Control of Inspection Behavior by Test-like Events. *American Educational Research Association Journal,* 3 (1966), 241-249.

Ruddell, R. The Effect of Oral and Written Patterns of Language Structure on Reading Comprehension. *The Reading Teacher,* 18 (1965), 270-275.

Rudorf, E. What Sounds and What Symbols? A paper presented at the fifty-eighth annual convention of the National Council of Teachers of English, Milwaukee, November 29, 1968.

Russell, D., et al. *The Ginn Basic Readers.* Boston: Ginn, 1961.

Rutherford, W. Five Steps to Effective Reading Instruction. *The Reading Teacher,* 24 (1971), 416-421, 424.

Sanders, N. *Classroom Questions: What Kinds?* New York: Harper and Row, 1966.

Scarry, R. *Best Word Book Ever.* New York: Golden Book, 1963.

————. *Storybook Dictionary.* New York: Golden Book, 1966.

Science Research Associates. *Reading Laboratory I: Word Games.* Chicago: Science Research Associates, 1968.

Seuss, Dr. *Cat in the Hat.* New York: Random House, 1957.

————. *Green Eggs and Ham.* New York: Random House, 1960.

Silberman, C. *Crisis in the Classroom.* New York: Random House, 1970.

Smith, B. O. A Study of the Logic of Teaching. Bureau of Educational Research, The University of Illinois, 1962. (mimeographed)

Smith, N. B. *Reading Instruction for Today's Children.* Englewood Cliffs, N.J.: Prentice-Hall, 1963.

_____. The Many Faces of Reading Comprehension. *The Reading Teacher,* 21 (1969), 249-259.

Spache, G. *Diagnostic Reading Scales.* California Test Bureau, 1963.

_____. *Toward Better Reading.* Champaign, Ill.: Garrard Press, 1963.

_____, and E. Baggett. What Do Teachers Know about Phonics and Syllabication? *The Reading Teacher,* 14 (1961), 326-330.

_____, and E. Spache. *Reading in the Elementary School,* second edition. Boston: Allyn and Bacon, 1969.

Spalding, R. *The Writing Road to Reading.* New York: Whiteside and William Morrow, 1962.

Staats, A., et al. Motivated Learning Reading Treatment with Additional Subjects and Instructional Techniques. *ERIC ED 015-110, 1968.*

Stauffer, R. "A Study of the Prefixes in the Thorndike List to Establish a List of Prefixes That Should Be Taught in Elementary School." *Journal of Educational Research*, 35 (Feb. 1942), 453-458.

_____. *Teaching Reading as a Thinking Process.* New York: Harper and Row, 1969.

Strickland, R. The Language of Elementary School Children: Its Relationship to the Language of Reading Textbooks and the Quality of Reading of Selected Children. *Indiana University,* Bulletin of the School of Education (1962).

_____. The Contribution of Structural Linguistics to the Teaching of Reading, Writing, and Grammar in the Elementary School. Indiana University, *Bulletin of the School of Education* (January 1964).

_____. A Challenge to Teachers of Reading. Indiana University, *Bulletin of the School of Education* (March 1969).

Taba, H. The Teaching of Thinking. *The Elementary English Review,* 42 (1965), 534-542.

Tannenbaum, A. An Evaluation of STAR: A Non-professional Tutoring Program. Teachers College, Columbia University, *The Record,* 69 (1968), 433-448.

Taylor, S., et al. Norms for the Components of the Fundamental Reading Skills. Research Bulletin, No. 3. Huntington, N.Y.: Educational Development Laboratories, 1960.

Taylor, W. Cloze Procedure: A New Tool for Measuring Readability. *Journalism Quarterly,* 40 (1953), 414-438.

Thomas, J. Tutoring Strategies and Effectiveness: A Comparison of Elementary Age Tutors and College Age Tutors. Unpublished Ph.D. dissertation, University of Texas at Austin, 1970.

Thorndike, E. Reading as Reasoning: A Study of Mistakes in Paragraph Reading. *Journal of Educational Research* (1917), 323-332.

_____. *The Teaching of English Suffixes.* New York: Teachers College, Columbia University, 1941.

_____, and C. Barnhart. *Thorndike-Barnhart Beginning Dictionary.* Chicago: Scott, Foresman, 1968.

Thorpe, L. E., et al. *SRA Achievement Series: Reading.* Chicago: Science Research Associates, 1964.

Tiegs, E. W., and W. W. Clark. *California Reading Tests.* California Test Bureau, 1963.

Tinker, M. A. *Teaching Elementary Reading.* New York: Appleton-Century-Crofts, 1952.

_____. *Bases for Effective Reading.* Minneapolis: University of Minnesota Press, 1965.

Trace, A. *What Ivan Knows That Johnny Doesn't.* New York: Random House, 1961.

Tunley, R. Johnny Can Read in Joplin. *Saturday Evening Post,* October 26, 1957.

Turner, R., and N. Fattu. Skill in Teaching Assessed on the Criterion of Problem Solving. Indiana University, *Bulletin of the School of Education,* 1961.

Veeatch, J. *Reading in the Elementary School.* New York: Ronald, 1966.

Vernon, M. D. Major Approaches to Word Perception. *Education,* 86 (1966), 459-463.

Wade, E. W. The Construction and Validation of a Test of Ten Teacher Skills Used in Reading Instruction. Unpublished Ph.D. dissertation, University of Indiana, 1961.

Walbesser, H. H. *Constructing Behavioral Objectives.* College Park, Md.: Bureau of Educational Research, University of Maryland, 1966.

Walcutt, C. *Tomorrow's Illiterates: The State of Reading Today.* Boston: Little, Brown, 1961.

Weintraub, S. The Question as an Aid in Reading. *The Reading Teacher,* 22 (1969), 751-755.

Wells, C. The Value of an Oral Reading Test for Diagnosis of the Reading Difficulties of College Freshmen of Low Academic Performance. *Psychological Monographs,* 60 (1950), 1-35.

Wepman, J. *Wepman Auditory Discrimination Test.* Chicago: Wepman, 1958.

Winkley, C. Which Accent Generalizations Are Worth Teaching? *The Reading Teacher,* 20, 3 (December 1966), 219-224.

Winterhaven Lions Research Foundation. *Perceptual Achievement Forms.* Winterhaven, Fla.: Winterhaven Lions Research Foundation, 1964.

Wittes, G., and N. Radin. *Ypsilanti Home and School Handbook, Helping Your Child Learn: The Reinforcement Approach.* San Rafael, Calif.: Dimension Publishing Company, 1969.

Wolf, W., et al. *Critical Reading Ability of Elementary School Children.* Project No. 5-1040, U.S. Office of Education, 1967.

Worley, L. *Coordinator of the Junior Great Books Program.* Royal Oak, Mich.: n.d.

Wortman, A., and D. Kurtz. *The Classroom Management Project.* A film prepared for the Neighborhood Service Organization, Detroit, Michigan, 1969.

Index

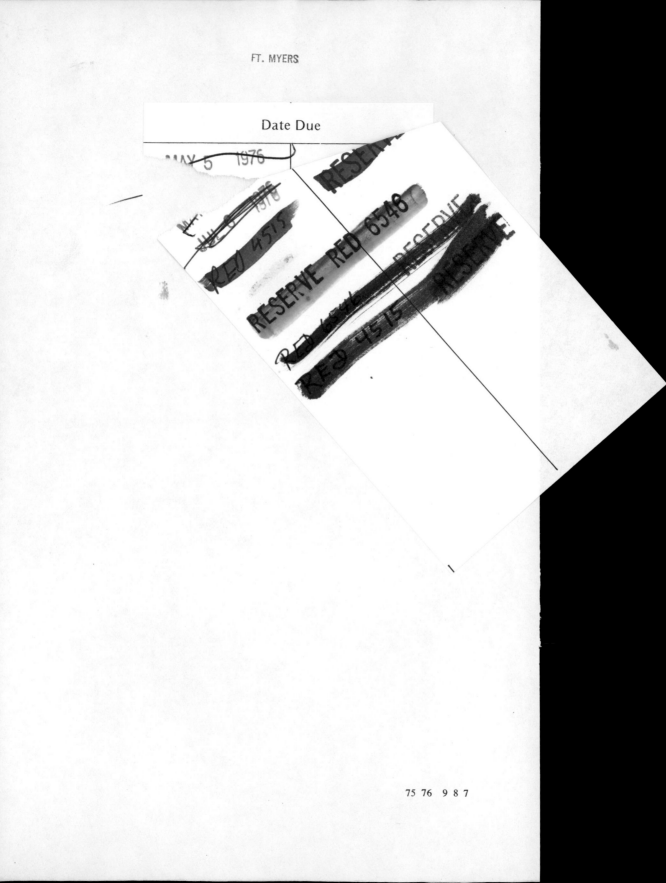

Date Due

MAY 5 1976